RICHARD ARROW SMITH

OF
WAKE COUNTY NORTH CAROLINA
AND
HIS DESCENDANTS

SMITH AND RELATED FAMILIES
BROUGHTON, BAGWELL AND STANCIL
OF
WAKE AND JOHNSTON COUNTIES
NORTH CAROLINA

Compiled by
Rebecca L. Blackwell
and
Crama Smith Graham

HERITAGE BOOKS
2007

HERITAGE BOOKS
AN IMPRINT OF HERITAGE BOOKS, INC.

Books, CDs, and more—Worldwide

For our listing of thousands of titles see our website at
www.HeritageBooks.com

Published 2007 by
HERITAGE BOOKS, INC.
Publishing Division
65 East Main Street
Westminster, Maryland 21157-5026

Copyright © 1993 Rebecca L. Blackwell
and Crama Smith Graham

Other Heritage Books by Rebecca L. Blackwell:
Descendants of John Michael Kreider of Montgomery County, Pennsylvania, Kentucky, and Tennessee

All rights reserved. No part of this book may be reproduced or transmitted in any form or by any means, electronic or mechanical, including photocopying, recording or by any information storage and retrieval system without written permission from the author, except for the inclusion of brief quotations in a review.

International Standard Book Number: 978-1-55613-763-1

Descendants of Richard Arrow Smith

This book is dedicated
to my father,
E. Vernon Smith, Jr.,
who suggested to me
a few years ago,
"Why don't you try to find out
about our Smiths?"

and to
Crama Smith Graham
whose energetic collection of data
enlarged our
Smith family tree.

Descendants of Richard Arrow Smith

Table of Contents

Preface..iii
Arrowsmith Families of the Southern United States.......v
Contributors..viii
Descendants of Richard Arrow Smith
    First Generation......................................1
    Second Generation.....................................8
    Third Generation.....................................17
    Fourth Generation....................................35
    Fifth Generation.....................................68
    Sixth Generation.....................................84
    Seventh Generation...................................95
Unidentified A. Smith Relatives.........................112
Descendants of Richard Johnson
    First Generation....................................114
    Second Generation...................................116
Descendants of Phereby Johnson Sauls
    First Generation....................................119
    Second Generation...................................121
    Third Generation....................................122
Descendants of Joseph Broughton
    First Generation....................................127
    Second Generation...................................129
    Third Generation....................................133
    Fourth Generation...................................142
Descendants of John Stancil
    First Generation....................................143
    Second Generation...................................144
    Third Generation....................................145
    Fourth Generation...................................148
Descendants of Daniel Bagwell
    First Generation....................................150
    Second Generation...................................154
    Third Generation....................................157
    Fourth Generation...................................161
Descedants of John Baucom
    First Generation....................................173
    Second Generation...................................175
    Third Generation....................................182
    Fourth Generation...................................187
    Fifth Generation....................................193

Descendants of George Poole
  First Generation..................................194
  Second Generation.................................196
  Third Generation..................................198
  Fourth Generation.................................200
Family Charts
  Smith...203
  Johnson...210
  Sauls...211
  Broughton...214
  Stancil...215
  Bagwell...217
  Baucom..220
  Poole...222
Bibliography..224
Index...227

Richard Arrow Smith

Researching this Smith family back to its progenitor led to some surprises. Crama S. Graham and I noticed that most of our known Smith relatives had the same middle initial--the letter A--even prior to the early 19th century when middle names were not used. In addition, both males and females used the same initial before their surnames.

Then the marriage bond for William A. Smith, dated 1794, showed his full name to be William Arrow Smith. This led to the discovery of Richard Arrow Smith who left a will dated 1819 in Wake County. Richard signed his name "Richard Ar. Smith" and named his executor as Samuel Ar. Smith, witnessed by Calvin Ar. Smith. William and Samuel turned out to be brothers, and Calvin the son of Samuel. It is clear that Ar. stands for Arrow, and that it is not a middle name but rather a part of the surname.

While working on another Smith family, I happened upon a Revolutionary War pension application of "James A. Smith (alias James Arrowsmith" of Fauquier County, Virginia. Further investigation indicated this James was a descendant of the Westmoreland County family of Arrowsmiths. Richard Arrow Smith may be a descendant of the same Virginia family.

Thus, I came to the conclusion that our first known Smith ancestor was actually descended from

Descendants of Richard Arrow Smith

an Arrowsmith family. The prefix, Arrow, was first separated from the name Smith, then abbreviated Ar., then shortened to A., then dropped altogether in the mid-1800s.

Richard's ancestors have not been ascertained, but a dissertation on the known Arrowsmith families of early colonial America is included in this book. It is hoped additional information will surface in the future to assist in new discoveries.

                        Rebecca L. Blackwell

Descendants of Richard Arrow Smith

Arrowsmith Families of the Southern United States

The name "Arrowsmith" comes from the Old English and literally means a maker of iron arrowheads. In England the name is most common in the North and in the Midlands. It is still a rather unusual name in the United States, only a handful of known families making the voyage to the new land. I have concentrated on two Arrowsmith families that seem the most likely progenitors of our Richard Arrow Smith.

Samuel Arrowsmith immigrated to Maryland from England about 1740, dying there in 1742. His wife was Elizabeth Fishpaw. Their only known offspring was son Samuel, born near Baltimore, Maryland in 1742 and died in Ross County, Ohio, 1826. He married Mary Millard who died in Mason County, Kentucky in 1794. They were the parents of Ezekiel, Hannah, John, Mary, Elizabeth, Ann, Katherine, and Samuel Arrowsmith. Samuel and Elizabeth appear to be the right age to be parents of our Richard Arrow Smith, but due to Samuel's early death, the possibility seems remote.

Thomas Arrowsmith immigrated from Bristol, England, to Virginia between 1663 and 1670. Thomas Arrowsmith of Cople Parish appears frequently in Westmoreland County, Virginia, records beginning about 1691. His wife's name was Grace, surname unknown. He may have been the father of Richard Arrowsmith of Upper Machotick in Westmoreland County who married the widow of John Holland, Mary, before 1 November 1677. Richard died about 1688, leaving at least one son, William, born in 1687. Mary married secondly Thomas Russell. William was then "bound out" to John Moon at the age of three in January 1690/91. Richard's estate was settled in 1695 when Thomas Russell made a bond of 20,000 pounds

Descendants of Richard Arrow Smith

of tobacco to the "orphans" of Richard Arrowsmith. No further records have been found for William Arrowsmith as well as no sure evidence of siblings.

However, on 13 May 1718 a Richard Arrow Smith was a witness to the will of Joseph Smith of Westmoreland County. He may be another son of Richard Arrowsmith or Thomas Arrowsmith, above. This Richard Arrowsmith died in Westmoreland County in 1752. In his will he mentioned wife Elizabeth, son Thomas, grandchildren William Arrowsmith and Elizabeth Arrowsmith, William Bittey and Mary Bittey. Apparently, Richard also had a daughter who married a Mr. Bittey.

A Thomas Arrowsmith appears in the Stafford County Tax Lists of 1783. He is shown with two white males over sixteen years of age. In 1785 Thomas has only one white male over sixteen and a Richard Arrowsmith is living nearby, a single man. Another list, the same year, shows Thomas has eight persons in the household, Richard has only himself. It appears that Richard is the eldest son of Thomas. In 1786 a James Arrowsmith appears, also a single man under age 21. Richard is no longer listed. Thomas and James also appear in the 1787, 1789 and 1790 tax lists. James appears to be another son of Thomas. Richard's disappearance is intriguing, but the date is too late for him to be our Richard Arrow Smith.

A William Arrowsmith appears in the Fauquier County tax list, 1787, living in the home of George Easum. There are many references to a Thomas A. Smith in Stafford County, 1790s. There are no Arrowsmiths listed in the 1800 census, but in 1810 James Arrowsmith appears in Fauquier. This is the James A. Smith who is listed in his Revolutionary War pension application as "alias James Arrowsmith." He served in the 3rd Virginia Regiment, Continental

Descendants of Richard Arrow Smith

Line. His descendants are named in the pension record, and son Charles was living in Fauquier in 1830. Also, a William Arrowsmith served in the 8th Virginia Regiment, Continental Line, as a Drummer and Fife. He married Susanna McBee in Fauquier County, September 14, 1789.

No Arrowsmith or A. Smith families have been found in early North Carolina prior to Richard's appearance. It would seem he probably traveled south from either Virginia or Maryland. The evidence seems to lean toward Virginia.

Thus, we have several interesting possibilities, but no definite connection between the Arrowsmith families of the south and our Richard Arrow Smith. Due to the destruction of county records over the years we may never know the names of his parents.

R.L.B.

Contributors

The following contributors are hereby acknowledged and sent sincere gratitude:

Elaine Boyette
Wilson's Mills, North Carolina

Christine Bagwell Costine
Raleigh, North Carolina

Linda Smith Creech
Zebulon, North Carolina

Albert Earle Garrett, Sr.
Danville, Virginia

E. Vernon Smith
Troy, Virginia

Clyde S. Stallings
Frederick, Maryland

Descendants of Richard Arrow Smith

First Generation

1   Richard ARROW SMITH, born about 1745; died after 13 January 1819 at Wake County, North Carolina.

Our Richard Smith first appears in the Court Minutes of Cumberland County, North Carolina. On May 18, 1763 he was among grand jury members fined for not appearing in court, along with a Sterling Carroll. August 16 of the same year William Pace deeded land to Richard, proven by John Bettis.

The first record concerning our Richard Smith in Johnston was a notation in the Johnston County Court Minutes in April, 1767: "Ordered that Richard Smith's mark be recorded which is Crop & Slit in the right ear & Nick under the left." At this date, Richard was still a single man and probably in his early twenties.

No marriage bond has been found, but we know that Richard married Esther Johnson between 1769 and 1772 when their first child was born. (Richard Johnson, Esther's father, mentioned her as Esther Johnson in his will, dated 1769.) Richard A. Smith is mentioned in the will of mother-in-law, Phereby Johnson Sauls, as the husband of her daughter Esther (Phereby married neighbor Abner Sauls after Richard's death).

December 3, 1773 John Smith of Bladen County, Planter, deeded 100 acres of land in Johnston County to Richard Smith of Cumberland County. This land was on the south side of Black Creek bordering Joseph Johnston (Deed Bk H, p. 109). Five years later, in August of 1778, Richard Smith of Cumberland County deeded this same 100

Descendants of Richard Arrow Smith

acres to Rubin Johnson, his wife's relation. Richard signed his name "Richard A. Smith." (Deed Bk I, p. 109).

Several land entries in Cumberland County refer to our Richard Smith. Feb. 2, 1778 he entered 100 acres on Neills Creek bordering "..land where he lives." Neills Creek was in the northern corner of the county near the border with Wake County. On April 27 of the same year Francis Smith of Cumberland County deeded land to Richard Smith, proved by William Rand (Minutes of the Court of Pleas and Quarter Sessions of Cumberland Co.) Francis Smith entered 400 acres on the "..upper prong of Buies Creek" Feb. 5, 1778. Buies Creek is near Neills Creek, miles from the Wake County border. The original deed has not been found as many Cumberland County records have not survived. The relationship between Francis Smith and Richard Smith has not been determined, if indeed there was a relationship. Samuel Hart deeded land to Richard Smith on July 27, 1778. Hart's land was also on Neills Creek. August 8 and 11, 1778, Richard entered an additional 210 acres on the south side of Neills (Nulls) Creek, bordering Simon Johnston and Benjamin Wamock. August 21 Richard Smith entered 300 acres on Black River bordering his own land. Black River meanders up from its mouth on the South River bordering Sampson County to where it hugs the borders of Johnston and Wake Counties. December 3, 1778 Theophilius Hunter (of Johnston Co.) entered 320 acres on both sides of Buies Creek "on both sides of path from widow Cutts to Richard Smith's old place." In February of the following year, a Hardy Smith and an Alexander Smith entered land adjoining Richard Smith and "Up the river." Richard entered another 100 acres on the waters of Buies Creek on the same date, bordering Simon Johnston and Samuel Hart. This is the last entry made by Richard Smith in Cumberland County. It is believed that this is our Richard due to the reference wherein

Descendants of Richard Arrow Smith

Richard A. Smith, of Cumberland Co., deeded land to Rubin Johnson. The other Smiths mentioned are accounted for as members of the family who founded Smithfield, the county seat of Johnston County, with the exception of Francis and Hardy. Their possible connection to Richard will continue to be researched.

An interesting notation occurs on May 28, 1783 when Caleb Penny, planter, purchased 106 acres of land in Johnston County. This land on Bushey Branch adjoined the property of said Caleb Penny, Richard Aperson, Ephraim Ferrell, Abner Sauls and Richard Arrow Smith. This is one of several records wherein Richard gave his name as "Arrow Smith" (Bk N, No. 1, p. 106).

Richard A. Smith appears in the 1790 census of North Carolina in Wake Co. with four sons and four daughters, no slaves. In 1794 he participated in the laying of a road beginning "...at the Johnston County line at or near the lands whereon Richard A. Smith now lives so as to cross the road leading from Smithfield to Col. Hunter's at or neary Henry Hubbard's road that leads out of the same so as to go into the said Hubbard's road." Later that year, he was involved in the laying of another road "...from the line of Johnston County on or near the lands of Richard A. Smith to Aaron Sugg's, Esq." The following year he received a deed from John McCullers, proven by Samuel (A.) Smith. In 1796 another road was laid between "White Oak Creek and Marlow's Creek and from the Newburn Road leading from Raleigh down by Aaron Sugg's to the Johnston's line near to Richard A. Smith." Also, in 1797, he was a member of the Jury involved in re-routing the "...road that leads from the City of Raleigh to Fayetteville, and if they think proper, to turn the same so as to cross Swift Creek below the Mouth of Steep Hill Creek so as to make one bridge answer instead of the two which are now kept up." Also on this jury were

Descendants of Richard Arrow Smith

Jonathan Smith and Turner Smith of Johnston County. That same year he was on the Jury in the cases of The State vs. Moses Bledsoe, and Henry Buffalow and Thomas Jinks vs. Roadham Atkins.

In May of 1803, Richard A. Smith deeded land to William A. Smith, proven by John White (husband of Clary), according to the Wake County Court Minutes. In addition, Richard deeded land to son Samuel A. Smith in August of the same year (ibid.). Both original deeds were apparently destroyed in a fire.

[Richard Smith (no relation), owner of the store formerly belonging to William Hill, was also made County Registrar in 1807. For his own convenience, he kept the deed books in his storeroom in order to avoid making the trek to the courthouse one block away. When employee Benjamin F. Seaborn set a fire in the storeroom to cover up his theft in September, 1832, the inventory and half of the deed books were destroyed. Ben was was caught and tried to blame his deed on a black man, to no avail. He was hanged for his crime. This Richard wrote his will in 1816, leaving wife Penelope and daughter Mary Anne. Penelope left her holdings to her nephew, Richard S. Pullen (see Orrin A. Smith deed), known for his benefactions to the city. Mary Ann died in 1861 and left money to the University of North Carolina.]

Richard became the executor of the estate of son-in-law John White in August, 1803, when John's wife, Clary, relinquished her right. Richard returned the inventory of John's estate in November, 1803. Later, in the month of February, 1807, Richard became the guardian of his grand-daughter, Elizabeth White.

Richard wrote his will January 13, 1819, mentioning only his wife, Esther, leaving her to dispose of his estate upon her death. He signed

Descendants of Richard Arrow Smith

his name, "Richard Ar.Smith." The executor was Samuel Ar. Smith, witnesses (grandson) Calvin Ar. Smith, Rigdon Johnson (son of Sill Johnson, nephew of wife Esther), and Elizabeth White (granddaughter).

♥ Richard ARROW SMITH married Esther JOHNSON about 1770 at North Carolina. Esther was born about 1752 at Johnston Co., North Carolina; died after 17 October 1820 at Wake Co., North Carolina.

Esther Johnson is mentioned in the will of her father, Richard Johnson, who died in 1769. She is also mentioned in her mother's (Phereby) will as Esther A. Smith, wife of Richard A. Smith, dated 9 October 1813. No marriage bond exists for Esther Johnson and Richard A. Smith, but as their first child, William, was born in 1772, we can assume they were married between 1769 and 1772.

Esther's will is dated 17 October 1820 in Wake County and probated in November of 1821. She mentions daughters February Etheridge, Elizabeth Slaughter, Clary White, and Winny Powell, as well as granddaughter Elizabeth White. She also mentions sons Samuel A. Smith (Executor), David Smith and Aaron Smith. Witnesses were Reynold Johnson and Becky Hill (granddaughter).

Descendants of Richard Arrow Smith

They had the following children:

```
+ 2   i     William ARROW SMITH.
+ 3   ii    Samuel A. SMITH.
+ 4   iii   John A. SMITH.
+ 5   iv    Richard A. SMITH Jr..
+ 6   v     Clary A. SMITH.
  7   vi    David A. SMITH, born about 1784 at
```
Wake Co., North Carolina; died before 1830 at Wake Co., North Carolina.

David A. Smith appears in the 1820 Tax List for St. Mary's District, Wake Co. However, he does not appear in the 1830 census; his wife, Theny, is living with three sons and two daughters. We can assume the younger four were David's offspring.

♥ David A. SMITH married Parthena "Theney" ROGERS on 17 August 1809 at Wake Co., North Carolina. Theney was born about 1790 at Wake Co., North Carolina.

Theney Rogers was charged with having an illegitimate child, born shortly before 19 February 1808, fathered by Hutson Yearby (*Wake Co. Bastardy Bonds*). Bondsmen were Samuel A. Smith (brother of David A. Smith) and Alexander Penny. Theney married David A. Smith in April of the following year. Hutson Yearby married Elizabeth Penny on 13 August 1816 at Johnston County. Was she a daughter or niece of Alexander Penny?

```
        8   vii   February A. SMITH, born about 1785
```
at Wake Co., North Carolina.

♥ February A. SMITH married William ETHERIDGE on 10 February 1807 at Wake Co., North Carolina. William was born about 1785 at Wake Co., North Carolina.

Descendants of Richard Arrow Smith

      9   viii Winny A. Smith, born about 1786 at Wake Co., North Carolina.

Winny is referred to as "Winny Powell" in her mother's will, 1820.

♥ Winny married Mr. POWELL before 1820 at Wake Co., North Carolina.

+ 10 ix   Elizabeth A. Smith

    11 x   Aaron A. Smith, born about 1797 at Wake Co., North Carolina. Aaron was living in Johnston County in 1820.

♥ Aaron A. SMITH married Gilly ELLIS on 4 June 1818 at Wake Co., North Carolina. She was born about 1800 at Wake Co., North Carolina.

Descendants of Richard Arrow Smith

Second Generation

2 William ARROW SMITH, born in 1772 at Wake Co., North Carolina; died before February 1833 at St. Mary's Township, Wake Co., North Carolina; buried at Wake Co., North Carolina.

William's marriage bond lists his name as "William Arrow Smith," 2 August 1794 in Wake County. His wife's name was Fereby (Phereby) Ferrell. The bondsman was Robert Johnston.

The exact children of William and Phereby may never been determined due to a lack of records. William mentioned only his youngest child, William Jr., in his will. Phereby did the same in her will. Son Benjamin was named in a deed from William that survived the fire of 1832. Therefore, all the other children who are listed here are not proven but are believed to be his offspring. In addition, there are other A.Smiths in the neighborhood who may be descended from William or his brothers John, David or Aaron who have not been successfully traced. These would include Kimbrough A. Smith, Wesley A. Smith and Ransom A. Smith.

William A. Smith was deeded land from Thomas Busbee, May Session, 1803, Wake County Court. The witness was John White, his brother-in-law (*Wake County Court Minutes*). The original deed has not been found and was probably destroyed.

Richard A. Smith deeded land to William A. Smith, May Session, 1803, Wake County Court. The witness again was John White. This Richard is assumed to be the father of William A. Smith, though the original deed has not been found. It was destroyed in the fire in Smith's storeroom in 1832 (see notes for Richard Arrow Smith).

8

Descendants of Richard Arrow Smith

December 15, 1807, William A. Smith attended the estate sale of Henry Johnson in Johnston County, along with Richard A. Smith and Samuel A. Smith, as well as many other friends and relatives.

The will of William A. Smith was written 6 November 1822. He mentions his "..loving wife Phereby Smith" who received all his land during her lifetime or widowhood and also all his property "of every description after paying my last debts." He mentions son William A. Smith who was to receive all his lands after the death of his mother. Phereby was named Executor and the Witness was Samuel A. Smith, brother of William. The will was proven in Wake County, May Term, 1837.

♥ William ARROW SMITH married Phereby FERRELL on 2 August 1794 at Wake Co., North Carolina, North Carolina. Phereby was born in 1776 at Wake Co., North Carolina; died after 1850 at St. Mary's Township, Raleigh, Wake Co., North Carolina; buried at Wake Co., North Carolina.

Phereby was called "Fereby" in her marriage bond. However, she is called "Phereby" in the will of her husband, William. She was probably the daughter of Richard Arrow Smith's neighbor, Ephraim Ferrell. Ephraim was shown to have three sons and six daughters in the 1790 census of Wake County, but he died intestate and his estate records mention only his son, Merritt, the executor. William A. Smith was the bondsman at the marriage of Ephraim Ferrell, Jr., and Nancy Britt 1806.

They had the following children:

+ 12 i   Edwin A. SMITH.
+ 13 ii   Benjamin A. SMITH.
+ 14 iii   Ephraim A. SMITH.
+ 15 iv   Bryant A. SMITH.

Descendants of Richard Arrow Smith

+ 16 v   Willey A. SMITH, born in 1814 at St. Mary's, Wake Co., North Carolina; died after 1850 at Wake Co., North Carolina.

Willey probably died unmarried. She was living with her mother, Phereby, in the 1850 census of St. Mary's Township, Wake County.

+ 17 vi   William A. SMITH.

3   Samuel A. SMITH, born about 1775 at Wake Co., North Carolina; died before November 1848 at St. Mary's, Wake Co., North Carolina.

Samuel A. Smith was deeded land by his father, Richard A. Smith, in August, 1803 (*Wake County Court Minutes*). The original deed apparently was destroyed in a fire.

Samuel A. Smith attended the estate sale of Henry Johnson in Johnston County, December 15, 1807, along with William A. Smith, Richard A. Smith, and others.

Samuel A. Smith was a bondsman in the matter of a "bastard" child born to Parthena (Theney) Rogers. Samuel and Alexander Penny both put up $50 bond, while the child's father, Hutson Yearby, put up $100, on January 30, 1808. The following year Theney married Samuel's younger brother, David A. Smith.

Reuben Sanders deeded land to Samuel A. Smith, proven by Calvin A. Smith, in 1822 (*Johnston Co. Court Minutes*).

Samuel died intestate shortly before November, 1848, when his widow, Sally A. Smith, filed a petition for support in Wake County.

♥ Samuel A. SMITH married Sarah Ann BAUCOM on 10 August 1798 at Wake Co., North Carolina. Sarah,

Descendants of Richard Arrow Smith

or Sally, was born in 1779 at Wake Co., North Carolina; died after 4 December 1850 at St. Mary's, Wake Co., North Carolina.

Sarah was the daughter of John Baucom of Johnston County (see Baucom Section).

Sarah, age 71, was living with Iano Bagwell, age 17, in the 1850 census of St. Mary's, Wake County. Sarah wrote her will 4 December 1850, mentioning sons Zachariah, Calvin, John, Abner, Richard, Caswell, and daughters Maria, Susan and Gilly.

They had the following children:

+ 18   i   Calvin A. SMITH.
  19 ii   Zachariah A. SMITH, born about 1802 at St. Mary's, Wake Co., North Carolina; died after November 1848.

Zachariah A. Smith was mentioned in the petition of his mother, Sally A. Smith for support following the death of her husband, Samuel, November, 1848. She states that son Zachariah is a "non-resident" of North Carolina.

♥ Zachariah A. SMITH married Elizabeth WALTERS on 13 May 1824 at Wake, North Carolina. She was born about 1800 at Wake Co., North Carolina.

  20 iii   Gilly A. SMITH, born about 1803 at St. Mary's, Wake Co., North Carolina.

♥ Gilly A. SMITH married Willie DODD at Wake Co., North Carolina. Willie was born about 1800 at Wake Co., North Carolina.

  21 iv   Susan A. SMITH, born about 1804 at St. Mary's, Wake Co., North Carolina.

♥ Susan A. SMITH married John W. ADAMS on 8 January 1838 at Wake Co., North Carolina.

Descendants of Richard Arrow Smith

+ 22 v Clement A. SMITH.
23 vi John A. SMITH, born about 1807 at St. Mary's, Wake Co., North Carolina; died after November 1848.

John A. Smith is mentioned in the petition of his mother, Sally A. Smith, for support following the death of her husband, Samuel, intestate, in November, 1848. She states that her son, John, is a "non-resident" of North Carolina.

+ 24 vii Abner A. SMITH.
25 viii Richard A. SMITH, born about 1810 at St. Mary's, Wake Co., North Carolina.
26 ix Sally Maria SMITH.
+ 27 x Caswell A. SMITH.

4   John A. SMITH, born about 1777 at St. Mary's, Wake Co., North Carolina.

John A. Smith was deeded land by his father, Richard A. Smith, 5 December 1816. This land was on Bushy Branch in Wake County, North Carolina.

♥ John A. SMITH married Elizabeth "Betsy" RIVERS on 18 February 1804 at Wake Co., North Carolina. The bondsman was Reddin Johnson.

They had the following children:

+ 28 i Eliza A. SMITH.

5   Richard A. SMITH Jr., born about 1779 at Wake Co., North Carolina; died before February, 1833 at Wake Co., North Carolina.

Richard was deeded land by his father, Richard A. Smith, Sr., December 5, 1816. This land was on Bushy Branch in Wake County, North Carolina (*Wake County Court Minutes*). The original deed was probably destroyed by fire.

Descendants of Richard Arrow Smith

Johnson Busbee deeded land in Wake County to Richard A. Smith on August 19, 1822. This land bordered the properties of Willis Holland, Isaac Hutchins, J. Busbee, Christopher Babb, and Jacob Ferrell and contained over 100 acres (Bk. 5, p. 476). Johnson Busbee sold him another 104 acres on the same date. This plot of land on White Oak Creek adjoined Jacob Ferrell, Christopher Babb, and William Ivey (Bk. 5, p. 489).

Richard A. Smith died intestate prior to February, 1833 when his estate was settled. He left a wife, Elizabeth A. Smith, and children Burchett, Esther, Oswell, Julia, Mary Ann, Simeon and Catherine. Estate records list children Mary Ann, Simeon and Catherine as minors whose guardian was Seth Jinks. Burchett is listed as the wife of Kinderick Johnson, Esther as married to Ben Herndon, and Julia as the wife of Anderson Yates.

♥ Richard A. SMITH Jr. married Elizabeth WREN on 21 March 1805 at Wake Co., North Carolina. Elizabeth was born about 1780; died after 1833 at Wake Co., North Carolina.

They had the following children:

  29 i Burchett SMITH, born about 1803 at Wake Co., North Carolina.

♥ Burchett SMITH married Kindred JOHNSON on 26 July 1824 at Wake Co., North Carolina.

  30 ii Esther SMITH, born about 1807 at Wake Co., North Carolina.

♥ Esther SMITH married Benjamin HERNDON before 1823 at North Carolina.

 + 31 iii Oswell A. SMITH.

Descendants of Richard Arrow Smith

      32 iv   Julia SMITH, born about 1809 at Wake Co., North Carolina.

♥ Julia SMITH married William Anderson YATES on 17 January 1831 at Wake Co., North Carolina. He was born about 1809 at North Carolina.

      33 v   Mary Ann SMITH, born about 1811 at Wake Co., North Carolina.

♥ Mary Ann SMITH married Gabriel BEASLEY on 14 July 1835 at Wake Co., North Carolina. Gabriel was born about 1805 at Wake Co., North Carolina.

      34 vi   Simeon A. SMITH, born about 1812 at Wake Co., North Carolina.

Simeon Smith enlisted in Co.D, 31st Reg. NC Troops, 4 April 1863. Captured at Fort Harrison, Virginia, 30 September 1864. Confined at Point Lookout, Maryland, 5 October 1864. Paroled at Point Lookout and transferred to Boulware's Wharf, James River, Virginia, where he was received 19 March 1865 for exchange. Paroled again at Raleigh 12 May 1865.

♥ Simeon A. SMITH married Maggie WOODS on 30 November 1865 at Wake Co., North Carolina. Maggie was born about 1815 at Wake Co., North Carolina.

      35 vii   Catherine A. SMITH, born about 1814 at Wake Co., North Carolina.

6   Clary A. SMITH, born about 1781 at Wake Co., North Carolina; died before November 1803 at Wake Co., North Carolina.

♥ Clary A. SMITH married John WHITE before 1800 at Wake Co., North Carolina. John was born about 1780; died before August 1802 at Wake Co., North Carolina.

Descendants of Richard Arrow Smith

Richard A. Smith took over as executor of John White after his wife (Richard's daughter) Clary relinquished her right. Richard was also appointed guardian of his granddaughter, Elizabeth White, February, 1807.

They had the following children:

36 i Elizabeth WHITE, born about 1800 at Wake Co., North Carolina.

10 Elizabeth A. SMITH, born about 1790 at Wake Co., North Carolina.

Elizabeth is referred to as "Elizabeth Slaughter" in her mother's will, dated 1820.

♥ Elizabeth A. SMITH married Mr. HILL about 1805 at North Carolina. He was born about 1785 at North Carolina; died before 1817 at Wake Co., North Carolina.

They had the following children:

37 i Rebecca HILL, born about 1806 at Wake Co., North Carolina.

Rebecca Hill was a witness to her grandmother's will (Esther Johnson Smith).

♥ Rebecca HILL married Bennett GOUCH on 16 February 1828 in Wake Co., North Carolina. The bondsman was Hutson Yearby (see notes for Samuel A. Smith #3).

Bennett Simon Gooch was the son of Pomfret Gooch who wrote his will on 28 February 1816 at Wake Co., North Carolina. He mentioned wife Patsy, son Bennett Simon, daughters Matilda, Betsy, Aley and Rachel. The will was probated in August of 1820 (Record Bk 16).

Descendants of Richard Arrow Smith

♥ Elizabeth A. SMITH married Samuel SLAUGHTER on 3 March 1817 at Wake Co., North Carolina. Samuel was born about 1790.

Descendants of Richard Arrow Smith

Third Generation

12   Edwin A. SMITH, born in 1797 at St. Mary's, Wake Co., North Carolina; died after 16 March 1866 at St. Mary's, Wake Co., North Carolina; buried at Wake Co., North Carolina.

Edwin is believed to be a son of William as his birthdate of 1797 is three years after the marriage of William and Phereby. No other A.Smith couple married prior to 1797, with the exception of Richard and Esther. In addition, the children of William's brothers, Samuel and Richard, were named in their wills and/or estate records and Edwin was not among them. Finally, Edwin is shown living among the other A.Smith families in St. Mary's Township in every tax or census record from 1820 onward.

Edwin A. Smith, age 30-40, was living next door to Samuel A. Smith, age 50-60, 1830 census. Living on the opposite side of Samuel, in order, were Zachariah A. Smith, age 20-30, Benjamin A. Smith, age 20-30, John Smith, age 40-50, Liddy Smith, female, age 40-50, and Kimbrough (Kimbreal) A. Smith, age 20-30.

Johnson Busbee deeded 125 acres to Edwin A. Smith on January 1, 1823. This land in Wake County bordered the properties of Richard A. Smith and Isaac Hutchins (Deed Bk. 5, p. 563). On October 8th of the same year Edwin purchased 87-1/2 acres from Samuel Slaughter, husband of his Aunt Elizabeth. That land, also in Wake County, bordered William Whitfield and William Polk (Bk. 5, p. 28).

John Lewis sold 35 acres to Edwin A. Smith on November 12, 1833. This land adjoined the properties of William Beasley on the waters of Beasley's Branch in Wake County (Bk. 11, p. 283).

Descendants of Richard Arrow Smith

On January 7, 1839, Edwin purchased 109 acres from John Griffis of Wake County. This land on Swift Creek bordered the farms of Calvin A. Smith, Elizabeth Griffis, John Lewis, Kimbrough A. Smith and Edwin's own property (Bk. 11, p.286).

Edwin deeded 82 acres in Wake County to Orrin A. Smith on December 9, 1847 "...for and in consideration of the natural love and affection which I have unto the said Orrin Smith (my son)..." This land bordered the farms of Calvin A. Smith, John Griffis, Marshall Beasley, and Allen Sturdivant (Bk. 29, p. 196).

Abner A. Smith, son of Samuel A. Smith, sold 45 acres to his cousin, Edwin, September 24, 1856. This land adjoined Edwin's own property (Bk. 29, p. 189).

Nathaniel G. Rand sold 135 acres to Edwin A. Smith on December 31, 1835. This land in Wake County adjoined Beasley's Branch, James Mitchener's corner, John Avera's line and Tabbs Branch (Bk. 29, p. 194).

Edwin A. Smith sold 233 acres to Lucius Smith, his son, May 20, 1862. This land bordered Orrin A. Smith (Edwin's son), Dr. Jones, and the Wilmington Road (Bk.29, p. 8). Lucius sold 49 acres on Bushey Branch, beginning on Daniel Beasley's line, to his father on May 19, 1871 (Bk. 32, p. 288).

The last deed in Wake County involving Edwin A. Smith is one dated January 18, 1873, wherein he sold 49 acres on Bushey Branch to his youngest son, Jefferson. This is the same land he bought from Lucius two years earlier (Bk. 35, p. 209).

A map of Wake County, dated 1870, by Fendol Bevers places E.Smith's property in St. Mary's Township (Auburn) just off Smithfield/Aversboro

Descendants of Richard Arrow Smith

Road leading eastward from New Bethel Church (where his son Rufus is buried). This would be the current state route 30 from Garner.

Edwin A. Smith's will, dated March 16, 1866 in Wake County, mentions his "beloved wife" (not named) who received "..the land I now reside on and afterwards (her death) I bequeath it to my son Jefferson Smith and all the stock...and at his death or marriage all the stock be sold and after paying for debts of the estate the remainder is to be divided between all my children except Nancy Smith and her part is to be given to her daughter Ellen Smith. I also bequeath Ellen Smith one bed and furniture." The witnesses were W.A. Busbee and Orrin Smith. The will was proven March 27, 1873.

♥ Edwin A. SMITH married Elizabeth TAYLOR on 3 September 1818 at Wake Co., North Carolina. She was born in 1796 at North Carolina; died before 1828 at St. Mary's, Wake Co., North Carolina; buried in Wake Co., North Carolina. The bondsman at the marriage was Richard A. Smith, either his uncle or his cousin (son of Samuel).

They had the following children:

+ 38 i   Orrin A. SMITH.
+ 39 ii   Larkin A. SMITH.

♥ Edwin A. SMITH married Eliza A. SMITH on 12 September 1828 at Wake, North Carolina. Eliza was born about 1804 at North Carolina; died about 24 December 1877 at Wake Co., North Carolina.

The *Raleigh Register* mentions the marriage of Edwin A. Smith to Eliza A. Smith, 25 September 1828. It refers to Edwin A. Smith as being "...of Johnston County". The bondsman at their marriage was Allen Jones.

Descendants of Richard Arrow Smith

Eliza A. Smith's obituary appeared in *The Biblical Recorder*, 26 December 1877. She was reported to be a member of Mt. Moriah Baptist Church (Auburn, NC), but she was apparently not buried there as no marker was found by this researcher.

They had the following children:

  40 iii Nancy Smith, born about 1830 at St. Mary's, Wake Co., North Carolina.

  Nancy apparently had a daughter out of wedlock named Ellen. Nancy received nothing in her father's will, but he bequeathed Ellen a bed and furniture and Nancy's share of his estate.

  41 iv Mary A. SMITH, born in 1832 at St. Mary's, Wake Co., North Carolina.
  + 42 v Rufus A. SMITH.
  + 43 vi Lucius A. SMITH.
  + 44 vii Edwin Jefferson SMITH.

13 Benjamin A. SMITH, born about 1800 at Wake Co., North Carolina; died at Johnston Co., North Carolina.

  Benjamin A. Smith was deeded land from William A. Smith, 14 January 1823: "...for and in consideration of the natural love, goodwill and affection which he has and doth bare to the said Benjamin A. Smith his son and for $40, "Northside of Swift Creek, Spanish oak at William Whitfield's corner, Beasley's corner and line, 50 acres, more or less. Witnesses: Calvin Jones, Jurat, and Samuel A. Smith (Wake Co. Deed Bk 5, p. 648).

 ♥ Benjamin A. SMITH married Susannah Ann BEASLEY on 29 January 1825 at Wake Co., North Carolina. She was born about 1800 at Wake Co., North Carolina. The bondsman was Daniel Beasley.

Descendants of Richard Arrow Smith

They had the following children:

  45 i Alfred SMITH, born in 1831 at Johnston Co., North Carolina.
  46 ii Catherine SMITH, born in 1832 at Johnston Co., North Carolina.
  47 iii Sophia SMITH, born in 1835 at Johnston Co., North Carolina.
  48 iv William SMITH, born in 1837 at Johnston Co., North Carolina.
 + 49 v Simeon Marion SMITH.

♥ Benjamin A. SMITH married Karen GOWER on 10 June 1847 at Johnston Co., North Carolina. Karen was born about 1808 at either Wake or Johnston County, North Carolina.

They had the following children:

 + 50 vi James Haywood SMITH.
  51 vii Ridley SMITH, born in 1848 at Johnston Co., North Carolina.
 + 52 viii Daniel Ruffin SMITH.

14 Ephraim A. SMITH, born about 1803 at Wake Co., North Carolina; died before November 1854 at Wake or Johnston Co., North Carolina.

Ephraim was 47 years old in the 1850 census of Johnston County, North Carolina. He was living 5 houses from Bryan(t) Smith and 8 houses from Benjamin A. Smith.

Ephraim's will, dated 7 February 1854 and probated in November of the same year, Johnston County, mentions wife Elizabeth who received all land and other property during her lifetime. At her death, to youngest son Levi. Levi also received 50 acres of land including the house. The remainder of the lands went to "two other sons and five daughters: Matthew Smith, William

Descendants of Richard Arrow Smith

Smith, Tranquella Smith, Phereby Smith, Perillia Smith, and Fanny Smith." The executor was Henry Blalock. No witnesses were named. (*Johnston County Will Abstracts, 1746-1870*, Elizabeth E. Ross).

He is tenatively included as a son of William A. Smith due to the fact of his close proximity to William's son, Benjamin A. Smith, his naming children William and Phereby, and the fact that his son Levi was married by William's descendant, J.E. Smith. This connection will be researched further.

♥ Ephraim A. SMITH married Elizabeth COLLINS on 28 June 1828 at Wake Co., North Carolina. She was born about 1804 at North Carolina; died after 1850 at Johnston Co., North Carolina. The bondsman was Uriah D. Collins.

They had the following children:

    53 i   Marcelia SMITH, born about 1830 at Johnston Co., North Carolina.
    54 ii   Matthew SMITH, born about 1833 at Johnston Co., North Carolina.
    55 iii   Tranquilla SMITH, born about 1835 at Johnston Co., North Carolina.
    56 iv   William SMITH, born about 1837 at Johnston Co., North Carolina.
    57 v   Phereby SMITH, born about 1839 at Johnston Co., North Carolina.
    58 vi   Perrilla SMITH, born about 1841 at Johnston Co., North Carolina.
    59 vii   Levi SMITH, born about 1843 at Johnston Co., North Carolina.

♥ Levi SMITH married C. KING on 1 December 1889 at Johnston Co., North Carolina. She was born about 1860 at North Carolina. They were married by Joseph Edwin Smith, Minister of the Gospel (son of Orrin A. Smith), at L.P. King's home.

Descendants of Richard Arrow Smith

C. King was said to be the daughter of O.B. Johnson (*Johnston County Marriages, Vol. II*, Elizabeth E. Ross).

      60 viii Fanny SMITH, born about 1845 at Johnston Co., North Carolina.

15   Bryant A. SMITH, born about 1804 at Wake Co., North Carolina; died after 1850 at Johnston Co., North Carolina.

The bondsman at the marriage of Bryant and Matilda was Clem A. Smith, son of Samuel A. Smith and Sarah Baucom.

Bryant Smith was 46 years of age in the 1850 census of Johnston County, North Carolina. He lived three houses from Benjamin A. Smith, son of William A. Smith brother of Samuel A. Smith).

Bryant is tentatively included as a son of William A. Smith due to his close proximity to Benjamin A. Smith, his eldest son being named William, and his wife being a Collins, possible sister of Elizabeth Collins who married Ephraim Smith. This connection will continue to be researched for verification.

In the 1880 census of Johnston County, B.A. Smith, father-in-law, was living in the household of his daughter, Tempy, and her husband Joseph Ogburn. Bryant was said to be 74 years old (76?) and "paralyzed." Bryant probably suffered a stroke(s), as did most other Smith males.

♥ Bryant A. SMITH married Matilda COLLINS on 1 January 1831 at Wake Co., North Carolina. Matilda was born about 1803 at North Carolina; died after 1850 at Johnston Co., North Carolina.

They had the following children:

Descendants of Richard Arrow Smith

      61 i   Luenza SMITH, born about 1834 at Johnston Co., North Carolina.

♥ Louinza (sic) SMITH married Ananias JORDAN on 17 October 1866 at Wake Co., North Carolina. The bondsman was J.B. Strain. Ananais Jordan was born in 1837.

Ananais Jordan was living in the home of Daniel Beasley in the 1850 census of St. Mary's Township, Wake County. Ananais was said to be a Mulatto.

   + 62 ii   Tempy SMITH.
     63 iii   William SMITH, born about 1840 at Johnston Co., North Carolina, according to the 1850 census.
     64 iv   James A. SMITH, born about 1842 at Johnston Co., North Carolina, according to the 1850 census.

♥ James A. SMITH married Mary J. WILLIAMS on 28 November 1866 at Wake Co., North Carolina. The bondsman was Daniel Beasley.

17   William A. SMITH, born in 1816 at Wake Co., North Carolina; died after 30 November 1854 at Wake Co., North Carolina.

This may be the William A. Smith who was Justice of the Peace in Johnston County, 1857 and 1864.

On 20 July 1854 William A. Smith Jr. sold land to his cousin, Oswell A. Smith, son of Richard A. Smith, Jr., and gave Fereby Smith, widow of William A. Smith, Sr., a lifetime right to the house and four acres of land. This deed was registered 30 November 1854 in Wake County. The 104 acres were described as follows: "..lying in the County of Wake and State of North Carolina, bounded as follows--beginning at a Maple on

Descendants of Richard Arrow Smith

Willie Broughton's, Spring Branch to James Stallings' lines running West to the second branch to a Maple, thence down said branch to Thomas Loring's corner, thence West to Loring's corner again. Thence nearly North to a pine bush in Sarah Rogers' line thence East to a Post Oak, thence East 105 poles to Stake Pointers Willie Broughton's Spring Branch, thence down and back to the beginning, enclosing one hundred four acres around the house now occupied by Fereby Smith, a dower her lifetime to him to hold.."

On 26 July 1842, William Jr. and his mother, Phereby, sold 172 acres on Bushy Branch left in the estate of William A. Smith, Sr., to John H. Jones. His relationship to the family, if any, is unknown at this time.

♥ William A. SMITH married Candis ELLIS on 22 November 1843 at Wake Co., North Carolina. Candis was born in 1824 at Wake Co., North Carolina.

They had the following children:

      65 i   Elizabeth SMITH, born in 1846 at St. Mary's, Wake Co., North Carolina.
+ 66 ii   Elender SMITH.
      67 iii   Delia SMITH, born in 1850 at St. Mary's, Wake Co., North Carolina.
+ 68 iv   William McRae SMITH.
      69 v   Hercelia SMITH, born in 1855 at Johnston Co., North Carolina.
      70 vi   Jesse A. SMITH, born in 1859 at Johnston Co., North Carolina.

♥ Jesse A. SMITH married Mollie L. PLEASANTS on 9 November 1877 at Johnston Co., North Carolina. Mollie was born about 1860 at North Carolina.

♥ Jesse A. SMITH married Lottie A. BRANHAM on 29 October 1879 at Johnston Co., North Carolina. She was born about 1855 at Johnston Co., North Carolina.

Descendants of Richard Arrow Smith

+ 71   vii   Sylvester A. SMITH.

18   Calvin A. SMITH, born about 1799 at St. Mary's, Wake Co., North Carolina; died before Febuary 1862 at St. Mary's, Wake Co., North Carolina.

Calvin Ar. Smith was a witness to his grandfather's will, 1819.

After Calvin died, his widow and children petitioned the court in February, 1862, to divide the slaves owned by Calvin among his heirs. Those slaves were Charles, Lizzy, Mitty, Harly, Hannah, Salisbury, Mary, Patsey, Amanda, and James. William R. Poole, Needham Bryant, and William Fort were appointed commissioners to divide the slaves.

♥ Calvin A. SMITH married Dolly CARROLL on 17 March 1820 at Johnston Co., North Carolina. Dolly was born about 1809 at Johnston Co., North Carolina; died after 1865 at St. Mary's, Wake Co., North Carolina. The bondsman at the marriage of Dolly and Calvin was Levi Ferrell of Wake County.

Dolly was 41 in the 1850 census of St. Mary's Township in Wake County, North Carolina. She was the daughter of John Carroll of Johnston County.

They had the following children:

72   i   John A. SMITH, born in 1825 at St. Mary's, Wake Co., North Carolina.

This may be the John A. Smith who was a Justice of the Peace in Johnston County, 1856.

+ 73   ii   James A. SMITH.

Descendants of Richard Arrow Smith

   74 iii Alexander A. SMITH, born in 1829 at St. Mary's, Wake Co., North Carolina; died in 1874.
   75 iv Samuel A. SMITH, born in 1839 at St. Mary's, Wake Co., North Carolina.
   76 v Richard A. SMITH, born in 1842 at St. Mary's, Wake Co., North Carolina; died on 23 March 1863 at Savannah, Chatham Co., Georgia.

  Richard A. Smith enlisted at age 20 in Co.D, 31st Regiment NC Troops as a Private. Present or accounted for until captured at Roanoke Island on 8 February 1862. Paroled at Elizabeth City on 21 February 1862. Returned to duty about 15 September 1862. Promoted to Corporal prior to 1 March 1863. Promoted to Sargeant in March 1863. Died in the hospital in Savannah, Georgia, 23 March 1863, of "typhoid fever".

  + 77 vi Esther A. SMITH.

22 Clement A. SMITH, born about 1808 at St. Mary's, Wake Co., North Carolina; died before November 1848 at St. Mary's, Wake Co., North Carolina.

  Ridley Smith is listed as the head of household in St. Mary's Township, Wake County, in the 1850 census taken beginning 15 July. Also in the home were Darius, age 16, and Eugene, age six.

  Clement is mentioned in the petition of Sally A. Smith, widow, for support after her husband, Samuel A., died intestate. Clement is mentioned as deceased, leaving a son, Dorris (Darius) Smith, and daughter, Lucetta, wife of Perrin Price.

  ♥ Clement A. SMITH married Ridley SMITH on 22 January 1831 at Wake Co., North Carolina. Ridley was born in 1810 at Wake Co., North Carolina;

Descendants of Richard Arrow Smith

died after 1850 at St. Mary's, Wake Co., North Carolina.

They had the following children:

       78 i   Lucetta A. SMITH, born about 1832 at St. Mary's, Wake Co., North Carolina.

♥ Lucetta A. SMITH married Perrin PRICE on 03 July 1847 at Wake Co., North Carolina. Perrin was born about 1830 at Wake Co., North Carolina.

       79 ii   Darius SMITH, born in 1834 at St. Mary's, Wake Co., North Carolina.

Darius Smith deeded land in Wake County to Rufus Smith on January 9, 1857 (Deed Bk. 21, p. 418).

       80 iii   Eugene SMITH, born in 1844 at St. Mary's, Wake Co., North Carolina.

24   Abner A. SMITH, born in 1809 at St. Mary's, Wake Co., North Carolina; died after 15 February 1866 at St. Mary's, Wake Co., North Carolina.

Abner apparently took his wife to Georgia after their marriage in 1829. All their children from Rufus (b. 1831) to Thomas (b. 1847) were born in Georgia. He had returned between 1847 and 1849 when their youngest child, Texanah, was born in Wake Co. They lived next to Wesley A. Smith and three houses from Ransom A. Smith. He lived next door, in the opposite direction, to Sarah Smith, age 71, his mother.

Sarah A. Smith's petition for support after the death of her husband, Samuel, dated November, 1848, mentions that son Abner is a "non-resident" of North Carolina. He apparently returned to Wake County after his father's death.

Descendants of Richard Arrow Smith

Abner A. Smith deeded land in Wake County to Caleb Penny on June 24, 1856 (Deed Bk. 21, p. 241).

Abner A. Smith deeded ten acres to Rufus W. Smith August 27, 1857. This land on Bushey Branch bordered the properties of Wesley Smith and Abner A. Smith (Deed Bk 25, p. 321).

Abner A. Smith wrote his will February 15, 1866 in Wake County. He mentions wife Willey, sons James and Thomas who were to receive the land after both parents were deceased. The witnesses were W.G. Williams and John A. Smith.

♥ Abner A. SMITH married Willey FERRELL on 17 October 1829 at Wake Co., North Carolina; born on 1812 at Wake Co., North Carolina; died after 1863 at St. Mary's, Wake Co., North Carolina.

They had the following children:

+ 81 i   Rufus W. SMITH.
  82 ii Burt E. SMITH, born in 1834 at Georgia.

Burt was 16 years old in the 1850 census of St. Mary's, Wake Co., North Carolina.

  83 iii Louisa SMITH, born in 1835 at Georgia.

Louisa was 15 years old in the 1850 census of St. Mary's, Wake Co., North Carolina.

  84 iv Sandal SMITH, born in 1838 at Georgia.

Sandal was 12 years old in the 1850 census of St. Mary's, Wake Co., North Carolina.

Descendants of Richard Arrow Smith

      85 v   Samuel A. SMITH, born in 1839 at Georgia; died on 24 March 1863 at Savannah, Chatham Co., North Carolina.

    Samuel A. Smith was residing in St. Mary's, Wake County, when he enlisted in Co. D, 31st NC Troops 18 September 1861. Present or accounted for until captured at Roanoke Island 8 February 1862. Paroled at Elizabeth City 21 February 1862. Returned to duty on or about 15 September 1862. Died on 24 March 1863 of disease. Place of death was not reported, but his cousin, Richard A. Smith of the same company died of typhoid fever on the previous day in Savannah, Georgia. It is thus assumed that Samuel was in the same hospital.

      86 vi   John A. SMITH, born in 1843 at Georgia.

    John was living in St. Mary's Township, Wake Co., North Carolina, in the 1850 census. He was 7 years old.

      87 vii   James A. SMITH, born in 1845 at Georgia.

    James was five years old in the 1850 census of St. Mary's, Wake Co., North Carolina. This is likely the James Smith of Garner whose son, James Smith, aged 17, drowned July 6, 1891, in W. Watt's fish pond in Auburn. He had a brother, two years younger, who survived him (*Death Notices, Raleigh State Chronicle,* Massengill and Tompkins).

      88 viii   Thomas A. SMITH, born in 1847 at Georgia according to the 1850 census of St. Mary's Township, Wake County, North Carolina.

      89 ix   Texanah A. SMITH, born in 1849 at St. Mary's, Wake Co., North Carolina according to the 1850 census.

Descendants of Richard Arrow Smith

26   Sally Maria SMITH, born in 1820 at St. Mary's, Wake Co., North Carolina; died in 1851 at Wake Co., North Carolina.

Sally was known by her middle name which was pronounced, and sometimes written, "Mariah."

Sally M. Pool, wife of Calvin Poole, was 30 years of age in the 1850 census of St. Mary's District, Wake County, North Carolina.

♥ Sally Maria SMITH married Calvin POOLE in 1841 at Wake Co., North Carolina. Calvin was born on 22 April 1822 at St. Mary's, Wake Co., North Carolina; died in 1908 at Garner, Wake Co., North Carolina.

Calvin Poole was 26 years of age in the 1850 census of St. Mary's Township, Wake County, North Carolina.

Calvin Poole, Private, resided in Wake County where he enlisted at age 40, 18 September 1861, in Co. D, 31st NC Troops. Discharged on or about 28 October, 1861 by reason of disability (back injury). He reportedly later served in Captain William D. Crowder's Company, 1st Regiment NC Militia.

Calvin was a member of Mt. Moriah Baptist Church from it's inception in 1832 to his death. He organized Bible study classes at the church and later became a deacon. In 1952 his descendants organized a family reunion at the church to dedicate a stained glass window there in honor of their ancestor. Reportedly, family reunions are still held at the church in May every alternate year (*Wake Co. Heritage*, p. 406-7).

They had the following children:

Descendants of Richard Arrow Smith

       90 i   Emeline POOLE, born about 1843 at Wake Co., North Carolina; died at Wake Co., North Carolina.

Emeline did not survive her infancy.

   + 91 ii   Paschal POOLE.

27   Caswell A. SMITH, born in 1821 at Auburn, Wake Co., North Carolina; died after February 1854 in Wake County.

   Caswell A. Smith sold 46 acres of land to his brother, Abner A. Smith, on 13 December 1853. This land was situated on Bushy Branch beginning "..at a Stake on Caleb Penny's line and running North with said Penny's line to a State in Willie Dodd's line. Thence ..along said Dodd's line across Bushy Branch to a Stake in John Jones' line and thence South along said Jones' line to Stake in John W. Adams's line, thence East along said Adams's line to the beginning."

   Caswell also sold 133 acres lying on Tate's Branch adjoining William A. Smith's corner and Calvin A. Smith's line, to Caswell Sturdivant, 4 August 1853 (Wake Co. Deed Bk. 20, p. 280).

♥ Caswell A. SMITH married Caroline POOLE on 19 September 1843 at Wake Co., North Carolina. Caroline was born in 1821 at Auburn, Wake Co., North Carolina.

   Caroline's mother, Aley Poole, was living with Caswell A. Smith in the 1850 census of St. Mary's Township, Wake County, North Carolina.

   They had the following children:

       92 i   Samuel SMITH, born on 1845 at St. Mary's, Wake Co., North Carolina.

Descendants of Richard Arrow Smith

    92 i   Samuel SMITH, born on 1845 at St. Mary's, Wake Co., North Carolina.
    93 ii   Salley SMITH, born on 1847 at St. Mary's, Wake Co., North Carolina.
    94 iii   William SMITH, born on 1849 at St. Mary's, Wake Co., North Carolina.

28   Eliza A. SMITH.
This individual's information has already been printed (daughter of John A. SMITH).

♥ Eliza A. SMITH married Edwin A. SMITH on 12 September 1828 at Wake, North Carolina.
This individual's information has already been printed (son of William A. SMITH).

31   Oswell A. SMITH, born on 1808 at Wake Co., North Carolina, North Carolina; died October 1886 at Wake Co., North Carolina.

Oswell was often erroneously called "Auswell" in the records.

Oswell A. Smith deeded 54 acres of land to his son, Yancey L. Smith February 13, 1867. This property bordered the lands of W.I. Busbee, James Stallings, and Billy Johnson (Wake County Deed Book 25, p. 179).

Oswell and his daughter-in-law Salina filed a complaint in 1886 against the other heirs of Joseph Broughton, Salina's father, for the rights to land that had been farmed by her husband, Yancey L. Smith, deceased. Yancey was Oswell's son.

Oswell's death notice appeared in the Raleigh State Chronicle, October 7, 1886.

Descendants of Richard Arrow Smith

♥ Oswell A. SMITH married Martha Patsy ROGERS on 19 December 1829 at Wake Co., North Carolina. Patsy was born in 1807 in Wake County and died after 1850.

They had the following children:

+ 95 i   Catherine SMITH.
  96 ii   Lucetta SMITH, born in 1833 at Auburn, Wake Co., North Carolina; died after 1884 at Wake Co., North Carolina.

♥ Lucetta SMITH married Rufus HONEYCUTT at Wake Co., North Carolina. Rufus was born about 1836 in Wake Co., North Carolina.

Rufus Honeycutt, Private, enlisted in Co.D., 31st Regiment of North Carolina Troops in Wake County, 19 September 1861. He was 25 years old. Present or accounted for until captured at Roanoke Island on 8 February 1862. Paroled at Elizabeth City 21 February 1862. Returned to duty on or about 15 September 1862. Deserted 4 December 1863. Returned to duty on 24 February 1864, deserted 13 August 1864.

+ 97   iii Yancy L. SMITH.
+ 98   iv   Marcellus A. SMITH.
  99   v   Kindrick SMITH, born in 1840 at Auburn, Wake Co., North Carolina.
+ 100 vi   Isabel SMITH.
  101 vii Richard A. SMITH, born in 1845 at Auburn, Wake Co., North Carolina.
  102 viii Martha A. SMITH, born in 1849 at Auburn, Wake Co., North Carolina.

Descendants of Richard Arrow Smith

Fourth Generation

38 Orrin A. SMITH, born on 2 September 1823 at St. Mary's, Auburn, Wake Co., North Carolina; died on 31 July 1891 at Raleigh, Wake Co., North Carolina; buried on 2 August 1891 at Auburn, Wake Co., North Carolina.

Orrin was deeded 82 acres of land in Wake County by his father, Edwin A. Smith, 9 December 1847. This land was bordered by the lands of John Griffis, Calvin A. Smith and Marshall Beasley. Orrin was living next door to Ridley Smith in the 1850 census. Ridley, widow of Clem, was two houses away from Caswell A. Smith. Larkin A. Smith, his brother, was two houses away from Caswell.

Orrin bought 75 acres of land adjoining his property from Allen Studivant December 14, 1853 (Wake Co. Deed Book 20, p. 576). This land also bordered the lands of John Griffis and Edwin A. Smith, Orrin's father. This places Orrin's property in the Auburn area about two miles south of Mt. Moriah Church and about one mile east of New Bethel Church in Garner.

Calvin A. Smith deeded 25 acres of land to Orrin October 3, 1857 (Wake Co. Deed Book 29, p. 382). This land bordered Orrin's own land and was therefore part of the same land Calvin owned in 1847 (see above).

Orrin A. Smith deeded 149 acres to John A. Smith April 3, 1861. This land adjoined the properties of Calvin A. Smith, Samuel Bryant and others, beginning on the West side of Wilmington Road. This is the same land mentioned in the previous deeds.

Orrin Smith enlisted in the Confederate Army on Sept. 18, 1861 at the age of 38. Seven other brothers and cousins also enlisted on that date, all in Co. D of the 31st North Carolina Troops. This entire company was captured at Roanoke Island on February 8, 1862. Orrin was paroled at Elizabeth City on or about February 21, 1862. He was discharged on September 15, 1862 after providing a substitute. It has been said that Orrin owned the largest general store in Raleigh (not proven). When he returned from the war, his manager had stolen all of his money. In the 1870 census Orrin is listed as a farmer with $2500 worth of property. By 1872 he was reportedly one of Raleigh's "leading merchants" (see obituary, below), retiring in 1875.

Family history states that Orrin's substitute was killed in the war. Records of the 31st N.C. Regiment indicate several soldiers who enlisted on 15 September 1862, but only one is indicated to have joined as a substitute. This was Daniel Warren, age 16, of Wake County. He was present or accounted for until December, 1864 and was paroled after 26 Apr 1865. It appears from these records that Daniel survived the war. He may or may not have been the correct substitute for Orrin Smith.

Phillip S. Smith, husband of Minerva Broughton and Orrin's brother-in-law, deeded him 55 1/2 acres on the south side of Marsh Creek December 10, 1867 for for the sum of $470. This property bordered the lands of Edward Chappel and Richard Justice (Deed Bk 25, p. 471). Orrin and his wife, Louisa, sold this land to W.H. Dean January 18, 1870 for $375 (Bk 29, p. 485).

William Jones purchased 64 acres from Orrin and Louisa December 13, 1872. These lands bordered James Smith, Henry Turner and Orrin's own land on Bushey Branch (Bk 35, p. 74). The following year Orrin and Louisa sold 300 acres to John S. Johns adjoining David Lewis, Caswell Sturdivant, Lucius Smith, Polly Williams, Jeff

Descendants of Richard Arrow Smith

Smith, Littleton Johnson and a corner of the land deeded to Orrin Smith from his father, Edwin. The deed was recorded December 20, 1873 (Bk 37, p.65). At this time, Orrin and Louisa were living in Raleigh and may have been trying to decrease expenses.

Orrin deeded 123 acres to his son, Albert, adjoining John (A.) Smith's line September 3, 1874 (Bk 38, p. 635).

April 20 of 1875 Orrin and Louisa took out a one-year mortgage from R.S. Pullen on property adjoining their own lot at the corner of Davie and Person Streets in Raleigh. They paid off the mortgage by 26 April 1876 (Bk 40, p. 421).

Apparently, Orrin continued to purchase farm land as he was deeded 181 acres from his son, Thaddeus (David Thaddeus), May 7, 1875. This property bordering Rufus Smith, dec'd, known as the Jackson Terrell land, descended to Thaddeus from his grandfather (the said Terrell), the father of his deceased mother, Elizabeth. Orrin paid Thaddeus $250 for the land.

Orrin's obituary appeared in the Raleigh *News and Observer*, 1 August 1891. He was reported to have died after a week-long paralysis at his home at 125 S. Bloodworth Street, 6:50 p.m. Friday night. He was 68 years old. He was said to be "...one of Raleigh's leading merchants" in the years 1872-73. (The city directory for 1881 states Orrin was a "dealer in wood.") He retired about 1875 and lived in the city until his death. "He was an exemplary Christian and enjoyed the high esteem and regard of all who knew him. ..He delighted in visiting and extending comfort to the poor and needy, by whom he will be greatly missed." He was buried at "..his old home in the lower edge of Wake County" at 3:00, Sunday, August 2, 1891. This would appear to be the land he received from his father, Edwin, in the Auburn

Descendants of Richard Arrow Smith

area. Another obituary appeared on the same date in the *Raleigh State Chronicle*. It includes the following information: "Mr. Smith was an old and esteemed citizen of Raleigh and was a native of Wake County, having been born 12 miles south of the city. For years he was a farmer and then a merchant in 1872 and '73...a member of the First Baptist Church in Raleigh...He was twice happily married. The interment will take place near his former home in the southern part of the county."

Like most other Smith males, Orrin died of a stroke and related paralysis.

The 1899 Raleigh City Directory lists Louisa Smith, widow of Orrin, living at 408 N. Person St. Also living at this address is Marcus M. Smith, Orrin and Louisa's second-born son. Marcus is listed as the Proprietor of the Southern Book Exchange, 127 Fayetteville Street. The Southern Book Exchange may be the store owned by Orrin A. Smith in family history. Also living at 408 N. Person St. are Miss Lula E. Smith, a clerk at the So. Book Exchange, Miss Carrie E. Smith, an operator at the Bell Telephone Co. (both sisters of Marcus), and Minerva Smith, widow of Philip S. Smith. Minerva, nee Broughton, was Louisa's sister, older by two years.

♥ Orrin A. SMITH married Elizabeth TERRELL on 12 January 1846 at Wake, North Carolina, North Carolina. Elizabeth was born in 1827 at Wake Co., North Carolina; died before 1866 at Raleigh, Wake Co., North Carolina; buried before 1866 at Raleigh, Wake Co., North Carolina.

Elizabeth was one of three daughters of Jackson Terrell who married Smith males.

They had the following children:

Descendants of Richard Arrow Smith

      103   i   Laura SMITH, born on 27 January 1847 at Raleigh, Wake Co., North Carolina.
+ 104   ii   Albert B. SMITH.
+ 105   iii   Mary O. SMITH.
      106   iv   David Thaddeus SMITH, born on 15 October 1852 at Raleigh, Wake Co., North Carolina.

David was known by his middle name, Thaddeus. Thaddeus inherited a parcel of land from his mother's father, Jackson Terrell, in 1870 (Wake Co. Deeds, Book 30, p. 218). He sold this land to his father five years later for the sum of $250. It bordered the property of Rufus Smith's children, also inherited from Mr. Terrell (Bk. 40, p. 360).

♥ David Thaddeus SMITH married Sally TURNER on 11 June 1879 at Wake Co., North Carolina. Sally was born in 1854.

      107   v   Roxanna SMITH, born on 04 September 1857 at Raleigh, Wake Co., North Carolina.
      108   vi   Alvin E. SMITH, born on 06 October 1858 at Raleigh, Wake Co., North Carolina.
      109   vii   Elizabeth O. SMITH, born on 17 January 1862 at Raleigh, Wake Co., North Carolina.

♥ Elizabeth O. SMITH married John COATES on 07 June 1884 at Wake Co., North Carolina. John was born about 1860.

♥ Orrin A. SMITH married Louisa BROUGHTON on 31 January 1866 at Raleigh, Wake Co., North Carolina. Louisa was born on 23 October 1842 at St. Mary's, Auburn, Wake Co., North Carolina; died on 15 November 1912 at Raleigh, Wake Co.,

Descendants of Richard Arrow Smith

North Carolina; buried November 1912 at Hargett St. Cemetary, Raleigh, Wake Co., North Carolina.

Louisa was married first to William Bryant of St. Mary's Township. They had no children and he died eight months after their marriage, fighting in the Civil War.

After Orrin's death in 1891, Louisa filed a petition for a Confederate Widow's Pension, May 29, 1911. The petition was initially filled out with the name of her first husband, William Bryant, and was corrected to read Orrin A. Smith. Louisa signed her name Louisa Bryant Smith. The witness was Joseph Melville Broughton, her brother. He filled in blank that read "Widow of:" with the name of her first husband. It is not known at this time whether Louisa received her widow's pension. It would appear she was entitled to two pensions as she was the widow of two Confederate veterans.

They had the following children:

+ 110   viii   Rev. Joseph Edwin SMITH.
  111   ix   Marcus M. SMITH, born on 28 August 1869 at Raleigh, Wake Co., North Carolina; died on 25 May 1942 at Richmond, Henrico Co., Virginia; buried May 1942 at Hargett St. Cemetary., Raleigh, Wake Co., North Carolina.

Marcus M. Smith was listed in the 1899 Raleigh City Directory as living at 408 N. Person St., along with Louisa, his mother, his sister Carrie, cousin Lula, and his aunt, Minerva (Louisa's sister and widow of Philip Smith). Marcus was also listed as the Proprietor of the Southern Book Exchange, 127 Fayetteville St. Later, he became the State Librarian in Raleigh.

Marcus reportedly did not continue to be an upstanding citizen. He opened up a home for "wayward girls," reportedly a house of ill-

Descendants of Richard Arrow Smith

repute, which was closed down by the city (Raleigh). He then moved to Richmond, Virginia and bought an apartment building during the depression, fixed it up and rented it to poor people. It has been reported that he carried a cane weighted with lead to discourage people from bothering him. Also, he owned a small plot of land in D.C. on which he claimed to have built a "Home for Foundling Children," convincing people he met to make donations. He was reportedly jailed in Boston and Philadelphia, talking himself out of serious consequences. Apparently, he and his first wife, Gussie, did not get along as he built her a separate house. He was married twice, but nothing is known about his second wife.

When his brother, Joseph, died, Marcus came by bus to the funeral and stayed several days. He brought no suitcases, only a few biscuits in a sack for lunch. He talked Joseph's congregation into letting him preach a sermon, which was apparently a great success.

On one of his trips to Chicago, he came to stay with his nephew, Vernon. Marcus got up in the middle of the night and left, without a word. All, in all, he was an usual character. Every family needs one. (To be fair, all these stories are family folklore and may not be entirely factual.)

He is buried next to his mother in City Cemetary, Hargett Street, in Raleigh. His marker reads: "IN LOVING MEMORY OF MARCUS M. SMITH, EVANGELIST, HE WALKED WITH GOD AND LOVED AND CARED FOR THE HOMELESS AND THE ORPHAN AND NEEDY CHILDREN 1869-1942."

♥ Marcus M. SMITH married Gussie LINCHON at Wake Co., North Carolina. She was born about 1870.

+ 112   x   William O. SMITH.

+ 113   xi   John W. SMITH.
+ 114   xii   Carrie Etta SMITH.
  115   xiii Benjamin F. SMITH, born on 03 October 1876 at Raleigh, Wake Co., North Carolina; died after 1927 at Mt. Rainier, Prince Georges Co., Maryland.

Ben Smith worked at the Government Printing Office in Washington, D.C. He and his wife had no children.

♥ Benjamin F. SMITH married Rosa Ellen SCHRIVER on 28 March 1901. She was born about 1880.

  116   xiv   Corrinna L. SMITH, born on 6 September 1879 at Raleigh, Wake Co., North Carolina.

♥ Corrinna L. SMITH married H. J. SATTERFIELD on 13 April 1898 at Wake Co., North Carolina. H.J. was born about 1875.

  117   xv   Henry Burgwyn SMITH, born on 16 October 1881 at Raleigh, Wake Co., North Carolina; died on 3 July 1883 at Raleigh, Wake Co., North Carolina; buried at Raleigh, Wake Co., North Carolina.

+ 118   xvi   Nellie May SMITH.

39   Larkin A. SMITH, born in 1827 at St. Mary's, Wake Co., North Carolina.

Larkin was listed as the guardian of his children's inheritance in the estate records of Jackson Terrell, his father-in-law.

Larkin was deeded 100 acres from Rufus A. Smith, his half-brother, December 3, 1873. This land in Wake County began on the "Waters of Guffy Swamp" adjoining Elijah Young, Joe Young, and

Descendants of Richard Arrow Smith

others and was originally purchased from F. Young.

Like so many other Smith men, Larkin suffered from strokes in his later years. His obituary appeared in the *Raleigh State Chronicle* June 22, 1892: "Smith, Larkin, Esq., June 21, 1892, in Mark's Creek Township, Wake County, in his 66th year. He had been totally paralyzed on his right side for more than six years. He was the father of Mrs. A.L. Ferrell of Raleigh. His funeral will take place at Bethlehem Church, and interment will be in the family burial ground. Charles H. Smith is the administrator of the estate" (*Death Notices 1882-1893, Raleigh State Chronicle,* Massengill and Tompkins).

♥ Larkin A. SMITH married Caroline TERRELL on 20 January 1847 at Wake Co., North Carolina. Caroline was born in 1824 at St. Mary's, Wake Co., North Carolina; died before May 1870 at Wake Co., North Carolina.

Caroline was a daughter of Jackson Terrell of Johnston County, North Carolina, sister of Elizabeth and Jane.

They had the following children:

+ 119   i   Sarah Jane SMITH.
  120   ii   Charles H. SMITH, born about 1857 at St. Mary's, Wake Co., North Carolina.

Charles H. Smith, age 45, registered to vote in St. Matthews Township, Wake County, October 18, 1902. His listed ancestor was Larkin Smith.

Charles was the administrator of his father's estate.

♥ Charles H. SMITH married Mattie E. HOOD on 05 March 1876 at Selma Baptist Church, Johnston Co., North Carolina. Mattie was born about 1860 at

Descendants of Richard Arrow Smith

Johnston Co., North Carolina; died at Johnston Co., North Carolina; buried at Selma City Cemetary, Johnston Co., North Carolina.

    121   iii Martha L. SMITH, born abt 1854 at Wake Co., North Carolina.
    122   iv Virginia SMITH, born abt 1856 at Wake Co., North Carolina.
    123   v Emma SMITH, born abt 1858 at Wake Co., North Carolina.
    124   vi Claudius SMITH, born abt 1860 at Wake Co., North Carolina.

♥ Larkin A. SMITH married Arthelia WILLIAMS on 4 February 1866 at Wake, North Carolina.

41   Rufus A. SMITH, born on 1 October 1832 at St. Mary's, Auburn, Wake Co., North Carolina; died on 23 December 1917 at Wake Co., North Carolina; buried at New Bethel Baptist, Garner, Wake Co., North Carolina.

    This is the Rufus A. Smith who enlisted, at the age of 27, in Co.D, 31st Reg. NC Troops on 18 September 1861. He mustered as a Private. Present or accounted for until captured at Roanoke Island 8 February 1862. Paroled at Elizabeth City 21 February 1862. Returned to duty about 15 September 1862. Promoted to Corporal on 1 May 1863. Promoted to Sargeant 9 March 1864. Present or accounted for through December, 1864.

    Rufus deeded 214 acres of the "..land whereon I now live known as the Sturdivant tract" to Solomon Terrell Sept. 5, 1862. This property bordered Esther Sturdivant, Caswell Sturdivant, and William Fort (Wake Co. Deed Bk 24, p. 326).

    Rufus wrote his will March 25, 1908 in Wake County (on Raleigh and Pamlico Sound Railroad Company stationery). He bequeathed to his wife, Elizabeth, "my home as long as she lives single;

Descendants of Richard Arrow Smith

my children shall have a home here as long as they live single. I give to my son Edwin E. Smith my land and premises after my death and after my wife (sic) death and he Edwin shall support me and my wife and children as long as they live single. I give to my son Frank R. Smith fourteen acres known as the Stevens Place. My Daughters Alma, Milly and Anna shall have a bed and fixtures and I give to my Daughter Alma my Organs (musical)." He ordered his personal property sold at his death in order to pay debts, if there were any. If Edwin had no heirs, his part should be divided among his daughters equally upon his death. "Said land is never to be sold until the third generation. I appoint my son Robert J. Smith Executor." Rufus wrote his own will, longhand. His witnesses were Y.E. Young and Melvin Hocutt.

♥ Rufus A. SMITH married Jane TERRELL on 09 February 1857 at Wake Co., North Carolina. Jane was born about 1835 at Wake Co., North Carolina; died before 1864 at Wake Co., North Carolina. The bondsman was Orrin A. Smith. The marriage was performed by W.J. Busbee, Justice of the Peace.

Jane was another daughter of Jackson Terrell of Johnston County, sister of Caroline and Elizabeth.

They had the following children:

      125   i   Benjamin SMITH, born in 1859 at Wake Co., North Carolina.

Benjamin is not mentioned in the division of the property of Jackson Terrell, his grandfather, in 1870. It could be that Benjamin died young.

      126   ii   Thomas SMITH, born after 1860 at Wake Co., North Carolina.
      127   iii   Elijah SMITH, born about 1864 at Wake Co., North Carolina.

Descendants of Richard Arrow Smith

128   iv   Leonora SMITH, born about 1866 at Wake Co., North Carolina.

♥ Rufus A. SMITH married Elizabeth YOUNG on 30 November 1865 at Wake Co., North Carolina. Elizabeth was born on 10 December 1842 at Wake Co., North Carolina; died on 21 June 1910 at Wake Co., North Carolina; buried at New Bethel Baptist, Garner, Wake Co., North Carolina.

They had the following children:

129   v   Robert J. SMITH, born on 1866 at Wake Co., North Carolina; died on 1928 at Garner, Wake Co., North Carolina; buried in 1928 at New Bethel Baptist, Garner, Wake Co., North Carolina.

Robert was the executor of his father's estate.

♥ Robert J. SMITH married Margaret Nancy BAGWELL on 25 November 1891 at Wake Co., North Carolina. Nancy was born about 1866 at Wake Co., North Carolina.

130   vi   Emma SMITH, born in 1868 at Wake Co., North Carolina; died in 1928.

♥ Emma SMITH married James M. STEVENS at Wake Co., North Carolina. James was born about 1868.

131   vii   Ella Elizabeth SMITH, born in 1870 at Wake Co., North Carolina; died in 1928 at Wake Co., North Carolina.

♥ Ella Elizabeth SMITH married Hardy Bryant BAGWELL at Wake Co., North Carolina. He was born about 1870 at Wake Co., North Carolina.

132   viii   Elizabeth Rufus SMITH, born in 1871 at Wake Co., North Carolina; died in 1953.

Descendants of Richard Arrow Smith

♥ Elizabeth Rufus SMITH married Henry Haywood KNIGHT at Wake Co., North Carolina. He was born 5 November 1842 in Wake Co., North Carolina; died 7 May 1904 at Knightdale, Wake Co., North Carolina.

Henry was the son of Peter and Mary Ann Knight.

133   ix   Acharel M. SMITH, born in 1873 at Wake Co., North Carolina; died in 1956.

Acral M. Smith (sic), age 28, registered to vote in St. Matthews Township, Wake County, October 24, 1902. His ancestor was listed as R.A. Smith.

♥ Acharel M. SMITH married Alma Grace GRIFFIN at Wake Co., North Carolina. Alma was born about 1873.

134   x   Alma SMITH, born in 1876 at Wake Co., North Carolina; died in 1960.

♥ Alma SMITH married Charlie GRIFFIN at Wake Co., North Carolina. Charlie was born about 1876.

135   xi   Cornelia Amanda SMITH, born in 1878 at Wake Co., North Carolina; died in 1970.

♥ Cornelia Amanda SMITH married S. Romelus SEYMOUR at Wake Co., North Carolina. He was born about 1878.

136   xii   Edwin E. SMITH, born on 12 July 1880 at Wake Co., North Carolina; died on 10 October 1932 at Garner, Wake Co., North Carolina; buried at New Bethel Baptist Church, Garner, Wake Co., North Carolina.

♥ Edwin E. SMITH married Hattie COWARD at Wake Co., North Carolina. She was born on 27 July 1893 at Wake Co., North Carolina; died on 11 January 1974 at Garner, Wake Co., North Carolina; buried

Descendants of Richard Arrow Smith

at New Bethel Baptist Church, Garner, Wake Co., North Carolina.

   137 xiii Frank Rufus SMITH, born on 1885 at Wake Co., North Carolina; died on 1956.

♥ Frank Rufus SMITH married Ethel May ATKINSON at Wake Co., North Carolina. She was born about 1885.

   138 xiv Anna SMITH, born in 1887 at Wake Co., North Carolina; died in 1981.

♥ Anna SMITH married James R. WILLIAMSON at Wake Co., North Carolina. He was born about 1887.

42 Lucius A. SMITH, born in 1836 at St. Mary's, Wake Co., North Carolina; died before 1880 at St. Mary's, Wake Co., North Carolina.

 Lucius Smith bought 233 acres from his father, Edwin A. Smith, May 20, 1862. This property in Wake County bordered the lands of Orrin A. Smith (his brother), Dr. Jones, and the Wilmington Road (Bk. 29, p. 8).

 Lucius A. Smith and wife Rebecca deeded 204 acres to Catherine Hicks, her sister, for the sum of one dollar. This land in Wake County bordered the properties of Weston Parker, William Snellings, Jos. A. Walton, Dallas Rand, O.R. Rand, and other. This land descended to Rebecca through her father, Jesse Broughton. In return, Catherine loaned Lucius $155 payable in two years with interest (Bk. 26, p. 405).

 In the settlement of Lucius's estate, 1884, he left a wife, Rebecca, and children Leonidas (Leonard), Ida, Stella and Walter, minors who had Jefferson Smith as their guardian, and Alonzo Smith, whose guardian was his uncle Joseph

Descendants of Richard Arrow Smith

Broughton. Lucius left land on "Jefferson Smith's line and Abraham McCullers' line."

♥ Lucius A. SMITH married Rebecca BROUGHTON on 12 December 1859 at Wake Co., North Carolina. Rebecca was born on 2 September 1837 at St. Mary's, Wake Co., North Carolina; died after 1884 at Wake Co., North Carolina.

Rebecca was referred to as being 61-1/3 years old at the settlement of her husband's estate in 1884. This is obviously an error.

After Lucius's death, Rebecca married her next-door-neighbor and brother-in-law, Jefferson Smith, as shown by the census of 1880. Jeff and wife Rebecca, age 44, were living with eleven children, a mixture of his and hers.

They had the following children:

+ **139** i Leonard SMITH.
140 v Alonzo SMITH, born about 1866 at St. Mary's, Wake Co., North Carolina.
141 ii Ida SMITH, born in 1867 at St. Mary's, Wake Co., North Carolina.
142 iii Stella SMITH, born in 1869 at St. Mary's, Wake Co., North Carolina.
143 iv Walter SMITH, born in 1871 at St. Mary's, Wake Co., North Carolina.

43 Edwin Jefferson SMITH, born in 1839 at St. Mary's, Wake Co., North Carolina; died after 22 April 1903 at Wake Co., North Carolina.

Edwin J. Smith, who was called Jefferson, enlisted with his brother, Rufus, in Co.D, 31st NC Troops at the age of 21, 18 September 1861. Present or accounted for until captured at Roanoke Island on 8 February 1862. Paroled at Elizabeth City 21 February 1862. Returned to duty

Descendants of Richard Arrow Smith

on or about 15 September 1862. Present or accounted for through December 1864.

On May 20, 1866, Jefferson Smith and wife Louisa A. Smith deeded to Caswell Pollard a lot in in the city of Raleigh on Wilmington Street between the lots of Jackson Overly and John Polk. This lot was bequeathed to Louisa from her father, S.W. Williams (Deed Bk. 32, p. 63).

On August 27th of the same year, Jefferson and Louisa sold another lot in the city of Raleigh to E.M. Flowers. This 1/4 acre adjoined the lots of Louisa's siblings, F.M. Williams and Polly Williams, on Holliman Road. Presumably, this is part of the land willed to the children of S.W. Williams. (Samuel W. Williams who married Mary Smith in Wake County.)

In the 1880 census of St. Mary's Township, Wake County, Jefferson Smith, aged 40, was living with second wife Rebecca, age 44, and eleven children. This Rebecca is the widow of Jeff's brother, Lucius, who died shortly before 1880. The children are a mixture of his and hers. This second marriage apparently did not produce any additional children.

Jefferson wrote his will April 2, 1903. He referred to himself as "..of Garner in the county of Wake and state of North Carolina." He directed his executor to sell "..my tract of 200 acres of land except 60 acres that part descended by my wife at the death of her first husband, using the proceeds therefrom in paying my funeral expenses and all my just debts and liabilities." He left all surplus funds, the 60 acres of land, and all personal property to his "dear wife Rebecca Smith for her maintenance and support during her life." At Rebecca's death, the 60 acres of land were to be sold and one quarter of the profits were to be given to Stella Hornbuckle (relationship unknown) and the remainder to be divided between "my

Descendants of Richard Arrow Smith

children Julia Beasley, Anner Beasley, A.J. Smith, Nat A. Smith, Silas Smith, Cora Wilson and Charles Smith." The executor was D. Henry Bryan. The witnesses were Geo. B. Montague and G.O. Barbee.

♥ Edwin Jefferson SMITH married Louisa A. WILLIAMS on 18 December 1860 at Wake Co., North Carolina. Louisa was born about 1840 at North Carolina and died before 1880. She was the daughter of Samuel W. Williams.

They had the following children:

    144   i   Alonzo J. SMITH, born in 1863 at Wake Co., North Carolina.

    145   ii   Cora SMITH, born in 1864 at Wake Co., North Carolina.

♥ Cora SMITH married Mr. WILSON before 1903 in North Carolina.

    146   iii   Silas SMITH, born in 1868 at Wake Co., North Carolina.
    147   iv   Julia SMITH, born in 1870 at Wake Co., North Carolina.

♥ Julia SMITH married Mr. BEASLEY before 1903 in North Carolina.

    148   v   Charlie SMITH, born in 1873 at Wake Co., North Carolina.
    149   vi   Annie SMITH, born in 1875 at Wake Co., North Carolina.

♥ Annie, or Anner, SMITH married Mr. BEASLEY before 1903 in North Carolina.

    150   vii   Nathaniel A. SMITH, born in 1877 at Wake Co., North Carolina.

Descendants of Richard Arrow Smith

♥ Edwin Jefferson SMITH married Rebecca BROUGHTON, widow of his brother Lucius, before 1880. They apparently had no children from this marriage.

48   William Gaston SMITH, born in 1837 at Johnson Co., North Carolina; died before 7 April 1904 at Johnston Co., North Carolina.

   William Gaston Smith wrote his will January 25, 1904, in Johnston County. He mentioned wife Margaret L., sons Oscar N., Larkin C., James B., and daughter Ella M. Smith. "Beloved son Oscar" received one dollar; however, Oscar was deceased by May, 1909. Larkin received 69 acres of land as per a deed written January 19, 1903, Lot #1. He also received six dollars in order to buy a bedstool out of his father's estate. Son James received 100 acres of land as per a deed given the same day as Larkin's, Lot #2, as well as William's double-barrel shotgun. Daughter Ella received 70 acres of land as per above, Lot #3, as well as her father's organ (musical). Wife Margaret received "...all my household and kitchen furniture of every description during her life or widowhood.." and at her marriage, to her daughter, Ella. The executors were Larkin and James.

♥ William Gaston SMITH married Margaret "Laney" before 1866 at Johnston Co., North Carolina.

   Margaret was refered to as "Laney" in the marriage register of her son, Oscar.

   They had the following children:

      151   i   Oscar N. SMITH, born in 1866, according to the 1880 census of Johnston County; died before May 1909 at Johnston Co., North Carolina.

Descendants of Richard Arrow Smith

♥ Oscar N. SMITH married Medoar "Dora" DODD on 10 February 1886 at Johnston Co., North Carolina. She was born in 1869 in Johnston Co., the daughter of Elender Smith Dodd and Henry Dodd. The marriage was performed by Rev. Joseph Edwin Smith, son of Orrin A. Smith, at the bride's home.

    152   ii   Larkin C. SMITH, born in 1868 at Johnston Co., North Carolina, according to the 1880 census of that county.
    153   iii   Ella M. SMITH, was born in 1871, according to the census of 1880.
    154   iv James B. SMITH, born in 1877, according to the 1880 census.

49   Simeon Marion SMITH, born on 1 February 1839 at Johnston Co., North Carolina; died on 13 July 1907 at Johnston Co., North Carolina.

♥ Simeon Marion SMITH married Nancy Emily CHAMPION in 1867 at Johnston Co., North Carolina. She was born on 1 February 1839 at Johnston Co., North Carolina; died on 20 March 1920 at Johnston Co., North Carolina.

They had the following children:

    155   i   Mary Susan SMITH, born on 11 September 1867 at Johnston Co., North Carolina.
    156   ii   Nancy Elizabeth SMITH, born on 7 August 1871 at Johnston Co., North Carolina.
+ 157   iii   Simeon Lonnie SMITH.
+ 158   iv   James Addison SMITH.
    159   v   Edy Elendor SMITH, born on 27 August 1877 at Johnston Co., North Carolina.
    160   vi   Rose Etta Florence SMITH, born on 7 July 1880 at Johnston Co., North Carolina.
+ 161   vii   Richard Henderson SMITH "Bud".
    162   viii William F. SMITH, born on 4 September 1883 at Johnston Co., North Carolina; died on 25 October 1924.

Descendants of Richard Arrow Smith

163 ix Ella Nettice SMITH, born on 17 August 1888 at Johnston Co., North Carolina; died on 22 September 1973.

♥ Ella Nettice SMITH married Caswell Putnam TEMPLE at North Carolina. He was born about 1888.

50 James Haywood SMITH, born on 18 September 1845 at Johnston Co., North Carolina; died on 27 January 1920.

♥ James Haywood SMITH married Martha Ann STEPHENSON in 1867 at Johnston Co., North Carolina. She was born on 29 January 1848 at North Carolina; died on 19 August 1926.

They had the following children:

164 i Richard A. SMITH, born on 15 September 1862 at Johnson Co., North Carolina; died on 29 May 1891.
165 ii Delia SMITH, born on 1 April 1870 at Johnston Co., North Carolina; died on 23 June 1884 at Johnston Co., North Carolina.
166 iii Matilda SMITH, born on 6 April 1872 at Johnston Co., North Carolina; died on 29 August 1932.
167 iv Martha SMITH, born in April of 1880 at Johnston Co., North Carolina.
168 v Emily SMITH, born on 16 June 1882 at Johnston Co., North Carolina; died on 31 October 1957.

♥ Emily SMITH married Haywood Isaac MATTHEWS on 22 September 1897 at Johnston Co., North Carolina.

52 Daniel Ruffin SMITH, born in 1849 at Johnston Co., North Carolina; died on 13 August 1917 in Franklin Co., North Carolina.

Descendants of Richard Arrow Smith

♥ Daniel Ruffin SMITH married Esther A. SMITH on 14 November 1867 at Johnston Co., North Carolina. Esther was the daughter of Calvin A. Smith.

Esther and Daniel, second cousins, were married at the home of Vina Carroll, widow of Labon Carroll. Labon was possibly the brother of Esther's mother, Dolly. Since Esther's father, Calvin, died before her marriage, it is possible that her uncle became her guardian.

Esther died after giving birth to a second child who did not survive.

They had the following children:

    169   i   Rozella SMITH, born about 1869 at Johnston Co., North Carolina.

♥ Daniel Ruffin SMITH married Julia JOHNSON on 21 February 1874 at North Carolina. Julia was born about 1853 at Wake Co., North Carolina; died before 1898 at Johnston Co., North Carolina.

They had the following children:

    170   ii   Elizabeth Jane SMITH, born in 1875 at Wake Co., North Carolina.
    171   iii   Lula Allen SMITH, born in 1887 at Wake Co., North Carolina.
    172   iv   Sallie SMITH, born in 1880 at Wake Co., North Carolina.
    173   v   Henrietta SMITH, born in July 1884 at Wake Co., North Carolina.
    174   vi   Mary Magdalene SMITH, born in April 1887 at Wake Co., North Carolina.
    175   vii   Minnie SMITH, born in September 1888 at Wake Co., North Carolina.

♥ Daniel Ruffin SMITH married Sarah CARLISLE on 22 September 1898 at Wake Co., North Carolina.

Descendants of Richard Arrow Smith

Co., North Carolina; died on 5 June 1954 at Wake Co., North Carolina.

They had the following children:

+ 176 viii William Alfred SMITH.
+ 177 ix Lonnie Hilliard SMITH.
+ 178 ix Haywood Thomas SMITH.

66   Elender SMITH, born in 1848 at St. Mary's, Wake Co., North Carolina.

♥ Elender SMITH married Henry DODD on 22 September 1867 at Johnston Co., North Carolina. He was born in 1847.

They had the following children:

179 i Medoar "Dora" DODD (see number 151).

♥ Medoar "Dora" DODD married Oscar N. SMITH on 10 February 1886 Johnston Co., North Carolina.
This individual's information has already been printed (son of William Gaston Smith).

180 ii Alonzo DODD, born in 1871 at Johnston Co., North Carolina.
181 iii Jenny DODD, born in 1873 at Johnston Co., North Carolina.
182 iv John DODD, born in 1876 at Johnston Co., North Carolina.
183 v Malissa DODD, born in 1879 at Johnston Co., North Carolina.

68   William McRae SMITH, born on 20 December 1854 at Johnston Co., North Carolina; died on 17 November 1894 at Johnston Co., North Carolina; buried at Smith Cemetary, Bethesda, Johnston Co., North Carolina.

Descendants of Richard Arrow Smith

♥ William McRae SMITH married Annie Maria JONES on 6 October 1872 at Johnston Co., North Carolina. She was born on 24 July 1853 at Johnston Co., North Carolina; died on 15 August 1907 at Johnston Co., North Carolina; buried at Smith Cemetary, Bethesda, Johnston Co., North Carolina.

They had the following children:

    184   i   Baby SMITH, born in 1876 at Johnston Co., North Carolina.
    185   ii   Rev. James W. SMITH, born in 1875 at Johnston Co., North Carolina.
+ 186   iii   Garner Arrista SMITH.
    187   iv   Ida SMITH, born in 1874 at Johnston Co., North Carolina.
    188   v   Leather B. SMITH "Lee", born in 1880 at Johnston Co., North Carolina.
    189   vi   Grover Thurman SMITH, born in 1888 at Johnston Co., North Carolina.
    190   vii   Coy SMITH, born in 1890 at Johnston Co., North Carolina.

71   Sylvester A. SMITH, born on 13 April 1862 at Johnston Co., North Carolina; died on 15 November 1954 at Clayton, Johnston Co., North Carolina; buried at Bethesda Baptist Church, Clayton, Johnston Co., North Carolina.

In the 1887 Raleigh City Directory, Sylvester Smith is listed as residing at 508 S. West St.

♥ Sylvester A. SMITH married Dezzie JONES on 14 August 1880 at Smithfield, Johnston Co., North Carolina. She was born on 28 March 1861 at Johnston Co., North Carolina; died on 6 April 1936 at Johnston Co., North Carolina, North Carolina; buried at Bethesda Baptist Church, Clayton, Johnston Co., North Carolina.

Descendants of Richard Arrow Smith

They had the following children:

   191 i Elizabeth Hawkins SMITH, born on 16 July 1881 at Johnston Co., North Carolina; died on 14 October 1909.

♥ Elizabeth Hawkins SMITH married Thomas J. TALTON at Johnston Co., North Carolina. Thomas was born on 1 November 1871 at Johnston Co., North Carolina; died on 19 November 1920.

   192 ii Hattie Idella SMITH, born on 21 January 1885 at Johnston Co., North Carolina; died on 28 October 1951 at Johnston Co., North Carolina, North Carolina; buried at Bethesda Baptist Church, Clayton, Johnston Co., North Carolina.
   193 iii Mattie V. SMITH, born in 1886 at Johnston Co., North Carolina.

♥ Mattie V. SMITH married Paul Edwin WHITLEY at Johnston Co., North Carolina. He was born about 1885; died in 1949.

   194 iv Vernon L. SMITH, born in 1888 at Johnston Co., North Carolina.
   195 v William Ivan SMITH, born on 13 February 1891 at Johnston Co., North Carolina; died on 24 November 1946 at Johnston Co., North Carolina, North Carolina; buried at Bethesda Baptist Church, Clayton, Johnston Co., North Carolina.

♥ William Ivan SMITH married Pauline BENSON at Johnston Co., North Carolina.

 + 196 vi Irene Lula SMITH.

73 James A. SMITH, born in 1825 at St. Mary's, Wake Co., North Carolina; died after 1874 at Jonesboro, Clayton Co., Georgia.

Descendants of Richard Arrow Smith

James was 25 years old in the 1850 Census of Johnston County, North Carolina.

James A. Smith deeded land in Wake County to William R. Poole on October 10, 1857 (Deed Bk. 21, p. 689).

This may be the James A. Smith who was Justice of the Peace in Johnston County, 1866-67.

James A. Smith sued Flora V. Byrd Smith and Esther P. Smith, heirs of Calvin A. Smith, over money for the land belonging to his father. He sent a postcard to Judge J.N. Bunting in Raleigh, dated 4 December 1875, which read, "Money for land should be divided in two shares for James Smith and Mary Smith. You will therefore please hold on to the money now in your possession until you hear from me again as I will establish my right." Signed, James A. Smith, Jonesboro, Georgia.

James A. SMITH married Martha BYRD on 13 July 1852 at Johnston Co., North Carolina. Martha was born about 1830.

They had the following children:

    197   i   Calvin A. SMITH, born about 1854 at Wake Co., North Carolina.

♥ Calvin A. SMITH married Jennie CREECH on 13 June 1876 at Johnston Co., North Carolina. She was born about 1855 at Johnston Co., North Carolina.

    198   ii   John B. SMITH, born about 1858 at Wake Co., North Carolina.

♥ John B. SMITH married Sarah S. LEE on 14 April 1881 at Johnston Co., North Carolina.

Descendants of Richard Arrow Smith

　　　　199　iii　James M. SMITH, born about 1860 at Wake Co., North Carolina.

♥ James M. SMITH married Elizabeth CLIFTON on 25 November 1886 at Johnston Co., North Carolina.

77　Esther A. SMITH.
This individual's information has already been printed (Daughter of Calvin A. Smith).

♥ Esther A. SMITH married Daniel Ruffin SMITH on 14 November 1867 at Johnston Co., North Carolina. This individual's information has already been printed (Son of Benjamin A. Smith).

Descendants of this couple have already been printed.

81　Rufus W. SMITH, born on 1831 at Georgia.

Rufus was 19 years old in the 1850 census of St. Mary's, Wake Co., North Carolina.

Abner A. Smith deeded land in Wake County to Rufus W. Smith August 22, 1867. This land, on Bushey Branch, bordered the properties of Wesley Smith and Abner A. Smith (Deed Bk. 25, p. 321).

♥ Rufus W. SMITH married Margaret JONES on 5 September 1853 at Wake Co., North Carolina.

They had the following children:

　　　　200　i　Irvin Lorenza SMITH, born about 1856 at Wake Co., North Carolina.

♥ Irvin Lorenza SMITH married Corinna JONES on 19 September 1876 at Johnston Co., North Carolina. Corinna was born about 1857 at Johnston Co., North Carolina.

Descendants of Richard Arrow Smith

91   Paschal POOLE, born on 22 February 1847 at St. Mary's, Wake Co., North Carolina; died on 24 October 1929 at Fuquay Springs, Wake Co., North Carolina.

Paschal Poole served at age 17 in the Confederate Junior Reserves (Co. D, 1st Regiment) which tried in vain to stop General Sherman's march through North Carolina to Raleigh after the Battle of Bentonville.

♥ Paschal POOLE married Henrietta PENNY on 8 December 1870 at Johnston Co., North Carolina. She was born in 1851 at Johnston Co., North Carolina; died in 1921 at Wake Co., North Carolina.

They had the following children:

201   i   William R. POOLE, born about 1872 at Wake Co., North Carolina; died August 1882 at Wake Co., North Carolina.

Willie died of influenza (*Calvin Pool, His Ancestors and Descendants*, Clyde M. Stallings, 1991).

202   ii   Sallie POOLE, born about 1874 at Auburn, Wake Co., North Carolina; died in August 1882 at Auburn, Wake Co., North Carolina.

Like her older brother, Sallie reportedly died of influenza in the same month as his death (ibid.).

+ 203   iii   Della POOLE.
  204   iv   Ava POOLE.
  205   v   Eulalia POOLE, born in 1880 at Auburn, Wake Co., North Carolina; died in 1895 at Auburn, Wake Co., North Carolina.

Descendants of Richard Arrow Smith

Eulalia reportedly died at the age of 15 (ibid.)

95 Catherine SMITH, born in 1831 at Auburn, Wake Co., North Carolina.

♥ Catherine SMITH married Green POOLE on 24 July 1859 at Wake Co., North Carolina; born about 1821 at Wake Co., North Carolina.

Green Poole, Private, enlisted in Co. D, 31st NC Troops, in Wake County, 18 September 1861. Discharged on or about 28 October, 1861. Reason for discharge was not reported, however his relative, Calvin, was also discharged on the same date for "disability".

They had the following children:

    206   i   William POOLE, born about 1861 at Wake Co., North Carolina.
    207   ii   Martha POOLE, born in 1862 at Wake Co., North Carolina.

Martha, age 18, was living with her grandfather, Oswell Smith, in St. Mary's Township, Wake County, 1880 census.

97 Yancy L. SMITH, born in 1836 at St. Mary's Township, Wake Co., North Carolina; died February 1886 at Auburn, Wake Co., North Carolina.

Yancy was the bondsman at the marriage of Louisa Broughton and Orrin A. Smith in 1866. Yancy was the cousin of Orrin, and Louisa was the sister of Yancy's wife, Salina.

Y.L. Smith deeded 54 acres in Wake County to M.A. Smith (probably Marcellus) on December 7, 1870. This land bordered the properties of Dr.

Descendants of Richard Arrow Smith

W.I. Busbee, James Stallings, and Betty Johns (Bk. 31, p. 276).

On February 8, 1876, Yancy and wife deeded land in Wake County to Perrin Gower. This property began on the County Road and lay against a corner of the grove of Mt. Moriah Church, consisting of less than an acre (Bk. 43, p.328).

In the 1881 Raleigh City Directory, Yancy was listed as a farmer in Auburn, North Carolina. Yancey was deceased by 1888 as his wife as listed as Mrs. Salina Smith, widow, 538 E. Hargett Street, Raleigh.

♥ Yancy L. SMITH married Salina BROUGHTON on 31 July 1861 at Wake Co., North Carolina. Salina was born in 1845 at St.Mary's Township, Wake Co., North Carolina; died after 1896 at Raleigh, Wake Co., North Carolina.

Salina was a daughter of Joseph Broughton and Mary Bagwell.

Salina was widowed by 1888. By 1896 she had moved to 305 S. Person St. where she lived with her son, S.M. (Collector for J.M. Broughton & Co.), daughters Eva (Retoucher at Johnson's Gallery) and Lillie (Student). She lived for a brief period between 1888-1896 with her widowed sisters Louisa and Minerva at the home of Louisa and her son Marcus at 408 N. Person St.(now in the Historic Oakwood District).

They had the following children:

    208   i   Mollie L. SMITH, born about 1864 at Auburn, Wake Co., North Carolina; died after 1914 at Wake Co., North Carolina.

Mollie was 16 in the 1880 census of St. Mary's Township, Wake County.

Descendants of Richard Arrow Smith

♥ Mollie L. SMITH married Thomas GOWER before 1886 at Wake Co., North Carolina. He was born died after 1914 at Wake Co., North Carolina.

    209   ii   Leonora "Nora" SMITH, born in 1864 at St. Mary's, Wake Co., North Carolina; died before 1914 at Wake Co., North Carolina.

Nora was 14 years old in the 1880 census of Wake County. Leonora Smith was listed as a "Bookfolder" in the 1888 Raleigh City Directory. She probably worked at Edwards and Broughton Printing Company, owned by her uncle Needham B. Broughton.

    210   iii   Lillie SMITH, born about 1868 at St. Mary's, Wake Co., North Carolina; died after 1914 at Wake Co., North Carolina.

Lillie was listed in the 1896 Raleigh City Directory as a student.

♥ Lillie SMITH married Thomas MILLER at Wake Co., North Carolina.

    211   iv   Lula B. SMITH, born about 1869 at St. Mary's, Wake Co., North Carolina; died after 1914.

Lula was 11 years old in the 1880 census. Lula B. Smith worked as a "Bookfolder," probably at Edwards and Broughton Printing Company owned by her uncle Needham B. Broughton (1888 Raleigh City Directory).

♥ Lula B. SMITH married Mr. MEDLIN at Wake Co., North Carolina.

    212   v   Minerva SMITH, born in 1872 at St. Mary's, Wake Co., North Carolina; died after 1914.

Descendants of Richard Arrow Smith

Minerva was 8 years old in the 1880 census of St. Mary's Township, Wake Co. Minerva, like her sisters Lula and Leonora, worked as a "Bookfolder," probably for her uncle Needham B. Broughton (Edwards and Broughton Printing Company).

♥ Minerva SMITH married Louis GORE at Wake Co., North Carolina.

213 vi Lonnie SMITH, born about 1873 at Auburn, Wake Co., North Carolina; died after 1914 at Wake Co., North Carolina.

Lonnie was 7 years old in the 1880 census.

♥ Lonnie SMITH married Mamie at Wake Co., North Carolina.

214 vii Virginia "Jennie" SMITH, born about 1875 at Auburn, Wake Co., North Carolina; died after 1914 at Wake Co., North Carolina.

Virginia was five years old in the 1880 census.

♥ Virginia "Jennie" SMITH married Thomas JOHNSON at Wake Co., North Carolina.

215 viii Ola SMITH, born about 1878 at Auburn, Wake Co., North Carolina; died after 1914 at Wake Co.,North Carolina.

♥ Ola SMITH married George RUSLIN at Wake Co., North Carolina.

216 ix Eva SMITH, born April 1880 at Auburn, Wake Co., North Carolina; died after 1914 at Wake Co., North Carolina.

Eva was one month old in the 1880 census of St. Mary's Township, Wake County. Her birth month was given as April.

Descendants of Richard Arrow Smith

Eva was listed as a "Retoucher at Johnson's Gallery" in the 1896 Raleigh City Directory.

♥ Eva SMITH married David KING at Wake Co., North Carolina.

217   x   Minnie SMITH, born in about 1882 at Auburn, Wake Co., North Carolina; died after 1914 at Wake Co., North Carolina.

♥ Minnie SMITH married Lester HUNNICUTT at Wake Co., North Carolina.

98   Marcellus A. SMITH, born in 1838 at Auburn, Wake Co., North Carolina; died before 1920 at Wake Co., North Carolina.

In his will, dated 13 January 1913 in Wake County, Marcellus mentions his "beloved wife" but does not call her by name. He also mentions his eleven children: Ernest, Marcus, Norman, Early, Alton, Valley, Rufus Millard, Vernon, Macy, Herman, and Margarette.

The estate records of Marcellus Smith, dated 1920, list his widow as Mattie A. Smith, and children Alton, Vallie, Rufus M., Vernon, Macy, Margaret, and Herman. Ernest, Marcus, Norman, and Margarette are not mentioned.

Marcellus A. Smith served in Co. D, 31st NC Troops in the Civil War.

♥ Marcellus A. SMITH married Mattie A. at Wake Co., North Carolina.

They had the following children:

218   i   Ernest SMITH, born at Wake Co., North Carolina; died after 1912.

Descendants of Richard Arrow Smith

219 ii Marcus SMITH, born at Wake Co., North Carolina; died after 1912.
220 iii Norman SMITH, born at Wake Co., North Carolina; died after 1912.
221 iv Early SMITH, born at Wake Co., North Carolina; died after 1912.
222 v Alton SMITH, born at Wake Co., North Carolina; died after 1912.
223 vi Valley SMITH, born at Wake Co., North Carolina; died after 1912.
224 vii Rufus Millard SMITH, born at Wake Co., North Carolina; died after 1912.
225 viii Vernon SMITH, born at Wake Co., North Carolina; died after 1912.
226 ix Macy SMITH, born at Wake Co., North Carolina; died after 1912.
227 x Herman SMITH, born at Wake Co., North Carolina; died after 1912.
228 xi Margaret SMITH, born at Wake Co., North Carolina; died after 1912.

100 Isabel SMITH, born in 1843 at Auburn, Wake Co., North Carolina.

♥ Isabel SMITH married Mr. TODD at Wake Co., North Carolina.

They had the following children:

229 i Otho TODD, born before 1886 at Wake Co., North Carolina.
230 ii Fannie TODD, born before 1886 at Wake Co., North Carolina.

Descendants of Richard Arrow Smith

Fifth Generation

104 Albert B. SMITH, born on 31 August 1847 at Raleigh, Wake Co., North Carolina; died on 18 September 1911 at Auburn, Wake Co., North Carolina; buried at Mt. Moriah Baptist Church, Auburn, Wake Co., North Carolina.

Albert B. Smith, age 55, registered to vote October 22, 1902, in the Auburn Precinct of Wake County.

♥ Albert B. SMITH married Sandal D. YOUNG on 16 October 1872 at Wake Co., North Carolina. Sandal was born in 1853 at Wake Co., North Carolina; died in 1926 at Auburn, Wake Co., North Carolina; buried at Mt. Moriah Baptist Church, Auburn, Wake Co., North Carolina.

Sandal and her sister, Frances, were twins, daughters of Francis Young and Lucy Ogburn Young. Sandal's birth and death dates were taken from her marker in Mt. Moriah Baptist Church Cemetary, Auburn, Wake County.

They had the following children:

    231 i   Lucy SMITH, born in 1874 at St. Mary's, Wake Co., North Carolina.
    232 ii   Gertrude SMITH, born about 1876 at Wake Co., North Carolina; died before 1910 at Wake Co., North Carolina.
    233 iii   Troy Gaston SMITH, born on 12 May 1878 at Wake Co., North Carolina; died on 22 April 1953 at Auburn, Wake Co., North Carolina; buried at Mt. Moriah Baptist Church, Auburn, Wake Co., North Carolina.
    234 iv   Harlan SMITH, born about 1880 at Wake Co., North Carolina.
    235 v   Lula SMITH, born about 1884 at Wake Co., North Carolina.

Descendants of Richard Arrow Smith

  236   vi   Eva SMITH, born about 1885 at Wake Co., North Carolina; died before 1910 at Wake Co., North Carolina.
  237   vii   Eppie SMITH, born on 28 September 1886 at Wake Co., North Carolina; died on 21 July 1907 at Auburn, Wake Co., North Carolina; buried at Mt. Moriah Baptist Church, Auburn, Wake Co., North Carolina.

105   Mary O. SMITH, born on 17 February 1850 at Raleigh, Wake Co., North Carolina.

♥ Mary O. SMITH married George H. BROUGHTON on 2 June 1867 at Wake Co., North Carolina. George was born about 1845 at Wake Co., North Carolina.

They had the following children:

  238   i   Leonard G. BROUGHTON, born about 1870 at Wake Co., North Carolina.

  Len G. Broughton was a reknown Baptist Minister of the Atlanta Baptist Tabernacle, which he built. He later went to serve as the pastor of a church in London, England.

110   Rev. Joseph Edwin SMITH, born on 3 September 1867 at Auburn, Wake Co., North Carolina; died on 11 July 1938 at Trafalger, Johnson Co., Indiana; buried at Calumet Park Cemetary, Gary, Lake Co., Indiana.

  Joseph Edwin Smith got "the calling" for the ministry as a young boy. He recalled that fateful day in the following sermon excerpt: "The Lord is pleased to meet us anywhere. He received me at the church. In old Mt. Moriah Church, near Auburn, North Carolina. All of the people had gone out of the church during a protracted meeting and were preparing to go home except old Uncle Calvin Pool. I remained seated on the bench where I had been a mourner for about two days. As he passed out he put his hand upon my head and (said) to me, "Can't you trust Jesus as your Savior?" I said, "Yes." I meant it and there Jesus saved me. I got up and went out of the house so happy. As I passed down toward the well, I passed old Mr. Gower and Mr. Troy Baucom walking together. Mr. Gower looked at me and said, "That boy's got religion," and I knew he was telling the truth." Rev. Smith went on to say, "Just before we left, Mr. Pool came down to the carriage and asked father to let me go home with his boys to spend the night. I went and at family prayers he gave me a place right by his side and prayed most affectionately for me. I was baptised by old brother Johnson Olive in Pool's millpond about the first Sunday in September, 1884. This was in Wake County, North Carolina." Uncle Calvin Pool(e) married as his first wife Sally Maria Smith, daughter of Samuel A. Smith, brother of Joseph's great-grandfather, William A. Smith. Samuel's wife was Sarah Baucom, aunt of Troy Baucom (son of her brother Urias Baucom).

The notes following the entry for his wife, Mary Blanche Blackwell, contain a detailed summary of Joseph's education and career moves (there were many).

Joseph Smith's sermon books and scrapbook are in the possession of his great-granddaughter, Rebecca Smith Blackwell (this researcher). They contain numerous photographs, clippings, and memories collected by Joseph and his wife, Mary Blanche. In his youth, Joseph was the "spitting image" of his grandson, E. Vernon Smith, although smaller in stature. His photos graced many newpapers and advertising flyers whenever he visited a town in Indiana and gave a public sermon. As State Evangelist for the state of Indiana, he received reviews that praised his "..pleasing personality which quickly wins, and (he) is a strong and effective preacher...has an

Descendants of Richard Arrow Smith

original way of putting things which, while at times exciting a ripple of amusement, drives home and clinches what he wishes to say. He comes to the city highly recommended, both as a preacher and successful soul winner" (15 April 1909, Bedford, Indiana).

In addition to being responsible for the construction of the First Baptist Church in Gary, Indiana (1908), Joseph did general construction work in his spare time. He and his sons built many homes in Gary.

Joseph died of a "cerebral vascular incident" (stroke) at home, in the arms of his son-in-law Robert Tranter with his wife, Blanche, by his side. He had been paralyzed for some time before his death. He was much loved and respected by all who knew him.

♥ Rev. Joseph Edwin SMITH married Mary Blanche BLACKWELL on 13 July 1892 at Townsville, Vance Co., North Carolina. Blanche was born on 20 April 1873 at Townsville, Vance Co., North Carolina; died on 19 October 1943 at Franklin, Johnson Co., Indiana; buried at Calumet Park Cemetary, Gary, Lake Co., Indiana.

Mary Blanche Blackwell was born in the home of her grandfather, John Pomfret Blackwell, in Townsville, North Carolina. At the age of 5 she began school in Townsville; her teacher was Miss Clementine Wilson and classes were held in the home of Dr. William R. Wilson. She boarded here and went home on the weekends. When she traveled home, she went on horseback, accompanied by Mary Blackwell, a black servant of her father's. Her horse's name was "Fannie"; it was given by her grandfather, Richard Jordan Wortham, to her mother, Sallie Green Wortham, as a wedding present. After one year, she then went to public school near her grandfather's home. Two years later, she went to school in Townsville, boarding

Descendants of Richard Arrow Smith

at Ed Taylor's for five months. Afterwards, she walked to and from home in Townsville to school. Her teacher, Carr Moore, was a Presbyterian minister. She attended that school until she was sixteen. She continued her education at Greensboro Female College for two years, graduating when she was nineteen.

Blanche and Joseph Edwin Smith were married at the home of J.P. Blackwell, Jr., by Rev. John R. Hall, the paster of Marrow's Chapel (Methodist). She and her husband, a Baptist minister, lived first at Mt. Olive, North Carolina, where she taught school for nine months. Then they moved back to her father's home where their son Ralph was born. They moved to Henderson, North Carolina for three months, then back to her home until her mother's death in 1893. Their next stop was Stem, North Carolina for one year, then to Creedmoor for two years. Carl was born there. Then they moved to Louisville, Kentucky, while Joseph attended the Southern Baptist Theological Seminary. Roy was born at West 9th St. After one year, they went to Mt. Vernon, Indiana. Joseph commuted to-and-from Louisville to attend classes and preach sermons on Sunday. After a year there, the next stop was Letts, Indiana where Vernon was born. They remained there for three-and-a-half years. Concord, NC was their next home and the birthplace of Edwin. Then on to Charlotte, NC for three months of evangelistic work. Mt. Airy was next, along with the birth of Mary. After three years, they moved to Franklin, Indiana for three months of evangelistic work. There Joseph was hired by the State Board. Next stop, Gary, Indiana, where Joseph was instrumental in the building of Central Baptist Church. They remained in Gary for 22 years. They made one last move back to Franklin in 1929 where they lived at 550 West Jefferson St. After their deaths, they were buried in Gary at the Calumet Park Cemetary.

Descendants of Richard Arrow Smith

Blanche began working on her family genealogy in the 1930s when she joined the Daughters of the American Revolution, claiming descent from Lt. Col. John Webb, her gr-gr-grandfather, who fought five years in the 7th and 5th Virginia Regiments, Continental Line.

Blanche was also an accomplished artist. A few of her watercolors and oil paintings are still in the possession of family members.

She died of "chronic leukemia."

They had the following children:

+ 239 i Ralph Payne SMITH.
240 ii Carl Taylor SMITH, born on 23 January 1895 at Creedmoor, Granville Co., North Carolina; died on 19 October 1918 at Marine Hospital; buried at Calumet Park Cemetary, Gary, Lake Co., Indiana.

Carl Smith died falling into a hatch of the ship William S. Corey during World War I. Ironically, he had been taking photographs and did not see where he was stepping. His camera and Navy notebook are in the possession of Rebecca Blackwell, his grandniece.

Carl's middle name of Taylor is probably in remembrance of his great-grandmother Elizabeth Taylor, wife of Edwin A. Smith.

+ 241 iii Roy Pomfret SMITH.
+ 242 iv Elmer Vernon SMITH.
+ 243 v Joseph Edwin SMITH II.
+ 244 vi Mary Blanche SMITH.

112 William O. SMITH, born on 7 February 1871 at Auburn, Wake Co., North Carolina; died on 25 May 1921 at Washington, D.C.; buried in May 1921.

Descendants of Richard Arrow Smith

♥ William O. SMITH married Helen BURGE on 21 December 1892 at Wake Co., North Carolina.

They had the following children:

    245   i   Henry SMITH, born about 1894 at Wake Co., North Carolina.
    246   ii   Jimmy SMITH, born about 1896 at Wake Co., North Carolina.
    247   iii   Helen SMITH, born about 1898 at Wake Co., North Carolina.

113   John W. SMITH, born on 7 June 1873 at Auburn, Wake Co., North Carolina; died on 25 November 1936 at Norfolk, Virginia; buried November 1936.

John W. Smith was employed as an overseer at the North Carolina State Prison in the 1899-1900 Raleigh City Directory. Sometime later, he moved his family to Norfolk, Virginia. A photograph of John, wife Daisy, and his three young children is in the possession of Rebecca Blackwell.

John W. SMITH married Daisy TURNER on 19 October 1896 at Wake Co., North Carolina. Daisy was born about 1875.

They had the following children:

    248   i   Muriel SMITH, born about 1898.
    249   ii   Esther SMITH, born about 1900.
    250   iii   Palmer SMITH, born about 1902.

114   Carrie Etta SMITH, born on 2 October 1874 at Auburn, Wake Co., North Carolina; died after 1959 at Norfolk, Virginia.

In the 1899 Raleigh City Directory, Miss Carrie E. Smith is listed as living at the home

Descendants of Richard Arrow Smith

of her mother, 408 N. Person St., and employed as an operator at the Bell Telephone Company.

♥ Carrie Etta SMITH married William H. KUESTER on 29 March 1899 at Wake Co., North Carolina. He was born about 1870; died at Norfolk, Virginia.

They had the following children:

   251 i Raymond L. KUESTER, born about 1901 at Wake Co., North Carolina.
   252 ii Louise Elizabeth KUESTER, born about 1903 at Wake Co., North Carolina.

118 Nellie May SMITH, born on 31 August 1885 at Raleigh, Wake Co., North Carolina; died after 1959 at Norfolk, Virginia.

Nellie May SMITH married Claude L. PARKER on 22 October 1902 at Wake Co., North Carolina. Claude was born about 1880; died at Norfolk, Virginia.

In 1959 this family was residing at 519 Carolina Avenue, Norfolk, Virginia.

They had the following children:

   253 i Lewis PARKER, born about 1904.
   254 ii Evelyn PARKER, born about 1906.
   255 iii Virginia PARKER, born about 1908.
   256 iv Bernard PARKER, born about 1910.
   257 v Robert PARKER, born about 1912.

119 Sarah Jane SMITH, born November 1849 at St. Mary's, Wake Co., North Carolina, according to the 1850 census.

Descendants of Richard Arrow Smith

♥ Sarah Jane SMITH married Alphious Lucian Ferrell on 7 December 1870 at Wake Co., North Carolina. A.L. was born on 18 September 1845 at Wake Co., North Carolina; died on 9 November 1893 at Wake Co., North Carolina.

Alphious Lucian Ferrell was the son of Laban Ferrell and wife Ailey. Laban was the son of James Ferrell and wife Anna (Anner).

They had the following children:

    258   i   Alice Catherine FERRELL, born in 1872 at Wake Co., North Carolina.

♥ Alice Catherine FERRELL married John Knox HAIR on 27 December 1917 at Wake Co., North Carolina.

    259   ii   Maggie Dent FERRELL, born on 11 January 1874 at Wake Co., North Carolina.
    260   iii   Hattie Helen FERRELL, born in March of 1877 at Wake Co., North Carolina.
    261   iv   Emma Rosa FERRELL, born on 9 February 1878 at Wake Co., North Carolina.

♥ Emma Rosa FERRELL married Frederick Earl MITCHELL on 23 April 1902 at Wake Co., North Carolina.

    262   v   Nellie FERRELL, born about 1878 at Wake Co., North Carolina.
    263   vi   Waylan Lucian FERRELL, born on 3 September 1879 at Wake Co., North Carolina.

140   Leonard W. SMITH, born about 1861 at St. Mary's, Wake Co., North Carolina; died after 1900 at Raleigh, Wake Co., North Carolina.

In the 1896-97 Raleigh City Directory, Leonard W. Smith is listed as a Printer at Edwards and Broughton, residing at 308 N. Dawson.

Descendants of Richard Arrow Smith

♥ Leonard SMITH married Sarah at Wake Co., North Carolina. Sarah was born about 1861 at Wake Co., North Carolina.

They had the following children:

    264   i   Leonard SMITH, born at Wake Co., North Carolina.

In the 1896-7 Raleigh City Directory, Leonard is listed as a student, living at home at 308 N. Dawson.

158   Simeon Lonnie SMITH, born on 3 April 1873 at Johnston Co., North Carolina; died on 4 July 1944.

♥ Simeon Lonnie SMITH married Everlina Elendor TEMPLE on 10 Dec 1893 at Middle Creek, Wake Co., North Carolina. She was born about 1880 at North Carolina.

They had the following children:

    265   i   Grover Artimas SMITH, born on 14 May 1898 at Wake Co., North Carolina; died on 29 September 1981 at Harnett Co., North Carolina.

♥ Grover Artimas SMITH married Carrie Elizabeth MESSER on 8 July 1917 at Harnett Co., North Carolina. Carrie was born on 9 November 1901 at Wake Co., North Carolina; died on 28 July 1963 at Harnett Co., North Carolina.

159   James Addison SMITH, born on 10 December 1876 at Johnston Co., North Carolina; died at Raleigh, Wake Co., North Carolina; buried at Oakwood Cemetary, Raleigh, Wake Co., North Carolina.

Descendants of Richard Arrow Smith

♥ James Addison SMITH married Amelia MYATT on 20 September 1883 at Myatt's Mill, Wake Co., North Carolina. She was born about 1860 at North Carolina.

They had the following children:

  263 i Myrtle SMITH, born about 1885 at North Carolina.
  264 ii Addison Glenn SMITH, born about 1887 at North Carolina.
  265 iii Margaret SMITH, born about 1900 at North Carolina.

Maggie died before she reached adulthood.

  266 iv Paul L. SMITH, born in 1904 at North Carolina.
  267 v Chester B. SMITH, born in 1906 at North Carolina.
  268 vi Harvey Moody SMITH, born about 1907 at North Carolina.

162 Richard Henderson SMITH "Bud", born on 13 March 1881 at Johnston Co., North Carolina; died on 16 May 1961 at Johnston Co., North Carolina.

♥ Richard Henderson SMITH "Bud" married Alvie Healon TEMPLE on 6 August 1907 at Fuquay Springs, Wake Co., North Carolina. She was born on 6 June 1896 at North Carolina; died on 7 April 1936.

They had the following children:

  269 i Corina Maude SMITH, born on 1 July 1900 at North Carolina.

Corina was adopted. Her biological parents are unknown.

  270 ii Mayton SMITH, born on 26 November 1905 at North Carolina.

Descendants of Richard Arrow Smith

  271 iii Avis SMITH, born on 15 December 1907 at North Carolina.
  272 iv Gladys SMITH, born on 22 July 1909 at Johnston Co., North Carolina.
  273 v Irene SMITH, born on 26 December 1911 at Johnston Co., North Carolina.
  274 vi Melvin H. SMITH, born on 25 June 1916 at Johnston Co., North Carolina.

176 William Alfred SMITH, born on 8 November 1899 at North Carolina; died on 2 December 1975 at Raleigh, Wake Co., North Carolina; buried at Franklin Co., North Carolina.

  William died of respiratory failure caused by acute bronchopneumonia while trying to recover from injuries sustained in a car accident.

 ♥ William Alfred SMITH married Pattie MOYE in North Carolina. Pattie died on 17 January 1926 at Franklin Co., North Carolina.

  They had the following children:

  + **275** i Alfred Daniel SMITH.
  + **276** ii Lawrence Odell SMITH.

 ♥ William Alfred SMITH married Bessie Gray PRIVETTE after 1926 at Franklin Co., North Carolina. Bessie died on 23 October 1929 at Franklin Co., North Carolina.

  They had the following children:

  277 iii Willie Gray SMITH, born after 1926 at Franklin Co., North Carolina.

  Willie died as an infant.

 ♥ William Alfred SMITH married Irma Mae BAKER after 1929 at Franklin Co., North Carolina. She

Descendants of Richard Arrow Smith

was born on 6 July 1909 at Franklin Co., North Carolina.

They had the following children:

+ 278 iv James Maylon SMITH.
+ 279 v Patricia Mae SMITH.

177 Lonnie Hilliard SMITH, born on 17 September 1902 at Franklin Co., North Carolina; died on 28 November 1988 at Raleigh, Wake Co., North Carolina; buried on 30 November 1988 at Gethsemane Memorial Cemetary, Zebulon, Wake Co., North Carolina.

Lonnie Hilliard Smith was considered to be an excellent tobacco farmer until he was stricken by a series of strokes which left him paralyzed on the left side. He spent the last ten years of his life in a nursing home.

♥ Lonnie Hilliard SMITH married Lillie Irene MITCHELL on 15 October 1924 at North Carolina. She was born on 4 April 1906 at Franklin Co., North Carolina; died on 22 August 1986 at Raleigh, Wake Co., North Carolina; buried at Gethsemane Memorial Cemetary, Zebulon, Wake Co., North Carolina.

They had the following children:

+ 280 i Betty Frances SMITH.
+ 281 ii Jesse Willard SMITH.
+ 282 iii Crama Lee SMITH.
+ 283 iv Lonnie Ruffin SMITH.
+ 284 v Jasper Glenn SMITH.
+ 285 vi Linda Carol SMITH.

178 Haywood Thomas SMITH, born about 1904 at Franklin Co., North Carolina.

Descendants of Richard Arrow Smith

♥ Haywood Thomas SMITH married Mary Gray PACE at Franklin County, North Carolina. Mary was born on 21 March 1910 at Franklin Co., North Carolina; died on 31 May 1933 at Pine Ridge, Franklin Co., North Carolina.

They had the following children:

+ 286 i Billy Thomas SMITH.
287 ii Baby SMITH, born on 3 June 1932 at Franklin Co., North Carolina; died on 3 June 1932 at Franklin Co., North Carolina.

Baby died before she was given a name.

288 iii Ernest Gray SMITH, born on 1 May 1933 at Franklin Co., North Carolina; died on 5 June 1981; buried at Pine Ridge, Franklin Co., North Carolina.

Earnest Gray Smith was stricken with polio at the age of eighteen months.

♥ Haywood Thomas SMITH married Willie Lee STONACHER as his second wife, date unknown.

198 Garner Arrista SMITH, born on 5 August 1878 at Johnston Co., North Carolina; died on 20 Augist 1962 at Clayton, Johnston Co., North Carolina; buried at Maplewood Cemetary, Clayton, Johnston Co., North Carolina.

♥ Garner Arrista SMITH married Myrtie Irene JONES on 31 May 1909 at Selma, Johnston Co., North Carolina. She was born on 13 December 1887 at Johnston Co., North Carolina; died on 8 November 1963 at Clayton, Johnston Co., North Carolina; buried at Maplewood Cemetary, Clayton, Johnston Co., North Carolina.

They had the following children:

Descendants of Richard Arrow Smith

      289   i   Annie Estelle SMITH, born on 21 March 1910 at Johnston Co., North Carolina.

♥ Annie Estelle SMITH married Roger BARBOUR at Johnston Co., North Carolina.

      290   ii   Dock Garner SMITH, born on 10 December 1913 at Johnston Co., North Carolina; died on 3 July 1950 at Clayton, Johnston Co., North Carolina; buried at Maplewood Cemetary, Clayton, Johnston Co., North Carolina.

♥ Dock Garner SMITH married Helen Gold RAINES at Johnston Co., North Carolina. Helen was born about 1915.

      291   iii   Grace SMITH, born on 14 November 1915 at Johnston Co., North Carolina.
      292   iv   Delia Irene SMITH, born on 17 November 1921 at Johnston Co., North Carolina.

♥ Delia Irene SMITH married J. C. BLAKE at Johnston Co., North Carolina.

205   Ava POOLE, born on 29 October 1886 at Auburn, Wake Co., North Carolina; died 4 January 1974 at Winston-Salem, Forsyth Co., North Carolina.

♥ Ava POOLE married Santford W. MARTIN on 23 October 1910 at Wake Co., North Carolina. He was born about 1880.

    Santford W. Martin was a noted newspaper publisher in Winston-Salem, North Carolina.

    They had the following children:

        + 293   i   Edwina MARTIN.
        + 294   ii   Santford Wingate MARTIN.

Descendants of Richard Arrow Smith

208 Irene Lula SMITH, born on 1893 at Johnston Co., North Carolina.

♥ Irene Lula SMITH married Norman Gaston JONES before 1919 at Johnston Co., North Carolina. Norman was born on 30 March 1890 at Johnston Co., North Carolina; died on 13 January 1963 at Bethesda, Johnston Co., North Carolina; buried at Bethesda Cemetary, Johnston Co., North Carolina.

They had the following children:

    295   i   Norman Woodrow JONES, born on 9 September 1919 at Johnston Co., North Carolina; died on 16 November 1964 at Bethesda, Johnston Co., North Carolina.
    296   ii   Geraldine JONES, born May 1924 at Johnston Co., North Carolina.

216 Della POOLE, born on 18 May 1876 at Auburn, Wake Co., North Carolina.

♥ Della POOLE married William Bonnie DAUGHTRY on 27 November 1901 at Mt. Moriah Baptist, Auburn, Wake Co., North Carolina. He was born about 1875.

They had the following children:

    297   i   William Bonnie DAUGHTRY Jr., born on 19 February 1905 at Blackstone, Nottoway Co., Virginia.
    298   ii   Miriam DAUGHTRY, born on 16 January 1909 at Meherrin, Brunswick Co., Virginia; died in May 1979 at North Carolina.

Descendants of Richard Arrow Smith

Sixth Generation

239 Ralph Payne SMITH, born on 20 August 1893 at Townsville, Vance Co., North Carolina.

♥ Ralph Payne SMITH married Isabelle Maude CLEVELAND on 17 June 1916. She was born about 1895. They were divorced before 1935.

They had the following children:

    299 i   Helen Arlyne SMITH, born in 1917 at Gary, Lake Co., Indiana.

♥ Ralph Payne SMITH married Viola Hagerman HANES in 1935 at Gary, Lake Co., Indiana.

They had the following children:

    300 ii   Carl Taylor SMITH II, born in 1937 at Gary, Lake Co., Indiana.

241 Roy Pomfret SMITH, born on 29 March 1897 at Louisville, Jefferson Co., Kentucky; died in 1972 at Ft. Myers, Lee Co., Florida.

Roy Pomfret Smith was born Pomfret LeRoy Smith. He apparently did not like that name and made the change. Roy was a dentist.

♥ Roy Pomfret SMITH married Elsie Loraine JORS on 30 June 1923 at Gary, Lake Co., Indiana. She was born about 1900.

They had the following children:

    301 i   Glenn Carl SMITH, born in 1924 at Gary, Lake Co., Indiana.
    302 ii   Roy Pomfret SMITH Jr., born in 1928 at Gary, Lake Co., Indiana; died in 1930 at Gary, Lake Co., Indiana.

Descendants of Richard Arrow Smith

      303   iii   Gail Ruth SMITH, born in 1932 at Gary, Lake Co., Indiana.

242   Elmer Vernon SMITH, born on 27 May 1899 at Letts, Decatur Co., Indiana; died on 27 July 1973 at Gary, Lake Co., Indiana; buried at Lehigh Acres, Lee Co., Florida.

    Vernon's nickname was "Deak," short for Deacon, a moniker earned in his youth for reasons unknown.

    Vernon worked in the steel mills of Gary, Indiana, before moving to Franklin and being co-owner of Turney's Shoe Store on Main Street, along with his brother-in-law, Bob Tranter. They changed the name to Smith and Tranter. When Vernon bought out Bob's half of the business, it became Smith's Shoe Store. Hazel and Vernon worked side-by-side, making a good living. Their home was at 1021 E. King Street.

    After retirement, Vernon and Hazel moved to Lehigh Acres, Florida where they lived happily until Hazel's death in 1971.

    After Hazel's death, Vernon was contacted by an old friend from high school, Ethel Teeples. They were married in 1972 and Vernon moved back to Gary, which was her home. Although Vernon continued to call Ethel "Hazel" by mistake, she loved him dearly and took excellent care of him till his death of arteriosclerosis. She died a few months later.

    Vernon was a good man and a kind-hearted soul who is missed by all who knew him. His son, E.V., calls him, "The finest man I ever knew."

♥ Elmer Vernon SMITH married Hazel Muriel BUNDY on 19 December 1927 at Indianapolis, Marion Co., Indiana. Hazel was born on 17 October 1899 at

Descendants of Richard Arrow Smith

Salem, Washington Co., Indiana; died on 27 March 1971 at Ft. Myers, Lee Co., Florida; buried at Lehigh Acres, Lee Co., Florida.

Hazel was the daughter of Willam Grant Bundy and Mollie Susan Fultz Bundy of Washington County, Indiana. Hazel was a teacher before she married Vernon. She worked most of her life, helping Vernon run Smith's Shoe Store in Franklin, Indiana. She was a loving, consciencious mother and grandmother who always tried to do her best. Her Quaker upbringing was evident in her strong code of moral behavior. At the time of her death, Hazel was a Deacon of her Presbyterian church in Lehigh Acres, Florida.

She died of lung cancer after having given-up smoking years before. She is missed by her wide circle of family and friends.

They had the following children:

+ 304   i   E. Vernon SMITH
   305   ii   David William SMITH, born on 10 March 1940 at Gary, Lake Co., Indiana; died on 19 April 1940 at Gary, Lake Co., Indiana; buried April 1940 at Calumet Park Cemetary, Gary, Lake Co., Indiana.

David Smith reportedly died of Sudden Infant Death Syndrome. He was born in Methodist Hospital.

   306   iii   Richard Bundy SMITH, born in 1941 at Gary, Lake Co., Indiana; died in 1941 at Gary, Lake Co., Indiana; buried on 1941 at Calumet Park Cemetary, Gary, Lake Co., Indiana.

Richard Smith's exact birthdate is unknown, but he lived only one day. He was born, and died, in Methodist Hospital.

Descendants of Richard Arrow Smith

243 Joseph Edwin SMITH II, born on 12 November 1902 at Concord, North Carolina.

Joseph Edwin Smith, II, was known as "Eddie". He was an attorney at law in Gary, Indiana.

♥ Joseph Edwin SMITH II married Isabel CURTIS in 1926.

They had the following children:

    307 i Barbara Isabel SMITH, born on 1929.

    308 ii Curtis Blackwell SMITH, born on 22 May 1931 at Gary, Lake Co., Indiana; died on 29 May 1950 at Memphis, Shelby Co., Tennesee; buried June 1950 at Gary, Lake Co., Indiana.

Curtis Blackwell Smith attended Castle Heights Military Academy, Morgan Park Military Academy, and graduated from high school while he was living with his grandfather in Orlando, Florida. He entered Great Lakes Naval Training Station in July of 1949 and went into aviation training at Memphis, Tennessee.

While in Memphis, he had an altercation with a man named Ellroy Union Barefield of 347 Union Street. Barefield, 53, claimed Curtis and he had met in a bar, had a drink together, then Barefield went home. He reported that Curtis knocked on his door at 1:30 a.m. Monday, May 29, asking to sleep in Barefield's apartment. Barefield claimed Curtis struck him, then taking $3.00 in cash and a watch. Barefield took out a case knife and stabbed Curtis in the chest, neck and ear, killing him. He was arrested and charged with murder. Curtis was 19 years old.

    309 iii Joseph Edwin SMITH III, born in 1933 at Gary, Lake Co., Indiana.

Descendants of Richard Arrow Smith

244   Mary Blanche SMITH, born on 17 August 1908 at Mt. Airy, Surrey Co., North Carolina.

♥ Mary Blanche SMITH married Robert Reece TRANTER on 15 July 1929 at Chicago, Cook Co., Illinois. Bob was born on 9 June 1906 at Swayzee, Grant Co., Indiana; died 20 August 1979 at Franklin, Johnson Co., Indiana; buried at Greenlawn Cemetary, Franklin, Johnson Co., Indiana.

Bob Tranter was holding his father-in-law, Joseph Smith, in his arms when he died.

They had the following children:

+ 310   i   Robert Reece TRANTER II.
+ 311   ii   Mary Anne TRANTER.

275   Alfred Daniel SMITH, born on 30 October 1923 at Franklin Co., North Carolina.

♥ Alfred Daniel SMITH married Sally Lou MURRAY on 11 January 1946 at Franklin Co., North Carolina.

They had the following children:

+ 312   i   Rexie Jane SMITH.
  313   ii   Danny Marcus SMITH, born on 28 March 1950 at Franklin Co., North Carolina.

♥ Danny Marcus SMITH married Ann ALLEN on 14 February 1980 at Franklin Co., North Carolina. She was born on 8 September 1953 at Wake Co., North Carolina.

+ 314   iii   Peggy Lou SMITH.
+ 315   iv   Brenda Joyce SMITH.

Descendants of Richard Arrow Smith

276 Lawrence Odell SMITH, born March 1926 at Franklin Co., North Carolina; died on 5 March 1976 at Wilson Co., North Carolina.

♥ Lawrence Odell SMITH married Judy PERRY in March 1946.

They had the following children:

+ 316 i Lawrence Glenn SMITH.
+ 317 ii Russel Keith SMITH.

278 James Maylon SMITH, born on 25 January 1944 at Franklin Co., North Carolina.

♥ James Maylon SMITH married Janice LaRue BROWN at Franklin Co., North Carolina. Janice was born on 9 August 1946 at Johnston Co., North Carolina.

They had the following children:

318 i Timothy Wayne SMITH, born on 17 April 1972 at Wake Co., North Carolina.

279 Patricia Mae SMITH, born on 22 December 1948 at Franklin Co., North Carolina.

♥ Patricia Mae SMITH married Dan Thomas BURNETTE. Dan was born on 11 August 1944 at Nash Co., North Carolina.

They had the following children:

319 i Michael Dale BURNETTE, born on 17 October 1968 at Wake Co., North Carolina.

280 Betty Frances SMITH, born on 27 December 1925 at Franklin Co., North Carolina.

Descendants of Richard Arrow Smith

Betty worked as an electronics technician with ITT Corporation. She retired in 1991.

♥ Betty Frances SMITH married Charles George CLARK on 10 June 1944 at Wake Co., North Carolina; born on 22 November 1925 at Zebulon, Wake Co., North Carolina.

They had the following children:

+ 320   i   Gloria Jean CLARK.
+ 321   ii   Charles Richard CLARK.
+ 322   iii   Pamela Lynn CLARK.

♥ Betty Frances SMITH married Alfred Weldon ADAMS 8 December 1962 at Wake Co., North Carolina. Alfred was born 14 May 1914 at North Carolina.

They had the following children:

323   iv   Robin Frances ADAMS, born on 26 August 1963 at Anson Co., North Carolina.

♥ Robin Frances ADAMS married Linwood Sherrill PIPER on 2 April 1983 at Wake Co., North Carolina. He was born on 30 July 1964.

281   Jesse Willard SMITH, born on 5 February 1927 at Franklin Co., North Carolina.

Jesse moved to Nashville, Tennessee as a young man and obtained a job as an electrician lineman with Tennessee Power and Light Company. Before retiring, he had advanced to a management position.

♥ Jesse Willard SMITH married Sarah Gwendolyn KITCHENS at South Carolina.

They had the following children:

Descendants of Richard Arrow Smith

    324   i   Deborah Lynn SMITH, born on 24 December 1959 at Nashville, Davidson Co., Tennessee.

    325   ii   Kenneth Alan SMITH, born on 8 May 1968 at Nashville, Davidson Co., Tennessee.

♥ Jesse Willard SMITH married Evelyn Louise HORNER after 1968 at Nashville, Davidson Co., Tennessee.

282   Crama Lee SMITH, born on 22 May 1929 at Franklin Co., North Carolina.

    Crama worked as an assistant cashier at North Carolina State University, Raleigh, North Carolina for three years prior to marriage. After marriage she and her husband moved to Yorktown, Virginia, where she secured a Federal Civil Service job at the Naval Weapons Station. She started work as a Clerk-Typist and moved up the ladder to the position of Budget Officer (GS-13) before retirement. She was the first woman to hold that position at the Naval Weapons Station.

♥ Crama Lee SMITH married Billy Ross GRAHAM on 20 January 1951 at Hampton, Virginia. He was born on 28 March 1926 at Star, Montgomery Co., North Carolina.

    They had the following children:

+ 326   i   Steven Ross GRAHAM.

283   Lonnie Ruffin SMITH, born on 30 June 1931 at Franklin Co., North Carolina.

    Lonnie enlisted in the U.S. Army at the age of 18. He served in Germany, Korea and Viet Nam. He earned the rank of Master Sergeant (E-9) before retiring. Since that time, he has worked at the following jobs: bowling alley manager, truck driver, construction worker and a planner and estimator for a roofing contractor.

♥ Lonnie Ruffin SMITH married Katrina ALFORD on 2 October 1954 at Raleigh, Wake Co., North Carolina. Katrina was born on 4 August 1931 at Wake Co., North Carolina.

They had the following children:

+ 327   i   Kitty Sue SMITH.
+ 328   ii   Donnie Ruffin SMITH.
+ 329   iii   Kathy Ann SMITH.

284 Jasper Glenn SMITH, born on 26 November 1933 at Franklin Co., North Carolina.

Jasper enlisted in the U.S. Army, Transportation Corps. After he was discharged, his occupation was that of a tractor-trailer truck driver.

Jasper Glenn SMITH married Rachel ROGERS on 1956 at Wake Co., North Carolina.

They had the following children:

   330   i   Tammy Phyllis SMITH, born on 5 May 1957 at North Carolina.

♥ Tammy Phyllis SMITH married Michael PARKER.

♥ Jasper Glenn SMITH married Clara Lee Blackburn HOPE on 21 February 1961.

They had the following children:

+ 331   ii   Sonya Irene SMITH.

Descendants of Richard Arrow Smith

285 Linda Carol SMITH, born on 2 April 1945 at Franklin Co., North Carolina.

Linda is employed (1992) as a teacher's assistant in Zebulon, North Carolina.

♥ Linda Carol SMITH married Grady Ray CREECH on 13 October 1963 at Zebulon, Wake Co., North Carolina. Grady was born on 9 December 1941 at Wake Co., North Carolina.

They had the following children:

    332   i   Timothy Ray CREECH, born on 12 December 1965 at Wake Co., North Carolina.

♥ Timothy Ray CREECH married Demetrae Lynn HOLIFIELD on 28 July 1990 at North Carolina.

    333   ii   Wanda Joy CREECH, born on 12 January 1968 at Wake Co., North Carolina.
    334   iii   Rodney Alan CREECH, born on 20 August 1970 at Wake Co., North Carolina.
    335   iv   Anthony Scott CREECH, born on 21 February 1972 at Wake Co., North Carolina.

286 Billy Thomas SMITH, born on 29 July 1929 at Franklin Co., North Carolina.

♥ Billy Thomas SMITH married Carol Ann COX on 17 December 1955 at Jones Co., North Carolina. Carol was born on 3 February 1935.

They had the following children:

    + 336   i   Donna Lynn SMITH.
    337   ii   Donald Duane SMITH, born on 9 February 1964 at Wayne Co., North Carolina.

293 Edwina MARTIN, born on 26 August 1911 at Wake Co., North Carolina; died on 12 March 1983.

Descendants of Richard Arrow Smith

Ted was born on 20 November 1908; died on 16 August 1976 at Treasure Island, Pinellas Co., Florida.

♥ Edwina MARTIN married Edward A. CROWTHER on 6 December 1937.

They had the following children:

+ 338 i Sandra F. CROWTHER.
+ 339 ii Edward A. CROWTHER, Jr.

294 Santford Wingate MARTIN, born on 22 February 1922 at Winston-Salem, Forsyth Co., North Carolina.

♥ Santford W. MARTIN, Jr., married Frances HARRELL on 26 June 1948 in North Carolina. Frances was born on 26 April 1926 at Marshville, Union Co., North Carolina.

They had the following children:

340 i Miriam Frances MARTIN, born on 6 November 1954 at Raleigh, Wake Co., North Carolina.
341 ii Santford Frank MARTIN, born on 22 January 1956 at Raleigh, Wake Co., North Carolina.

♥ Sandy MARTIN married Corinna WILLIAMS on 29 October 1988 at Wake Co., North Carolina.

Descendants of Richard Arrow Smith

Seventh Generation

304 E. Vernon SMITH, born on 14 May 1932 at Gary, Lake Co., Indiana.

Vernon, E.V.'s dad, never liked his first name, Elmer. When he named his son after himself, he skipped the name Elmer, using only the initial E. in its place.

E.V., as he has always been called, has worked for the state of Virginia for 30 years. He is currently (1992) employed by the University of Virginia as the Associate Director of Business Affairs of the Housing Division.

He graduated from Indiana University as a Distinguished Military Graduate in 1954, majoring in Accounting. He began his military career as a Lieutenant, serving as a paratrooper in the 82nd Airborne Division and in Korea (1956).

He resigned from active service in 1959, continuing to serve in the Army Reserves. He retired as a Major.

His hobbies revolve around music and history. E.V. is a charter member of the Richmond (Virginia) Concert Band where he plays the trumpet, an instrument he played in his youth and picked up again in his 40's. Also, his interest in the Civil War has kept him busy collecting relics and researching. He is a co-author of *Rio Hill: Happenings and Relics* (Battle in Charlottesville, Virginia in 1864).

E.V. is an active, loving father who keeps young raising his two daughters from his third marriage.

♥ E. Vernon SMITH married Christine Joyce JONES on 14 June 1951 at Columbus, Lownes Co.,

Descendants of Richard Arrow Smith

Mississippi. Christine was born on 23 June 1932 at Corinth, Alcorn Co., Mississippi.

Christine is the third of six daughters of Hubert C. Jones and Anita Crider Jones of Corinth, Mississippi. She went to Judson College for one year where she met E.V. Smith (he was attending a nearby military academy). After her marriage, she attended Indiana University in Bloomington, majoring in Home Economics, until her first child was born.

Christine has been employed by the City of Dayton, Ohio, for many years. She is currently (1992) employed in the Office of Redevelopment where she purchases properties for the city. She also works part-time at Hyatt Legal Services.

They had the following children:

342 i Rebecca Lynn (Smith) BLACKWELL, born on 21 July 1952 at Corinth, Alcorn Co., Mississippi.

Rebecca, being young and not fond the surname Smith, adopted her great-grandmother Blanche's surname, Blackwell, in 1977. In her research she has since discovered the Smith family originally carried the surname Arrowsmith, abbreviating it in the early 1800s. Arrowsmith being a much more unusual name, Rebecca is disappointed her ancestors dropped the prefix.

Rebecca graduated from the University of South Florida in 1973 with a degree in Psychology and went on to graduate work at the Universities of Virginia and Washington.

She has been a special education teacher since 1976, and she is currently employed in Maryland. She has also taught in: Newport, Kentucky; Dayton, Ohio; Denver, Colorado; Wyoming (Wind

Descendants of Richard Arrow Smith

River Indian Reservation); Seattle, Washington and Devon, England.

Rebecca is the newest generation to continue the genealogical research begun by her great-grandmother, Blanche. She is indebted to her father, as well, for his work done in the late 1950s.

+ 343   ii   Clay Blackwell SMITH.

♥ E. Vernon SMITH married Roberta HEIMBACH December 1960 at Indianapolis, Indiana. Roberta was born on 19 April 1934 at Quakertown, Pennsylvania.

♥ E. Vernon SMITH married Linda Louise SCHWARZENBOECK on 14 February 1976 at Charlottesville, Albemarle Co., Virginia. Linda was born on 29 May 1944 at Brooklyn, Kings Co., New York.

Linda is the daughter of August Schwarzenboeck and Maria Gar Schwarzenboeck of Bavaria, Germany. August emigrated first in November of 1828, sending for Maria in April of 1930. They were married that year in New York and lived at E.69th Street. Later, they moved their large family to Albemarle County, Virginia, in 1949 and started a dairy farm near Ash Lawn, James Monroe's home.

They had the following children:

    344   iii   Jennifer Bundy SMITH, born on 26 September 1983 at Charlottesville, Albemarle Co., Virginia.
    345   iv   Katherine Gar SMITH, born on 28 May 1986 at Charlottesville, Albemarle Co., Virginia.

Descendants of Richard Arrow Smith

310 Robert Reece TRANTER II, born on 19 January 1931 at Franklin, Johnson Co., Indiana.

♥ Robert Reece TRANTER II married Jo Ann "Jody" FRIDDLE on 2 December 1953 at Franklin, Johnson Co., Indiana. Jody was born on 7 March 1934 at Washington, Davies Co., Indiana.

Jody is the daughter of Burl Rush Friddle and Anna Margaret Whitesides Friddle. Burl was born Burl Ellis Rush and was adopted by his mother and her second husband.

Bob and Jody live in Franklin, Indiana.

They had the following children:

+ 346 i Cynthia Ann TRANTER.
+ 347 ii Debra Jo TRANTER.
+ 348 iii William Robert TRANTER.
+ 349 iv John Richard TRANTER.

311 Mary Anne TRANTER, born on 14 March 1941 at Franklin, Johnson Co., Indiana.

♥ Anne TRANTER married Robert Martin MALINKA on 22 August 1965 at Franklin, Johnson Co., Indiana. Bob was born on 10 January 1939 at Gary, Lake Co., Indiana.

Anne is trained as a public school teacher, while Bob is the Superintendent of Schools in Franklin, Indiana.

They had the following children:

350 i Julia Ann MALINKA, born on 30 July 1966 at Franklin, Johnson Co., Indiana.
351 ii Amy Lynn MALINKA, born on 12 December 1968 at Franklin, Johnson Co., Indiana.
352 iii Mary Laura MALINKA, born on 12 December 1968 at Franklin, Johnson Co., Indiana.

Descendants of Richard Arrow Smith

312 Rexie Jane SMITH, born on 4 March 1947 at Franklin Co., North Carolina.

♥ Rexie Jane SMITH married Stephen Walter LYE on 29 March 1969 at Franklin Co., North Carolina. Stephen was born on 4 September 1946.

They had the following children:

353 i Kevin Daniel LYE, born on 24 January 1973 at Indianapolis, Marion Co., Indiana.
354 ii James LYE, born on 7 September 1977 at Indianapolis, Marion Co., Indiana.

314 Peggy Lou SMITH, born on 21 October 1954 at Franklin Co., North Carolina.

♥ Peggy Lou SMITH married Steve HICKS in 1977 at South Carolina.

♥ Peggy Lou SMITH married Richard MATHEU on 16 August 1986 at Franklin Co., North Carolina.

They had the following children:

355 i Patty Smith MATHEU, born on 26 July 1989 at Charlottesville, Albemarle Co., Virginia.

315 Brenda Joyce SMITH, born on 6 January 1958 at Franklin Co., North Carolina.

♥ Brenda Joyce SMITH married Ronald Clayton DAVIS on 11 August 1984 at Forsyth Co., North Carolina. He was born in 1956 at Forsyth Co., North Carolina.

They had the following children:

Descendants of Richard Arrow Smith

   356 i Robert Sanders DAVIS IV, born on 20 June 1989 at Forsyth Co., North Carolina.

316 Lawrence Glenn SMITH, born on 2 July 1947 at Wake Co., North Carolina.

♥ Lawrence Glenn SMITH married Iris Sue HILTON in 1968 at Forsyth Co., North Carolina.

 They had the following children:

   357 i Olivia Jean SMITH, born on 3 November 1975 at Forsyth Co., North Carolina.
   358 ii Jason Odell SMITH, born on 24 July 1979 at Pontiac, Oakland Co., Michigan.

♥ Lawrence Glenn SMITH married Mary Lynn HIGHTOWER on 12 June 1971. She was born on 24 August 1950.

317 Russell Keith SMITH, born on 8 June 1954 at Forsyth Co., North Carolina.

♥ Russel Keith SMITH married Kathy, surname unknown.

 They had the following children:

   359 i Anna Christena SMITH, born at Forsyth Co., North Carolina.

320 Gloria Jean CLARK, born on 15 June 1945 at Wake Co., North Carolina.

♥ Gloria Jean CLARK married William Frederick PRIVETTE on 17 June 1963 at Wake Co., North Carolina. He was born on 8 December 1942 at Franklin Co., North Carolina.

Descendants of Richard Arrow Smith

They had the following children:

+ 360 i Debbie Lorraine PRIVETTE.
361 ii Nancy Michelle PRIVETTE, born on 30 December 1974.
362 iii Cindy Evonne PRIVETTE, born on 15 January 1977.

321 Charles Richard CLARK, born on 5 October 1947 at Wake Co., North Carolina.

♥ Charles Richard CLARK married Tuyet Thi BUI on 23 December 1970. She was born on 5 Aug 1948 at South Vietnam.

They had the following children:

363 i Frances Tuyet CLARK, born on 17 June 1972 at North Carolina.
364 ii Victor Alan CLARK, born on 24 October 1973 at North Carolina.

322 Pamela Lynn CLARK, born on 25 April 1954 at Anson Co., North Carolina.

♥ Pamela Lynn CLARK married James Pinkney CARROLL on 10 November 1975 at Wake Co., North Carolina. James was born on 25 May 1954 at Houston, Harris Co., Texas.

They had the following children:

365 i Jason Michael CARROLL, born on 13 June 1978.
366 ii Jonathan Wayne CARROLL, born on 13 June 1980.
367 iii Jamie Lynn CARROLL, born on 17 April 1983.

Descendants of Richard Arrow Smith

326   Steven Ross GRAHAM, born on 7 November 1951 at Louisburg, Franklin Co., North Carolina.

♥ Steven Ross GRAHAM married Patricia Ann WINSLOW on 14 February 1976 at Newport News, Virginia. Patricia was born on 8 August 1951 at Newport News, Virginia.

They had the following children:

     368   i   Steven Ross GRAHAM, born on 4 May 1979 at Newport News, Virginia.

     369   ii   William Watson GRAHAM, born on 3 October 1981 at Newport News, Virginia; died on 25 September 1988 at Iowa City, Johnson Co., Iowa; buried at Pen. Mem. Park, Newport News, Virginia.

William was diagnosed as having Acute Lymphocytic Leukemia at the age of eight months. He was treated at the Medical College of Virginia Leukemia Clinic, Richmond, Virginia, with chemotherapy and radiation therapy. He underwent a bone marrow transplant at John's Hopkins University Hospital, Baltimore, Maryland at the age of four. He underwent another bone marrow transplant at the University of Iowa Hospital, Iowa City, Iowa, at the age of 6. His father, Steve Ross Graham, was the marrow donor. After nearly four months he lost his fight against leukemia one week prior to his seventh birthday. He made a notable contribution to the leukemia research efforts. He completed the first grade at Seaford Elementary School, York County, Virginia. He lived life to the fullest, he had a tremendous personality and everyone he met loved him.

327   Kitty Sue SMITH, born on 4 October 1955 at Wake Co., North Carolina.

♥ Kitty Sue SMITH married Marshall ANDREWS on 18 June 1977.

Descendants of Richard Arrow Smith

♥ Kitty Sue SMITH married James Hardwick ROBINS on 27 November 1986.

They had the following children:

    370   i   Joshua James ROBINS, born on 12 August 1983 at Wilson Co., North Carolina.

Joshua was born prior to his parents' marriage.

328 Donnie Ruffin SMITH, born on 13 August 1957 at Nuremberg, West Germany.

♥ Donnie Ruffin SMITH married Jackie HEIGHT on 27 September 1975.

♥ Donnie Ruffin SMITH married Paula Mae BYRD on 15 April 1977.

They had the following children:

    371   i   Jason Ruffin SMITH, born on 18 June 1980 at Raleigh, Wake Co., North Carolina.

Jason was adopted by his mother's second husband, Douglas Bass.

♥ Donnie Ruffin SMITH married Anita Beth TRULOVE on 15 May 1987.

They had the following children:

    372   ii   Amanda Brooke SMITH, born on 26 September 1990 at Raleigh, Wake Co., North Carolina.

329 Kathy Ann SMITH, born on 19 September 1959 at Wake Co., North Carolina.

Descendants of Richard Arrow Smith

Kathy Ann SMITH and Paul LEWIS of Pilot, North Carolina, had the following child:

 373 i Michael Loren SMITH, born on 16 January 1979 at Raleigh, Wake Co., North Carolina.

♥ Kathy Ann SMITH married Wayne PEARSON in April 1986.

♥ Kathy Ann SMITH married Phil SMITH on 1 August 1987.

♥ Kathy Ann SMITH married Arlie KELLY on 28 April 1989.

They had the following children:

 374 ii Brandon Todd KELLY, born on 29 August 1990 at Chesapeake, Virginia.
 375 iii Crystal Grace KELLY, born on 28 August 1991 at Chesapeake, Virginia.

331 Sonya Irene SMITH, born on 4 December 1962 at Wake Co., North Carolina.

♥ Sonya Irene SMITH married Mark OLIVER in 1981.

♥ Sonya Irene SMITH married Eddie ATWOOD before 1987.

They had the following children:

 376 i Christopher Brandon ATWOOD, born on 21 June 1987 at Wake Co., North Carolina.

336 Donna Lynn SMITH, born on 2 June 1960 at Forsyth Co., North Carolina.

Descendants of Richard Arrow Smith

♥ Donna Lynn SMITH married Kent JACKSON on 17 May 1987 at Raleigh, Wake Co., North Carolina. Kent was born at Raleigh, Wake Co., North Carolina.

They had the following children:

    377   i   Brittany Lynn JACKSON, born on 19 April 1989 at Raleigh, Wake Co., North Carolina.

338   Sandra F. CROWTHER, born on 27 July 1939 at Frederick Co., Maryland.

♥ Sandra F. CROWTHER married Paul N. FOX on 28 February 1956 at Frederick Co., Maryland. Paul was born on 2 November 1935 at Frederick, Maryland.

They had the following children:

  + 378   i   William E. FOX.
  + 379   ii   Henrietta Penny FOX.
    380   iii Paula Ann FOX, born on 23 August 1972 at Frederick, Frederick Co., Maryland.

339   Edward A. CROWTHER, Jr., born on 30 May 1941 at Frederick Co., Maryland.

♥ Edward A. CROWTHER, Jr. married Carla WISEMAN on 22 August 1964 at Wheatridge, Jefferson Co., Colorado. Carla was born on 19 April 1943 at Phoenix, Maricopa Co., Arizona.

They had the following children:

    381   i   Kristine CROWTHER, born on 1 November 1966 at Denver, Adams Co., Colorado.
    382   ii   Wayne Edward CROWTHER, born on 14 June 1968 at Denver, Adams Co., Colorado.

Descendants of Richard Arrow Smith

383　iii　Emily Edwina CROWTHER, born on 18 March 1971 at Denver, Adams Co., Colorado.

Descendants of Richard Arrow Smith

Eighth Generation

343 Clay Blackwell SMITH, born on 25 February 1956 at Ft. Bragg, Cumberland Co., North Carolina.

Like his mother's Crider ancestors, Clay has labored as a blacksmith. He was employed by the Colonial Williamsburg Foundation as a blacksmith in the Anderson Forge for a period of two years. He is now a fourth-year apprentice gunsmith in Colonial Williamsburg, which requires him to continuing using his blacksmithing skills (1992). His other jobs have included teaching Native American crafts to Native Americans on four reservations in Virginia.

Clay reports he has always felt he was born "in the wrong century." He seems to have found his niche in the 18th century.

♥ Clay Blackwell SMITH married Vara Holland BOTTOMS 17 January 1977 at Richmond, Henrico Co., Virginia. Holly was born on 31 March 1958 at Richmond, Henrico Co., Virginia.

Vara Holland Bottoms goes by the name "Holly". She is the only child of Vara S. Holland and William D. Bottoms of Richmond, Virginia. She is a Nursing Supervisor in the Neo-Natal Intensive Care Unit at the Medical College of Virginia.

In her spare time she enjoys various arts and crafts. She also accompanies her husband and family on primitive "rendezvous" or 18th century reinactments.

Holly's mother's Holland family is from Kenly, Johnston County, North Carolina.

They had the following children:

Descendants of Richard Arrow Smith

384 i Jessica Holland SMITH, born on 8 August 1977 at Richmond, Henrico Co., Virginia.
385 ii Jeremiah Blackwell SMITH, born on 21 August 1985 at Richmond, Henrico Co., Virginia.

346 Cynthia Ann TRANTER, born on 20 December 1954 at Ft. Belvoir, Fairfax Co., Virginia.

♥ Cynthia Ann TRANTER married Jeffrey Scott LYNN on 24 July 1976 at Franklin, Johnson Co., Indiana. Jeffrey was born on 30 May 1951 at Cleveland, Cuyahoga Co., Ohio.

Jeff Lynn is the son of Luther C. and Jan Lynn.

Cindy and Jeff live in Midland, Midland Co., Texas (1992).

They had the following children:

386 i Jason Matthew LYNN, born on 6 February 1980 at Columbus, Franklin Co., Ohio.
387 ii Ryan Michael LYNN, born on 7 July 1981 at Columbus, Franklin Co., Ohio.
388 iii Joshua Scott LYNN, born on 3 October 1984 at Oklahoma City, Oklahoma Co., Oklahoma.
389 iv Megan Elizabeth LYNN, born on 14 October 1986 at Oklahoma City, Oklahoma Co., Oklahoma.
390 v Robert Christopher LYNN, born on 14 October 1986 at Oklahoma City, Oklahoma Co., Oklahoma.

Megan and Robert are twins.

347 Debra Jo TRANTER, born on 22 May 1956 at Franklin, Johnson Co., Indiana.

Descendants of Richard Arrow Smith

♥ Debbie TRANTER married Clint Alan HALCOMB on 27 September 1980 at Franklin, Johnson Co., Indiana. Clint was born on 31 December 1956 at Indianapolis, Marion Co., Indiana.

Clint is the son of David Halcomb and Shirley May Adams Halcomb.

Debbie and Clint live in Indianapolis, Indiana.

They had the following children:

    391   i   Hilary Jo Ann HALCOMB, born on 4 February 1983 at Franklin, Johnson Co., Indiana.
    392   ii   Chad Alan HALCOMB, born on 13 March 1985 at Franklin, Johnson Co., Indiana.
    393   iii   Tyler "Ty" Burl HALCOMB, born on 17 July 1990 at Beech Grove, Marion Co., Indiana.

348   Robert William TRANTER, born on 17 August 1958 at Franklin, Johnson Co., Indiana.

♥ Bill TRANTER married Barbara Jo HOSKINS on 18 February 1977 at Trafalgar, Johnson Co., Indiana. Bobbie Jo was born on 8 May 1959 at Indianapolis, Marion Co., Indiana.

Bobbie Jo is the daughter of Bobby Joe Hoskins and Marcia Arlene Pogue Hoskins.

Bill and Bobbie Jo live in Franklin, Indiana.

They had the following children:

    394   i   Amanda "Mandy" Michele TRANTER, born on 23 September 1977 at Franklin, Johnson Co., Indiana.

Descendants of Richard Arrow Smith

395 ii Alison "Ali" Nicole TRANTER, born on 29 August 1981 at Franklin, Johnson Co., Indiana.

349 John Richard TRANTER, born on 17 August 1962 at Franklin, Johnson Co., Indiana.

♥ John TRANTER married Lisa Ann LITTLE on 17 March 1990 at Taylorsville, Bartholomew Co., Indiana. Lisa was born on 22 September 1967 at Franklin, Johnson Co., Indiana.

Lisa is the daughter of Dorman F. Little and Barbara Jean Stainbrook Little.

John and Lisa live in Franklin, Indiana.

They had the following children:

396 i Zachary William TRANTER, born on 2 October 1990 at Beech Grove, Marion Co., Indiana.

360 Debbie Lorraine PRIVETTE, born on 2 March 1965.

♥ Debbie Lorraine PRIVETTE married Perry Eugene KENNEDY. Perry was born on 27 October 1960.

They had the following children:

397 i Damian Jason KENNEDY, born on 17 November 1986 at North Carolina.
398 ii Krista Meagan KENNEDY, born on 19 June 1989 at North Carolina.
399 iii Rodney Jackson William KENNEDY, born on 31 October 1990 at North Carolina.

378 William E. FOX, born on 20 January 1959.

Descendants of Richard Arrow Smith

♥ William E. FOX married Katherine ROONEY on 5 February 1977. Katherine was born on 29 March 1958.

They had the following children:

  400 i Michael John FOX, born on 30 May 1977.
  401 ii Angela Marie FOX, born on 19 June 1979.

379 Henrietta Penny FOX, born on 24 December 1960. She goes by the name "Penny."

♥ Penny FOX married Ronald THOMAS on 4 February 1978. Ronald was born on 17 December 1950. They were divorced in 1982.

They had the following children:

  402 i Melissa THOMAS, born on 9 August 1978.
  403 ii Jessica Lynn THOMAS, born on 14 August 1981.

Descendants of Richard Arrow Smith

Unidentified A. Smith Relatives

The following persons are believed to be descendants of Richard Arrow Smith, but their exact parentage has not yet been determined. Any and all assistance is greatly appreciated.

Barthenia (Parthenia?) A. SMITH married Thomas H. AVERA on 5 August 1858 at Wake Co., North Carolina. The bondsman was A.J. Terrell. The marriage was performed by J.F. Ellington.

John A. SMITH married Louezur (Louisa?) JOHNSON on 13 October 1853 at Wake Co., North Carolina. The marriage was performed by H.H. Finch, J.P.

Kimbrael (or Kimbrough) A. SMITH married Rebecca TAYLOR on 29 December 1824 at Wake Co., North Carolina. The bondsman was Edwin A. Smith, son of William Arrow Smith. Was he a son of John A. Smith, or perhaps William A. Smith? Was Rebecca the sister of Elizabeth Taylor who married Edwin?

Philip S. SMITH married Minerva A. BROUGHTON on 2 November 1858 at Wake Co., North Carolina. The bondsman was W.M. Carter. The marriage was performed by Thomas E. Skinner. Minerva was the sister of Louisa Broughton who married Orrin A. Smith and Salina Broughton who married Yancey A. Smith.

Ransom A. SMITH married Emeline ROGERS on 19 September 1848 at Wake Co., North Carolina. The bondsman was Allen Jones.

Wesley A. SMITH married Menzia SMITH on 21 March 1836 at Wake Co., North Carolina. The bondsman was Rufus A. Smith, son of Orrin A. Smith.

Wesley A. SMITH married secondly Ugenia SMITH on 29 March 1863 at Wake Co., North Carolina. The bondsman was again Rufus A. Smith. The marriage was performed by Haywood Griffis, J.P.

Descendants of Richard Arrow Smith

Wesley O. SMITH married Vasti POOLE on 22 November 1847 at Wake Co., North Carolina. The bondsman was Henderson A. Cope.

William A. SMITH married Mary A. POOLE on 14 December 1853 at Wake Co., North Carolina. The bondsman was Wesley O. Smith. The marriage was performed by William R. Poole, J.P.

William A. SMITH married Julia Ann CROWDER on 30 December 1865 at Wake Co., North Carolina. The bondsman was B.A. Spence, J.P., who also performed the ceremony.

Descendants of Richard Arrow Smith

Descendants of Richard Johnson

First Generation

404 Richard JOHNSON, born about 1730 at Johnston Co., North Carolina; died before November 1769 at Johnston Co., North Carolina.

Richard Johnson's will, dated 1769 and probated 28 November 1769 in Johnston County, mentions wife Phereby Johnson who received the plantation, negro Lucy, household furniture, all during her life or widowhood. Son Samuel received land on both sides of White Oak (Branch). Son Sill Johnson received acreage on both sides of "_____ Swamp" (paper torn). Son (William) (paper torn) received 156? acres on both sides of _____. Son Richard received acreage on _____ Swamp. Son Philip Johnson received acreage on both sides of adjacent plantation "where I live". At wife's decease, estate to be divided among the children: Sill Johnson, Samuel Johnson, Esther Johnson, Richard Johnson, and Phereby Johnson, Jr. Son William was mentioned in the will of his mother, Phereby, who married secondly neighbor Abner Sauls.

♥ Richard JOHNSON married Phereby about 1750 at Johnston Co., North Carolina. Phereby was born about 1735 at Johnston Co., North Carolina; died after 9 October 1813 at Johnston Co., North Carolina.

In her will, dated 9 November 1813 and probated February, 1821, Phereby mentions granddaughter Phereby Sauls, d/o Redin Sauls, granddaughter Phereby Penny, d/o Alexander Penny (husband of daughter, Phereby, Jr.). She also stated that, "If son William Johnson comes home before 5 years, Negro Jesy to be sold and money divided equally between all my living children: Esther Smith, wife of Richard A. Smith, Sill

Descendants of Richard Arrow Smith

Johnson, William Johnson, Phillip Johnson, Redin Sauls, David Sauls, and Belle Poole, wife of Theophilous Poole." We can assume, therefore, that daughter Phereby and son Samuel were deceased before 1813. (*Johnston County Will Abstracts 1746-1870*, Elizabeth E. Ross).

They had the following children:

+ 405 i Esther JOHNSON.
406 ii Samuel JOHNSON, born about 1754 at Johnston Co., North Carolina; died before 1813.
+ 407 iii Phereby JOHNSON.
+ 408 iv Sill JOHNSON.
409 v William JOHNSON, born about 1763 at Johnston Co., North Carolina.

♥ William JOHNSON married Clary GALE on 27 February 1796 at Johnston Co., North Carolina. The bondsman was Charles Copeland.

410 vi Philip JOHNSON, born about 1765 at Johnston Co., North Carolina.

♥ Philip JOHNSON married Nancy GILES on 26 February 1792 at Wake Co., North Carolina. The bondsman was William Giles.

♥ Philip JOHNSON married Lucy COPELAND on 24 November 1818 at Wake Co., North Carolina. The bondsman was Samuel A. Smith.

Descendants of Richard Arrow Smith

Descendants of Richard Johnson

Second Generation

405 Esther JOHNSON.
This individual's information has already been printed (wife of Richard ARROW SMITH).

♥ Esther JOHNSON married Richard ARROW SMITH about 1770 at North Carolina.

Descendants of this couple have already been printed.

407 Phereby JOHNSON, born about 1760 at Johnston Co., North Carolina.

♥ Phereby JOHNSON married Alexander PENNY on 28 August 1787 at Johnston Co., North Carolina. The bondsmen were Caleb Penny and Jacob Penny.

Alexander was the son of Caleb Penny, Sr., who was a neighbor of Richard Arrow Smith.

They had the following children:

    411   i   Phereby PENNY.

408 Sill JOHNSON, born about 1761 at Johnston Co., North Carolina; died in May 1832 at Johnston Co., North Carolina.

Sill Johnson's will was dated 17 May 1832 and probated in the same month. He mentions wife Elizabeth, daughter Sarah Avera and son Richard Johnson, granddaughter Patsy Griffis, daughter of Richard Griffis whose wife was deceased, and son Rigdon Johnson.

♥ Sill JOHNSON married Elizabeth WATKINS on 10 December 1778 at Wake Co., North Carolina. The bondsman was Reece Watkins.

Descendants of Richard Arrow Smith

They had the following children:

    412   i   Richard JOHNSON, born at Johnston Co., North Carolina.

♥ Richard JOHNSON married Martha JOHNSON on 10 October 1795 at Johnston Co., North Carolina. The bondsman was Abner Sauls.

    413   ii   Sarah JOHNSON, born at Johnston Co., North Carolina.

♥ Sarah JOHNSON married Kedar AVERA on 8 October 1807 at Johnston Co., North Carolina. The bondsman was John Turner.

Kedar was the son of Thomas Avera and wife Mary. Thomas wrote his will in Johnston County on 9 March 1787. Kedar received "..all the land the plantation below Mill Branch" (Will Bk I, p. 7).

    414   iii   Rigdon JOHNSON, born in 1781 at Johnston Co., North Carolina; died after 1850 at Wake Co., North Carolina.

Rigdon Johnson was among the buyers at the estate sale of Henry Johnson, December 15, 1807, in Johnston County.

Rigdon Johnson was 69 years old in the 1850 census of St. Mary's Township, Wake County, North Carolina.

♥ Rigdon JOHNSON married Fanny BAUCOM on 13 April 1847 at Johnston Co., North Carolina. Fanny was born in 1795 at North Carolina; died after 1850 at Wake Co., North Carolina. The bondsman was Alsey Johnson.

Fanny Baucom was the daughter of Asa Baucom and Elizabeth Scott Baucom (see Baucom Section).

Descendants of Richard Arrow Smith

415 iv Daughter JOHNSON, born at Johnston Co., North Carolina; died before May 1832 at Johnston Co., North Carolina.

♥ Daughter JOHNSON married Richard GRIFFIS at Johnston Co., North Carolina. Richard died after May 1832.

Descendants of Richard Arrow Smith

Descendants of Phereby Johnson Sauls

First Generation

416 Phereby, surname unknown.
This individual's information has already been printed (wife of Richard Johnson).

♥ Phereby married Richard JOHNSON about 1750 at Johnston Co., North Carolina.

Descendants of this couple have already been printed.

♥ Phereby married Abner SAULS about 1771 at Johnston Co., North Carolina. Abner was born about 1740 at Warren Co., North Carolina; died on 28 April 1804 at Johnston Co., North Carolina.

Abner married the widow of Richard Johnson of Johnston County who died in 1769.

Abner Sauls and Richard Johnson were neighbors as shown by the following deed: "30 December 1779. North Carolina Survey Grant #422 to Abner Sauls, 300 acres on north side of White Oak Branch including his improvement beginning at a Pine near Richard Johnson's corner: East 160 paces to a Hickory: North 300 paces to a Post Oak: West 160 paces to a Pine in Richard Johnson's line near the upper corner, along his line South 300 paces to the beg., Wit: Richard Caswell, Gov. at Kingston, Wm. Sheppard, D. Secty." (Johnston County Deed Book M, #1, p.18).

On 31 December 1782, Abner deeded 150 acres of the above land to William Smith (relationship unknown), said to be on the "Southside of Neuse River on both sides of prong of Little Creek". Phereby Sauls surrendered, "all right or Dowrys to me belonging..." The Witnesses were James

Descendants of Richard Arrow Smith

Morris and Richard Johnston (Johnson). (Johnston Co. Deed Book N, #1, p. 26).

The William Smith mentioned above may be the brother of Benjamin Smith who married Mary Morse, both sons of John Smith and Elizabeth Hawkins of Franklin County, North Carolina. The Witnesses to the will of Benjamin Smith, dated 27 October 1827 in Johnston County, were Wm. Penny, Merritt Ferrell, and Redden (Reuben?) Sauls, son of Abner Sauls. (*Johnston County Will Abstracts 1746-1870*, Elizabeth Ross).

A notice in the *Raleigh Minerva* newspaper, Monday, May 7, 1804, reads, "A few days ago, Mr. Abner Sauls, of Johnston County, was found dead against a tree...supposed to have been thrown from his horse." Johnston County Deed Book D-2, page 227, shows a deed written July 21, 1804 stating, "Abner Sauls departed this life on or about the 28th of April in the year aforesaid..." He died intestate, leaving 800 or 900 acres adjoining the lands of Isaac Jones, Philip Johnson, Reuben Sanders and others.

They had the following children:

+ 417   i   Reuben or Redin SAULS.
   418   ii   Bellison SAULS, born about 1776 at Johnston Co., North Carolina.

♥ Bellison SAULS married Theophilous POOLE at North Carolina. He was born about 1770 at Johnston Co., North Carolina.

Theophilous Poole was one of the original trustees of Mt. Moriah Baptist Church, along with relative, William R. Poole.

+ 419   iii David SAULS.

Descendants of Richard Arrow Smith

Descendants of Phereby Johnson Sauls

Second Generation

417 Reuben or Redin SAULS, born at Johnston Co., North Carolina.

♥ Reuben or Redin SAULS married an unknown woman at North Carolina.

They had the following children:

+ 420 i Phereby SAULS.

419 David SAULS, born about 1778 at Johnston Co., North Carolina.

♥ David SAULS married Lydia PENNY on 3 December 1799 at Wake Co., North Carolina. Lydia was born about 1778.

Lydia Penny was the daughter of Charles Penny and Sarah Beddingfield Penny.

David and Lydia lived in Johnston County until about 1815 when they relocated to Chatham County, North Carolina.

They had the following children:

+ 421 i Abner SAULS, II.

Descendants of Richard Arrow Smith

Descendants of Phereby Johnson Sauls

Third Generation

420 Phereby SAULS, born about 1790 at Johnson Co., North Carolina; died after October 1853 at Johnson Co., North Carolina.

♥ Phereby SAULS married Willie JOHNSON at Johnson Co., North Carolina. Willie was born at Johnson Co., North Carolina; died after 29 October 1853 at Johnson Co., North Carolina.

Willie was the son of Amos Johnson and wife Mary. Willie wrote his will 29 October 1853 in Johnston County. He mentioned wife Phereby, sons Rigdon, Merritt, Osborne, Alec and his children Sidney and Larkin, daughter Leacy Griffis and her children, W.A., Rufus G., Lucretta G., and Jane, daughter Louise Johnson, sons Edmund and Carroll. The executors were son Rigdon and Lewis B. Sanders. The witnesses were H.H. Finch and Irby Stevens.

They had the following children:

    422   i   Rigdon JOHNSON, born at Johnston Co., North Carolina.

♥ Rigdon JOHNSON married Emily JOHNSON on 22 March 1823 at Johnston Co., North Carolina. The bondsman was Edmund Johnson, his brother.

    423   ii   Merritt JOHNSON, born at Johnston Co., North Carolina.

♥ Merritt JOHNSON married Mary HOLLAND on 20 September 1837 at Johnston Co., North Carolina. The bondsman was Alsey Johnson.

    424   iii Alexander "Alec" JOHNSON, born at Johnston Co., North Carolina.

Descendants of Richard Arrow Smith

♥ Alexander JOHNSON married Ally COTTON on 9 October 1824 at Johnston Co., North Carolina. The bondsman was Noel West.

  425 iv Osborne JOHNSON, born at Johnston Co., North Carolina.
  426 v Leacy JOHNSON, born at Johnston Co., North Carolina.
  427 vi Edmund JOHNSON, born at Johnston Co., North Carolina.

♥ Edmund JOHNSON married Wilsey JOHNSON on 7 May 1819 at Johnston Co., North Carolina. The bondsman was Benjamin Carroll.

♥ Edmund JOHNSON married Elizabeth LASSITER on 24 September 1839 at Johnston Co., North Carolina. The bondsman was Alfred Lassiter.

  428 vii Carroll "Carey" JOHNSON, born at Johnston Co., North Carolina.

♥ Carey JOHNSON married Polly WEST on 10 January 1835 at Johnston Co., North Carolina. The bondsman was Reuben Johnson.

  429 viii Louise JOHNSON, born at Johnston Co., North Carolina.

421 Abner SAULS II, born on 2 May 1802 at Johnston Co., North Carolina; died 28 May 1885 at St. Mary's Township, Wake Co., North Carolina.

 Abner moved from Chatham to Wake County between 1875 and 1880. All their children were born in eastern Chatham County.

 In the 1880 census of North Carolina, Abner and Nancy Sauls were living in the home of their son Rufus A. Sauls and his wife Elisa in Middle Creek Township in Wake County. Abner was listed as the keeper of a grist mill, and Rufus was a

Descendants of Richard Arrow Smith

farmer. Lydia and her husband were living next door. John William and his wife Annie were also living in Middle Creek. Josephus and his second wife were living in Buckhorn Township. David was residing in White Oak Township.

The Raleigh News and Observer reported on Friday, 29 May 1885 that "Mr. Abner Sauls, of St. Mary's Township, last Friday fell out of the door of his home, receiving injuries which yesterday proved fatal. He had for years been a cripple and used crutches. His age was eighty-three."

♥ Abner SAULS II married Nancy HORTON in Johnston Co., North Carolina.

They had the following children:

      430   i   Lydia SAULS, born about 1835 at Chatham Co., North Carolina.

♥ Lydia SAULS married Edward S. CERTAIN on 14 December 1873 at Chatham Co., North Carolina.

      431   ii   Sarah A. SAULS, born about 1836 at Chatham Co., North Carolina.

♥ Sarah A. SAULS married Thomas MITCHELL on 15 September 1856 at Wake Co., North Carolina.

      432   iii David SAULS, born in June 1837 at Chatham Co., North Carolina.

♥ David SAULS married Louisiana FORD on 17 October 1867 at Wake Co., North Carolina.

Louisiana was the daughter of Zack and Peggy Ford.

      433   iv Troy William SAULS, born about 1838 at Chatham Co., North Carolina.

Descendants of Richard Arrow Smith

♥ Troy William SAULS married Caroline JONES on 30 September 1865 at Wake Co., North Carolina.

    434   v   Reuben Seaton SAULS, born about 1839 at Chatham Co., North Carolina.
    435   vi   Rufus A. SAULS, born 14 June 1840 at Chatham Co., North Carolina.
    436   vii Theophilous Pope SAULS, born 3 August 1845 at Chatham Co., North Carolina.

♥ Theophilous Pope SAULS married Emiline FRANKS.

    437   viii Elizabeth Catherine SAULS, born in June 1846 in Chatham Co., North Carolina.

♥ Elizabeth C. SAULS married Daniel MATTHEWS on 30 March 1870 at Chatham Co., North Carolina.

    438   ix   Josephus SAULS, born 11 June 1847 at Chatham Co., North Carolina.

♥ Josephus SAULS married Isabella DENBY on 22 April 1869 at Wake Co., North Carolina.

♥ Josephus SAULS married Amanda ENNIS on 27 October 1875 at Wake Co., North Carolina.

♥ Josephus SAULS married Sarah MUNNS on 21 March 1889 at Wake Co., North Carolina.

    439   x   Ann Tilla SAULS, born about 1850 at Chatham Co., North Carolina.

♥ Ann Tilla SAULS married James HEARN on 14 February 1887 at Chatham Co., North Carolina.

    440   xi   John William SAULS, born 20 July 1853 at Chatham Co., North Carolina.

♥ John William SAULS married Annie Eliza ENNIS on 24 August 1875 at Wake Co., North Carolina. Annie Eliza was born in 1843 at Johnston Co.,

Descendants of Richard Arrow Smith

North Carolina, the daughter of Rayman (Raymond) Ennis and wife Sally.

    441   xii   Thomas Henry SAULS, born in May 1858 at Chatham Co., North Carolina.

♥ Thomas H. SAULS married Morning E. BRADY on 14 May 1882 at Wake Co., North Carolina.

♥ Thomas H. SAULS married Addie BAKER on 19 January 1901 at Lenoir Co., North Carolina.

Descendants of Richard Arrow Smith

Descendants of Joseph Broughton

First Generation

442 Joseph BROUGHTON, born in 1770 at Virginia or North Carolina; died in 1814 at Johnston Co., North Carolina; buried at Johnston Co., North Carolina.

Some sources have claimed Joseph Broughton is the son of Joshua **Boughton** of Essex County, Virginia. Joshua was the son of Joshua Boughton, Sr., who died in Essex County in 1731. His other children were John, Mary, Ann, Elizabeth, and Hannah. None of the daughters were married at the time of his death. Others have given Joshua, Jr., as the son of Reuben Broughton of Essex County, but no one of that name has been found by this researcher. Until more information can be located, we must begin our lineage with the first known Broughton ancestor, Joseph.

Death Date: *Johnston County Court of Pleas & Quarter Session Minutes*, N.C. Archives Microfilm #56.301.10.

♥ Joseph BROUGHTON married Mary Polly STANCIL on 23 March 1796 at Johnston Co., North Carolina. Polly was born on 22 May 1771 at Johnston Co., North Carolina; died on 13 January 1859 at Johnston Co., North Carolina; buried at Johnston Co., North Carolina.

Polly Stancil's birth and death dates were found in *Bible and Family Records*, Johnston County North Carolina Gen. Record Committee, Smith-Bryan Chapter, NSDAR, Smithfield, NC.

They had the following children:

Descendants of Richard Arrow Smith

     443   i   Elizabeth BROUGHTON, born on 7 January 1797 at Johnston Co., North Carolina.

♥ Elizabeth "Betsy" BROUGHTON married William EASON on 2 January 1819 at Johnston Co., North Carolina. The bondsman was Jonathan Stancil.

     444   ii   John BROUGHTON, born on 26 January 1799 at Johnston Co., North Carolina.

♥ John BROUGHTON married Martha Patsy BOYETTE on 8 February 1825 at Johnston Co., North Carolina. She was born about 1800 at Johnston Co., North Carolina.

     445   iii   Sallie BROUGHTON, born on 13 October 1801 at Johnston Co., North Carolina.

♥ Sallie BROUGHTON married William EASON on 28 March 1826 at Johnston Co., North Carolina. The bondsman was Jesse Eason. Was this William Eason the former husband of her sister Betsy?

     446   iv   Benjamin BROUGHTON, born on 9 April 1804 at Johnston Co., North Carolina.

Benjamin Broughton was the bondsman at the marriage of his brother Joseph and Mary Bagwell. Apparently, the clerk was confused and recorded Benjamin as the groom. I have not located a bride for Benjamin. Perhaps his name on the marriage bond caused him some legal barriers?

    + **447**   v   Jesse BROUGHTON.
    + **448**   vi   Steven BROUGHTON.
    + **449**   vii   Joseph BROUGHTON.

Descendants of Richard Arrow Smith

Descendants of Joseph Broughton

Second Generation

447 Jesse BROUGHTON, born on 7 November 1806 at Johnston Co., North Carolina; died on 1 August 1859 at Auburn, Wake Co., North Carolina.

♥ Jesse BROUGHTON married Susan BAGWELL on 3 March 1834 at Wake Co., North Carolina. Susan was born on 1806 at Wake Co., North Carolina; died on 13 May 1845 at Auburn, Wake Co., North Carolina.

Susan Bagwell Broughton died the same day she gave birth to her son, Joseph.

They had the following children:

    450 i   Martha BROUGHTON, born on 1 February 1835 at Auburn, Wake Co., North Carolina; died on 13 May 1845 at Auburn, Wake Co., North Carolina.
+ **451** ii   Rebecca BROUGHTON.
+ **452** iii   Catherine BROUGHTON.
    453 iv   William H. BROUGHTON, born on 9 April 1841 at Auburn, Wake Co., North Carolina; died on 14 October 1861 at Carolina City, Virginia.

William H. Broughton joined the Wake Guards, Company D, 26th Regiment of NC Volunteers under the command of Capt. Oscar R. Rand. While in training at Carolina City, Virginia, he contracted typhoid fever and died at the age of 20 (*Heritage of Wake County*, p. 147).

    454 v   Louisa M. BROUGHTON, born on 19 June 1842 at Auburn, Wake Co., North Carolina; died on 2 December 1860 at Auburn, Wake Co., North Carolina.

Descendants of Richard Arrow Smith

Louisa died at the age of 16 as a result of her clothing catching on fire as she stood warming herself by the open fireplace.

+ 455 vi Joseph Thomas BROUGHTON.

♥ Jesse BROUGHTON married Matilda STURDIVANT on 29 November 1845 at Wake Co., North Carolina. She was born about 1805 at Wake Co., North Carolina; died after 1859 at Garner, Wake Co., North Carolina.

They had the following children:

456 vii Mary Esther BROUGHTON, born on 25 December 1846 at Garner, Wake Co., North Carolina.

448 Steven BROUGHTON, born on 21 March 1809 at Johnston Co., North Carolina; died after 1850 at Wake Co., North Carolina.

The bondsman at the marriage of Stephen and Willey was Jesse Broughton, his brother.

♥ Steven BROUGHTON married Willey STALLINGS on 19 March 1833 at Wake Co., North Carolina. She was born in 1817 at Wake Co., North Carolina; died after 1850 at Wake Co., North Carolina.

They had the following children:

457 i Sally BROUGHTON, born in 1834 at St. Mary's, Wake Co., North Carolina.
458 ii Polly BROUGHTON, born in 1836 at St. Mary's, Wake Co., North Carolina.

♥ Polly BROUGHTON married James M. WALL on 6 January 1858 at Wake Co., North Carolina. The marriage was performed by Robert N. Gully, Justice of the Peace.

Descendants of Richard Arrow Smith

  459 iii Elizabeth BROUGHTON, born in 1839 at St. Mary's, Wake Co., North Carolina.
  460 iv Nancy BROUGHTON, born in 1842 at St. Mary's, Wake Co., North Carolina.

♥ Nancy BROUGHTON married James D. WALL on 24 July 1858 at Wake Co., North Carolina. The marriage was performed by Robert N. Gully, Justice of the Peace.

  461 v Tevilla BROUGHTON, born in 1846 at St. Mary's, Wake Co., North Carolina.
  462 vi James BROUGHTON, born December 9 at St. Mary's, Wake Co., North Carolina.

James was 7 months old in the July census of 1850.

449 Joseph BROUGHTON, born on 4 February 1812 at Johnston Co., North Carolina; died on 28 August 1853 at Auburn, Wake Co., North Carolina; buried at Mt. Moriah Baptist Church, Auburn, Wake Co., North Carolina.

♥ Joseph BROUGHTON married Mary BAGWELL on 25 February 1834 at Johnston Co., North Carolina. Mary was born on 1813 at Wake Co., North Carolina; died on 8 January 1892 at Raleigh, Wake Co., North Carolina; buried January 1892 at Oakwood Cemetary, Raleigh, Wake Co., North Carolina.

Mary died January 8, 1892, at the home her daughter, Salina, on South Person Street in Raleigh at the age of 79. She was one of the founders of the Baptist Tabernacle Church (*Death Notices 1883-1893, Raleigh State Chronicle*, Massengill and Tompkins).

She is buried in Oakwood Cemetary with her two sons, J.M. and Needham Broughton. Her husband lies by himself in Mt. Moriah Baptist Church cemetary in Auburn, Wake County.

They had the following children:

+ 463 i Gaston H. BROUGHTON.
  464 ii Minerva A. BROUGHTON, born in 1840 at St. Mary's Township, Wake Co., North Carolina.

♥ Minerva A. BROUGHTON married Phillip S. SMITH on 2 November 1858 at Wake Co., North Carolina. Phillip was born about 1840 at Wake Co., North Carolina. The bondsman was W.M. Carter. The marriage was performed by Thos. E. Skinner.

+ 465 iii Louisa BROUGHTON.
+ 466 iv Salina BROUGHTON.
+ 467 v Needham Bryan BROUGHTON.
+ 468 vi Zachariah T. BROUGHTON.
+ 469 vii Joseph Melville BROUGHTON.

Descendants of Richard Arrow Smith

Descendants of Joseph Broughton

Third Generation

451   Rebecca BROUGHTON.
This individual's information has already been printed (daughter of Jesse Broughton).

♥ Rebecca BROUGHTON married Lucius A. SMITH on 12 December 1859 at Wake, North Carolina.
This individual's information has already been printed (son of Edwin A. Smith).

Descendants of this couple have already been printed.

♥ Rebecca BROUGHTON married Edwin Jefferson SMITH about before 1880 in Wake Co., North Carolina.
This individual's information has already been printed (son of Edwin A. Smith, brother of Lucius, above).

452   Caroline BROUGHTON, born on 7 April 1839 at Auburn, Wake Co., North Carolina.

♥ Catherine BROUGHTON married Henry C. HICKS on 16 May 1865 at Wake Co., North Carolina. The bondsman was J.M. Taunt.

They had the following children:

   471   i   Henry Thomas HICKS, born 4 March 1866 at Wake Co., North Carolina.

Henry T. Hicks became a Raleigh druggist and maker of a headache remedy known as Hicks Capudine.

455   Joseph Thomas BROUGHTON, born on 13 May 1845 at Auburn, Wake Co., North Carolina; died on 15 January 1915 at Garner, Wake Co., North Carolina;

buried at Hayes Christian Chruch, Garner, Wake Co., North Carolina.

Joseph Thomas Broughton's mother, Susan Bagwell Broughton, died the day he was born. He was taken to the home of his uncle and aunt, Joseph and Mary Bagwell Broughton, to be nursed by Mary (his mother's sister) whose baby was still nursing.

Joseph T. Broughton enlisted as a Private in Co.D, 31st Regiment, NC Troops on 10 August 1863 at the age of 18 for the duration of the war. He was present or accounted for through December 1864. On 25 May 1865 he took the Oath of Allegiance at Raleigh.

♥ Joseph Thomas BROUGHTON married Martha Helen SNELLING on 1 November 1866 at Wake Co., North Carolina. She was born about 1845; died on 7 March 1930 at Garner, Wake Co., North Carolina; buried at Hayes Christian Church, Garner, Wake Co., North Carolina.

They had the following children:

  472 i Frances Susan BROUGHTON, born on 12 July 1868 at Garner, Wake Co., North Carolina.
  473 ii William F. BROUGHTON, born on 6 July 1870 at Garner, Wake Co., North Carolina.

William was Garner's first pharmacist.

  474 iii Thomas J. BROUGHTON, born on 12 March 1872 at Garner, Wake Co., North Carolina; died in 1891 at Garner, Wake Co., North Carolina.

Thomas died at the age of 19 of typhoid fever (*Wake Co. Heritage*, p.147).

  475 iv John F. BROUGHTON, born on 6 March 1874 at Garner, Wake Co., North Carolina.

Descendants of Richard Arrow Smith

        476   v   Marvin J. BROUGHTON, born on 25 March 1876 at Garner, Wake Co., North Carolina.
        477   vi   Numa R. BROUGHTON, born on 18 November 1881 at Garner, Wake Co., North Carolina.
        478   vii   Needham L. BROUGHTON, born on 6 April 1884 at Garner, Wake Co., North Carolina.
        479   viii Helen Irma BROUGHTON, born on 24 March 1887 at Garner, Wake Co., North Carolina.

463 Gaston H. BROUGHTON, born in 1838 at St.Mary's Township, Wake Co., North Carolina; died after 1896 at Raleigh, Wake Co., North Carolina.

    Gaston H. Broughton is listed as a "Nightwatchman," residence 312 E. Martin in the 1896 Raleigh Directory.

♥ Gaston H. BROUGHTON married Louisa FRANKS on 1 February 1859 at Wake Co., North Carolina.

    They had the following children:

        480   i   Charles BROUGHTON, born about 1860 at Wake Co., North Carolina.
        481   ii   J. Leonard BROUGHTON, born about 1862 at Wake Co., North Carolina.
        482   iii   Joseph BROUGHTON, born about 1863 at Wake Co., North Carolina.
        483   iv   Lillie BROUGHTON, born about 1865 at Wake Co., North Carolina.
        484   v   Anna BROUGHTON, born about 1856 at Wake Co., North Carolina.

465 Louisa BROUGHTON.
    This individual's information has already been printed (daughter of Joseph Broughton).

Descendants of Richard Arrow Smith

♥ Louisa BROUGHTON married William R. BRYANT on 20 October 1862 at Raleigh, Wake Co., North Carolina. William was born in 1842 at St. Mary's Township, Wake Co., North Carolina; died on 20 July 1863 at Charleston, Charleston Co., South Carolina.

William was the son of Needham and Sarah Bryant of St. Mary's Township, Wake County, North Carolina.

William R. Bryant enlisted in the Confederate Army, Co. D, 31st Regiment of the North Carolina Troops in Auburn, Wake County, on 18 September 1861. This was the same date Orrin Smith enlisted in this company, the day it was first raised. He was present or accounted for until captured at Roanoke Island on 8 February 1862. He was paroled at Elizabeth City on 21 February 1862 and returned to duty on or about 15 September 1862. On 18 July 1863 he was wounded at Fort Wagner, Charleston, South Carolina, and he died from his wounds two days later in or near Charleston. He was 21 years old when he died.

♥ Louisa BROUGHTON married Orrin A. SMITH on 31 January 1866 at Raleigh, Wake Co., North Carolina.
This individual's information has already been printed (son of Edwin A. Smith).

Descendants of this couple have already been printed.

466 Salina BROUGHTON.
This individual's information has already been printed (daughter of Joseph Broughton).

♥ Salina BROUGHTON married Yancy L. SMITH on 31 July 1861 at Wake Co., North Carolina.
This individual's information has already been printed (son of Oswell A. Smith).

Descendants of Richard Arrow Smith

Descendants of this couple have already been printed.

467 Needham Bryan BROUGHTON, born on 14 February 1848 at St. Mary's Township, Wake Co., North Carolina; died on 26 May 1914 at Raleigh, Wake Co., North Carolina; buried at Oakwood Cemetary, Raleigh, Wake Co., North Carolina.

Needham Bryan Broughton was a newpaper man, working first at the Raleigh Register until 1864, then moving to Washington to work on The Congressional Globe, and finally to New York where he set type in The Herald office. In 1872 he returned to Raleigh and engaged in the printing business with Mr. C. B. Edwards, establishing the firm of Edwards & Broughton, which continues to this day. After his death, his children sold the company to Dr. Charles Lee Smith. His grandchildren sold the business to the present owner.

In Raleigh a school was named after him: Needham B. Broughton High School, the first high school in the city and still in use as of 1992.

In the 1896 Raleigh Directory, Needham and his family were residing at 426 N. Person St., three doors north of the home of Marcus M. Smith, and his mother, Louisa Broughton Smith, widow of Orrin A. Smith.

Needham Bryan BROUGHTON married Caroline LOUGEE on 19 May 1869 at Wake Co., North Carolina. Caroline was born on 7 March 1850 at Wake Co., North Carolina; died on 10 June 1925 at Raleigh, Wake Co., North Carolina; buried at Oakwood Cemetary, Raleigh, Wake Co., North Carolina.

They had the following children:

Descendants of Richard Arrow Smith

   485 i Effie Lee BROUGHTON, born on 11 March 1870 at Raleigh, Wake Co., North Carolina; died on 25 September 1954 at Raleigh, Wake Co., North Carolina.

 ♥ Effie Lee BROUGHTON married Charles Benjamin PARK on 15 June 1892 at Wake Co., North Carolina.

   486 ii Edgar E. BROUGHTON, born about 1872 at Raleigh, Wake Co., North Carolina.

 Edgar E. Broughton was listed as a clerk at Edwards & Broughton, 1896 Raleigh Directory.

 Edgar sent a telegram to his cousin, Rev. Joseph Edwin Smith, on 26 May 1914 that read, "Papa died today."

   487 iii Rosa C. BROUGHTON, born 7 October 1874 at Raleigh, Wake Co., North Carolina; died on 25 March 1949 at Raleigh, Wake Co., North Carolina; buried at Oakwood Cemetary, Raleigh, Wake Co., North Carolina.
   488 iv Carrie Lougee BROUGHTON, born on 16 September 1879 at Raleigh, Wake Co., North Carolina; died on 27 January 1957 at Raleigh, Wake Co., North Carolina; buried at Oakwood Cemetary, Raleigh, Wake Co., North Carolina.

 Carrie L. Broughton was State Librarian of North Carolina, 1919-1957.

   489 v Mary N. BROUGHTON, born about 1882 at Raleigh, Wake Co., North Carolina.

 ♥ Mary N. BROUGHTON married S.O. GARRISON at Wake Co., North Carolina.

   490 vi Needham Bryan BROUGHTON, III, born about 1883 at Raleigh, Wake Co., North Carolina.

Descendants of Richard Arrow Smith

♥ Needham Bryan BROUGHTON,III, married Lorna BELL at Wake Co., North Carolina.

468   Zachariah T. BROUGHTON, born on 1850 at St. Mary's Township, Wake Co., North Carolina; died after 1896 at Raleigh, Wake Co., North Carolina.

Zachariah was six months old in the 1850 census of Wake County.

In the 1896 Raleigh Directory, Z.T. Broughton, printer, was residing at 117 W. Cabarrus. Also at that address was his wife, Mrs. M.J., son Phil H., daughters Ida, Ella, and Sadie, and son Zach T. Jr.

♥ Zachariah T. BROUGHTON married Miona J. PERRY at Wake Co., North Carolina. Miona was born about 1850; died after 1896 at Raleigh, Wake Co., North Carolina.

Mrs. M.J. Broughton, wife of Z.T., was listed in the 1896 Raleigh Directory as residing at 117 W. Cabarrus.

They had the following children:

491   i   Philip H. BROUGHTON, born at Wake Co., North Carolina.

Philip H., son of Z.T., was listed as a Pressman, Caucasian Office (Edwards & Broughton Printing Company?) in the 1896 Raleigh City Directory.

492   ii   Charles BROUGHTON, born at Wake Co., North Carolina.
493   iii   Ida M. BROUGHTON, born at Raleigh, Wake Co., North Carolina.
494   iv   Alma BROUGHTON, born at Raleigh, Wake Co., North Carolina.

Descendants of Richard Arrow Smith

  495 v Ella E. BROUGHTON, born at Raleigh, Wake Co., North Carolina.

  Ella E. Broughton, dau. of Z.T., was listed as a Book binder (Edwards & Broughton) in the 1896 Raleigh City Directory.

  496 vi Zachariah T. BROUGHTON, born at Raleigh, Wake Co., North Carolina; died at Durham, Durham Co., North Carolina.

  Zach T., son of Z.T., was listed as living at home (117 W. Cabarrus) in the 1896 Raleigh Directory. No occupation given.

♥ Zachariah T. BROUGHTON married Addie F. ROWLAND at Wake Co., North Carolina.

  497 vii Sadie A. BROUGHTON, born at Raleigh, Wake Co., North Carolina.

  Sadie A., daughter of Z.T., was listed as a student, living at home, in the 1896 Raleigh Directory.

469 Joseph Melville BROUGHTON, born on 15 February 1852 at St.Mary's Township, Wake Co., North Carolina; died on 21 December 1917 at Raleigh, Wake Co., North Carolina; buried at Oakwood Cemetary, Raleigh, Wake Co., North Carolina.

♥ Joseph Melville BROUGHTON married Sallie HARRIS on 5 May 1873 at Wake Co., North Carolina. Sallie was born on 7 January 1854 at Wake Co., North Carolina; died on 8 February 1910 at Raleigh, Wake Co., North Carolina; buried at Oakwood Cemetary, Raleigh, Wake Co., North Carolina.

  They had the following children:

+ 498   i   Joseph Melville BROUGHTON, Jr.

Descendants of Richard Arrow Smith

Descendants of Joseph Broughton

Fourth Generation

498 Joseph Melville BROUGHTON, Jr., born on 17 November 1888 at Raleigh, Wake Co., North Carolina; died on 6 March 1949 at Washington, D.C.; buried Raleigh, Wake Co., North Carolina.

Joseph Melville Broughton, Jr. was a Governor of North Carolina, inaugurated 9 January 1941. He began his term as United States Senator 3 January 1949 and died of a heart attack barely two months later.

♥ Joseph Melville BROUGHTON married Alice Harper WILSON on 14 Decembber 1916 at Wake Co., North Carolina.

They had the following children:

  499 i Alice Wilson BROUGHTON, born in 1920 at Raleigh, Wake Co., North Carolina; died on 27 July 1977 at Raleigh, Wake Co., North Carolina.
  500 ii Joseph Melville BROUGHTON, born about 1922 at Raleigh, Wake Co., North Carolina.
  501 iii Robert Bain BROUGHTON, born about 1924 at Raleigh, Wake Co., North Carolina.
  502 iv Woodson Harris BROUGHTON, born about 1926 at Raleigh, Wake Co., North Carolina.

Descendants of Richard Arrow Smith

Descendants of John Stancil

First Generation

503 John STANCIL, born about 1662 at England; died after 1704 at Nansemond Co., Virginia.

John Stancil migrated to Henry Neck, Virginia, aboard the ship "Mary," 6 November 1683. In 1704 he paid quit-rent for 500 acres of land in Nansemond County, Virginia (*Va. Mag. of History*, Vol. 29, p. 406).

♥ John STANCIL married Katherine HARDY who was born about 1670.

They had the following children:

+ **504** i John STANCIL, Jr.

Descendants of Richard Arrow Smith

Descendants of John Stancil

Second Generation

504 John STANCIL, Jr., born before 1700 at Nansemond Co., Virginia; died at North Carolina.

♥ John STANCIL, Jr., married Sarah SMITHWICK about 1720 at Nansemond Co., Virginia.

They had the following children:

+ 505   i   John STANCIL, III.

Descendants of Richard Arrow Smith

Descendants of John Stancil

Third Generation

505 John STANCIL,III, born about 1725 at Pitt Co., North Carolina; died before September 1795 at Johnston Co., North Carolina.

John Stancil's will, dated 17 February 1795 and probated September of the same year in Johnston County, mentioned a wife, not named, and children, also not named. He left 150 acres of land and a feather bed to Randolph Moore. The "Polly Stancil land" was to be sold to pay debts. The executors were John Stancil, Jr., Jonathan Stancil, and Nathan Stancil. The witnesses were Frederick Homes and Benjamin Homes.

The division of the estate of John Stancil, dec'd, dated August, 1807, lends more details on the heirs. Those listed were: John Stancil, Jonathan Stancil, Godfrey Stancil, Sally Duck, Elizabeth Moore, Polly Broughton, and Rebecca O'Neal. (*NC Archives Microfilm #56.501.5*, pg. 325).

♥ John STANCIL,III, married an unknown spouse.

They had the following children:

     506 i   John STANCIL,IV, born about 1770 at Johnston Co., North Carolina.

♥ John STANCIL,IV, married Zilpha GRICE on 29 August 1785 at Johnston Co., North Carolina.

  + *507* ii   Mary Polly STANCIL.
    508 iii Jonathan STANCIL, born about 1773 at Johnston Co., North Carolina; died before November 1847 at Johnston Co., North Carolina.

Descendants of Richard Arrow Smith

Jonathan Stancil was an executor of his father's will and named in the division of the estate.

Jonathan's will was dated 23 March 1844 and probated November 1847 in Johnston County, North Carolina. He mentions wife Priscilla, daughter Rebecca Whitley, and granddaughter Caroline. The executor was wife Priscilla. The witnesses were Josiah Batten, Patsey Batten, and L. Richardson.

   509 iv Nathan STANCIL, born about 1775 at Johnston Co., North Carolina.

♥ Nathan STANCIL married Clary TAYLOR on 17 February 1797 at Johnston Co., North Carolina. The bondsman was John Stancil, Nathan's brother.

♥ Nathan STANCIL married Nancy PENDER 27 February 1799 at Johnston Co., North Carolina. The bondsman was Frederick Homes.

   510 v Sally STANCIL, born about 1777 at Johnston Co., North Carolina.

♥ Sally STANCIL married John DUCK before 1795 at North Carolina.

John Duck received livestock from John Stancil in his will.

   511 vi Elizabeth STANCIL, born about 1779 at Johnston Co., North Carolina.

♥ Elizabeth STANCIL married Randolph MOORE on 10 June 1793 at Johnston Co., North Carolina.

  + 512 vii Godfrey STANCIL.
   513 viii Rebecca STANCIL, born about 1783 at Johnston Co., North Carolina.

♥ Rebecca STANCIL married Mr. O'NEIL before 1795 at North Carolina.

Descendants of Richard Arrow Smith

Descendants of John Stancil

Fourth Generation

507 Mary Polly STANCIL.
This individual's information has already been printed (daughter of John Stancil, II).

♥ Mary Polly STANCIL married Joseph BROUGHTON on 23 March 1796 at Johnston Co., North Carolina.
This individual's information has already been printed (son of Joshua Broughton).

Descendants of this couple have already been printed.

512 Godfrey STANCIL, born about 1781 at Johnston Co., North Carolina; died before May 1855 at Johnston Co., North Carolina.

Godfrey Stancil was mentioned in the division of the estate of John Stancil, Sr., as one of the heirs.

Godfrey's will, dated 20 April 1855 in Johnston County and probated the following month, mentions daughters Evelina Pearce, Polly Stot, Elizabeth Aycock, sons Godfrey Stancil, Willie Stancil, granddaughters Sarah Stancil and Meriah Stancil. Apparently Godfrey was rather well-off as he left each child two or more slaves, and the granddaughters $100 each. Son Godfrey also received 220 acres of land whereon his father lived. The executors were Godfrey and Willie. The witnesses were J.T. Kenyon and Simon Godwin. As no wife was mentioned, we must assume she was deceased.

♥ Godfrey STANCIL married an unknown spouse about 1805 at North Carolina.

They had the following children:

Descendants of Richard Arrow Smith

   514 i Polly STANCIL, born about 1812 at Johnston Co., North Carolina.

♥ Polly STANCIL married Alsey STOTT on 25 December 1837 at Johnston Co., North Carolina.

   515 ii Godfrey STANCIL,Jr., born in 1813 at Johnston Co., North Carolina.

♥ Godfrey STANCIL married Raney GODWIN on 7 September 1838 at Johnston Co., North Carolina.

   516 iii Evelina STANCIL, born in 1814 at Johnston Co., North Carolina.

  Evelina was 36 years old, single, living in the home of her father, Godfrey, Sr., in the 1850 census of Johnston County.

♥ Evelina STANCIL married Mr. PEARCE after 1850 at North Carolina.

   517 iv Elizabeth STANCIL, born about 1817 at Johnston Co., North Carolina.

♥ Elizabeth STANCIL married Daniel AYCOCK on 25 October 1844 at Johnston Co., North Carolina.

   518 v Willie STANCIL, born in 1815 at Johnston Co., North Carolina.

  Willie was 35 years old, living in the home of his father, Godfrey, Sr., in the 1850 census of Johnston County, North Carolina.

♥ Willie STANCIL married Martha STANCIL on 10 April 1852 at Johnston Co., North Carolina.

Descendants of Richard Arrow Smith

Descendants of Daniel Bagwell

First Generation

519 Daniel BAGWELL, born about 1735 at Brunswick Co., Virginia; died in 1802 at Wake Co., North Carolina.

Daniel Bagwell was in Brunswick Co., Virginia, as of 1758 and was old enough to have a child born by that time. He was notified to appear before the Court and show just cause why he should not be classified for militia duty. He did not appear, and was classified. There is no further record of him in Brunswick. His son, Frederick, claimed to have been born in Halifax County, Virginia (about 1759) in his Revolutionary War Pension application. Daniel was in Halifax County, North Carolina, in 1760 when he bought land there. John Bagwell, another son, claimed to have been born in Halifax County, North Carolina, about 1760-62, in his Revolutionary War Pension application. Perhaps Frederick was confused as to which Halifax it was? Daniel was in Bute-Warren County, North Carolina, before his move to Wake County.

[A Richard Bagwell in Brunswick County furnished supplies to the Continental Army during the Revolutionary War. Lunsford Bagwell was also living in Brunswick; his family moved to Rutherford County, North Carolina. These may be brothers of Daniel, but no proof has been found by this researcher.]

Daniel Bagwell purchased 640 acres of land in Wake County on 29 December 1778. This land "on the head of Gales Branch" adjoined the property of William Reynolds and the "improvement said Bagwell lives on" (*Wake Co. Court Minutes*). On 17 October 1780 Daniel bought 20 acres of land on the north side of Little River and on Tarborough

Descendants of Richard Arrow Smith

Road. He purchased the land from William Privitt. In 1783 Daniel bought another 500 acres of land on the north side of Little River from David Cooper. He made a request to the Secretary of State for a land grant on 20 June 1783, which was granted 15 May 1787. This grant of 414 acres was also on the head of Gales Branch in Wake County.

♥ Daniel BAGWELL married Elizabeth before 1759; born about 1737 at Virginia; died after 1802 at Wake Co., North Carolina.

They had the following children:

     520   i   Frederick BAGWELL, born in 1759 at Virginia; died on 13 February 1851 at Fayette Co., Alabama.

Frederick Bagwell entered the Revolutionary War as a substitute for his father, Daniel, who was drafted from Wake County. He served under Capt. Torrence and Gen. Butler. They marched from to Hillsboro, to Salisbury, Charlotte, and then down the Savannah River to Georgia. He was in the light infantry under Capt. Reynolds and in the battle of Stone. He was discharged in the summer of 1779. He later entered in April 1780 as a substitute for Jesse Richards, and was a part of Gen. Gates' defeat in South Carolina. Again, he was discharged and re-entered as asubstitute for Thomas Bunch in April 1781. He served under Capt. Blucker in South Carolina, finally serving the end of his service guarding prisoners in Hillsboro until October 1781. He served two more tours of duty, until he took sick in Salisbury and was in the hospital. While there he hired a man named Burn to take his place. He was discharged in August 1782 and returned home. He served a total of two years as a Private.

He owned land in Johnston and Wake Counties before and after the war, but moved his family south by 1803 when he owned land on the Saluda

Descendants of Richard Arrow Smith

River in Anderson Co., South Carolina. They later lived in Georgia, then settled permanently in Fayette Co., North Carolina.

♥ Frederick BAGWELL married Mary HILL on 27 March 1781 at Wake Co., North Carolina. Mary was born about 1760 at Wake Co., North Carolina; died after 1859 at Fayette Co., Alabama. The bondsman at the marriage was John Brewer.

Mary Hill lived to be at least 99 years old when she applied for her husband's Revolutionary War pension.

Frederick and Mary Bagwell are the probable parents of Frederick BAGWELL who married Winney ELLIS on 18 July 1803 in Wake Co., North Carolina. The bondsman was Nathan Bagwell.

They may also be the parents of Levy BAGWELL who married Eliza GARRISS on 21 August 1802 in Wake Co., North Carolina. The bondsman was again Nathan Bagwell.

    521 ii William BAGWELL, born in 1760 at Halifax Co., North Carolina; died after 1843 at Greenville Co., South Carolina.

William Bagwell served in the Revolutionary War. He was drafted from Bute Co., North Carolina for five months, serving with his brother, John, under Capt. John Cokely. They were engaged in three battles, marched to Elizabethtown, South Carolina and into Georgia. After being defeated by the British at Brier Creek, they retreated and joined Gen. Rutherford in South Carolina. He was discharged and returned home. Later that year he was drafted in Wake Co. for three months and served under Capt. Horton. They marched to Salisbury and remained there, guarding "Tories" until he was discharged. He served two more short tours of duty, the last at the end of the war. He served a total of one year and three months as a Private.

After the war he and his family remained in Wake County until at least 1790. He then moved his family to Greenville Co., South Carolina, and lived there the rest of his life. He owned land in Anderson Co., but their home was in Greenville. At the age of 83 he was living with Jesse Bagwell in Greenville Co., South Carolina.

+ 522   iii   John Daniel BAGWELL.
  523   iv   James BAGWELL, born about 1763 at Halifax Co., North Carolina; died after 1791.

This James Bagwell was old enough to have served in the Revolutionary War. There is no records of him living in North Carolina after 1794.

+ 524   v   Nathan BAGWELL.
  525   vi   Thomas BAGWELL, born about 1770 at Halifax Co., Virginia.

Thomas Bagwell was on the 1799 Tax Rolls of Wake County and on April 9, 1800 he bought 250 acres of land on the south side of Little River from Jesse Rhodes. This property was near Daniel Bagwell, his father. He sold this land 6 November 1801 and was at that time a resident of Wilkes County, North Carolina.

♥ Thomas BAGWELL married Sarah PRIVITT on 19 May 1798 at Wake Co., North Carolina.

Descendants of Richard Arrow Smith

Descendants of Daniel Bagwell

Second Generation

522 John Daniel BAGWELL, born in 1761 at Halifax Co., North Carolina; died on 15 April 1855 at Lawrenceville, Gwinnett Co., Georgia; buried at Sweetwater Church, Lawrenceville, Gwinnett Co., Georgia.

John Daniel Bagwell bought 100 acres of land in Wake County on the east side of Little River, 20 October 1785. This property was near or adjoining his father's land. He had moved his family to Anderson County, SC by 7 May 1798 when he bought land from Governor Pinckney. His land, along the Saluda River, near his brothers William and Frederick. Family history states that John Daniel moved to Georgia in 1851 to the vicinity of Lawrenceville. An old man of 89, he made the trip entirely by horseback. Perhaps he was going to live with relatives in that area. He died four years later.

John was reportedly drafted into Revolutionary War service from Bute County, North Carolina, at the age of 16 in 1778. He served five months under Col. Thos. Eaton, Major Blount, Captain John Cokely and 1st Lt. Philip Hawkins. He was discharged in 1778. Two years later he was drafted again. He served three months in Hillsboro, North Carolina. Two months later, in 1781 or 1782, he entered service under Col. Thomas Paster at Warrenton, North Carolina, and marched to Ashley Hill, South Carolina when they joined Gen. Greene. He remained with General Greene until the British left Charleston. After serving 12 months of an 18 month enlistment, he obtained a furlough and returned home. He was never "called out or discharged" His service was as a Private. (*Heritage of Wake County*, Wake Co. Historical Society, p. 110).

Descendants of Richard Arrow Smith

♥ John Daniel BAGWELL married Rachel CHAMBLEE on 27 January 1791 at Wake Co., North Carolina. Rachel was born about 1775 at Wake Co., North Carolina; died before 1837 at Anderson Co., South Carolina.

They had the following children:

    526   i   John Daniel BAGWELL Jr., born about 1793 at Wake Co., North Carolina.
    527   ii   Blake BAGWELL, born about 1795 at Wake Co., North Carolina.
    528   iii   Reed BAGWELL, born about 1797 at Wake Co., North Carolina.
    529   iv   William BAGWELL, born about 1798 at Wake Co., North Carolina.
    530   v   Robert BAGWELL, born in 1800 at Anderson Co., South Carolina.
    531   vi   Warren BAGWELL, born in 1802 at Anderson Co., South Carolina; died in 1843 at Anderson Co., South Carolina.

♥ Warren BAGWELL married Elizabeth STONE about 1825 at Wake Co., North Carolina.

    532   vii   Larkin BAGWELL, born in 1803 at Anderson Co., South Carolina.
    533   viii   Clara Kitty BAGWELL, born in 1805 at Anderson Co., South Carolina.

524 Nathan BAGWELL, born about 1833 at Wake Co., North Carolina; buried at Wake Co., North Carolina.

♥ Nathan BAGWELL married Sarah MAINOR on 7 March 1793 at Wake Co., North Carolina. Sally was born about 1770 in Wake Co., North Carolina; died before August 1833 at Wake Co., North Carolina; buried at Wake Co., North Carolina.

They had the following children:

Descendants of Richard Arrow Smith

+ 534 i Littleberry "Berry" BAGWELL.
+ 535 ii Clara BAGWELL.
+ 536 iii Bryant BAGWELL.
+ 537 iv Susan BAGWELL.
   538 v Rebecca BAGWELL, born about 1808 at Wake Co., North Carolina.

♥ Rebecca BAGWELL married Calvin JORDAN on 8 April 1828 at Wake Co., North Carolina.

+ 539 vi Nathaniel BAGWELL.
+ 540 vii Mary BAGWELL.

Descendants of Richard Arrow Smith

Descendants of Daniel Bagwell

Third Generation

534 Littleberry "Berry" BAGWELL, born in 1794 at Wake Co., North Carolina; died in 1884 at Raleigh, Wake Co., North Carolina; buried at Bagwell Cemetary, Raleigh, Wake Co., North Carolina.

Berry Bagwell was a farmer who lived all his life in Wake Co., buried at the Bagwell Cemetary six miles east of Raleigh on Rock Quarry Road.

♥ Littleberry "Berry" BAGWELL married Mary WALKER on 20 April 1816 at Wake Co., North Carolina; born about 1797.

They had the following children:

+ 541   i   William D. BAGWELL.
+ 542   ii   Green Berry BAGWELL.
+ 543   iii   Mary Willie BAGWELL.
+ 544   iv   A. Jack BAGWELL.
+ 545   v   Mason BAGWELL.
+ 546   vi   Needham Bryant BAGWELL.

534 Clara BAGWELL, born about 1798 at Wake Co., North Carolina.

♥ Clara BAGWELL married Jesse GREEN at Wake Co., North Carolina.

They had the following children:

+ 547   i   Catherine GREEN.

536 Bryant BAGWELL, born about 1805 at Wake Co., North Carolina.

Descendants of Richard Arrow Smith

♥ Bryant BAGWELL married Aisley BUNCH on 12 January 1828 at Wake Co., North Carolina.

They had the following children:

    548   i   Granberry Ross BAGWELL, born in 1829 at Wake Co., North Carolina.

♥ Granberry Ross BAGWELL married Barline BAUCOM on 3 January 1855 at Wake Co., North Carolina.

    549   ii   William Sidney BAGWELL, born in 1830 at Wake Co., North Carolina.

♥ William S. BAGWELL married Nancy BRITT on 27 November 1851 at Wake Co., North Carolina.

    + 550   iii   Sarah Ann BAGWELL.
    551   iv   Alcy BAGWELL, born in 1833 at Wake Co., North Carolina; died on 12 October 1915.

♥ Alcy BAGWELL married Edward GRAHAM on 18 September 1867 at Wake Co., North Carolina.

    552   v   Salivan BAGWELL, born in 1838 at Wake Co., North Carolina.

♥ Salivan BAGWELL married W. M. CARTER on 10 November 1858 at Wake Co., North Carolina.

    553   vi   Delaney BAGWELL, born in 1840 at Wake Co., North Carolina.

♥ Delaney BAGWELL married John V. WEATHERS on 18 January 1859 at Wake Co., North Carolina.

    554   vii   Nancy Catherine BAGWELL, born in 1843 at Wake Co., North Carolina.

♥ Nancy Catherine BAGWELL married T. J. BROOKS on 22 September 1866 at Wake Co., North Carolina.

Descendants of Richard Arrow Smith

555   viii Vashti Jackson BAGWELL, born in 1846 at Wake Co., North Carolina.

♥ Vashti Jackson BAGWELL married Sylvester CATLETTE on 6 April 1867 at Wake Co., North Carolina.

537 Susan BAGWELL.
This individual's information has already been printed.

♥ Susan BAGWELL married Jesse BROUGHTON on 3 March 1834 at Wake Co., North Carolina.
This individual's information has already been printed (son of Joseph Broughton).

Descendants of this couple have already been printed.

539 Nathaniel BAGWELL, born in 1810 at Wake Co., North Carolina.

It has been reported that Nathaniel owned land in both Johnston and Wake Counties, North Carolina, so the birthplace of his children is unknown. Also, he reportedly moved his family south to South Carolina or Georgia after 1850. (Christine Bagwell Costine, *Heritage of Wake County*, p. 104).

♥ Nathaniel BAGWELL married Phereby before 1832 at North Carolina. Phereby was born in 1814 at North Carolina.

They had the following children:

556   i   Eliza Ann BAGWELL, born in 1832 at North Carolina.

♥ Eliza Ann BAGWELL married George W. JOHNSON on 20 November 1867 at Wake Co., North Carolina.

Descendants of Richard Arrow Smith

  557 ii Cherry Cara BAGWELL, born in 1833 at North Carolina.
  558 iii Sally A. BAGWELL, born in 1836 at North Carolina.
  559 iv Nathan BAGWELL, born in 1838 at North Carolina.
  560 v John BAGWELL, born in 1840 at North Carolina.
  561 vi William G. BAGWELL, born in 1842 at North Carolina.
  562 vii Susan F. BAGWELL, born in 1844 at North Carolina.
  563 viii Henry B. BAGWELL, born in 1846 at North Carolina.
  564 ix Nancy BAGWELL, born in 1849 at North Carolina.

540 Mary BAGWELL.
 This individual's information has already been printed (daughter of Nathan Bagwell).

♥ Mary BAGWELL married Joseph BROUGHTON on 25 February 1834 at Johnston Co., North Carolina.
 This individual's information has already been printed (son of Joshua Broughton).

 Descendants of this couple have already been printed (see Broughton section).

Descendants of Richard Arrow Smith

Descendants of Daniel Bagwell

Fourth Generation

542 William D. BAGWELL, born in 1817 at Wake Co., North Carolina; died in 1853 at Wake Co., North Carolina.

♥ William D. BAGWELL married Martha POOLE on 30 December 1840 at Wake Co., North Carolina. Martha was born about 1820 in North Carolina.

They had the following children:

565 i Minerva H. BAGWELL, born in 1841 at Wake Co., North Carolina; died on 18 April 1931.

♥ Minerva H. BAGWELL married Jesse Bunion WALL on 25 April 1857 at Wake Co., North Carolina.

566 ii Martha H. BAGWELL, born in 1843 at Wake Co., North Carolina.

♥ Martha H. BAGWELL married Hancock POOLE on 30 April 1863 at Wake Co., North Carolina. The bondsman was Alonzo Poole.

567 iii Catherine B. BAGWELL, born on 1847 at Wake Co., North Carolina; died after 1866.

♥ Catherine B. BAGWELL married Sidney WILLIAMS on 26 December 1860 at Wake Co., North Carolina; born about 1845 at Wake Co., North Carolina; died before 1866.

Sidney Williams was killed in the Civil War.

542 Green Berry BAGWELL, born on 2 August 1818 at Wake Co., North Carolina; died on 18 January

Descendants of Richard Arrow Smith

1893 at Morrisville, Wake Co., North Carolina; buried at Morrisville, Wake Co., North Carolina.

♥ Green Berry BAGWELL married Ann C. KING on 23 March 1839 at Wake Co., North Carolina. Ann was born on 8 September 1825 at Wake Co., North Carolina; died on 21 May 1875 at Wake Co., North Carolina.

They had the following children:

    568   i   John G. BAGWELL, born on 20 October 1844 at Wake Co., North Carolina; died on 17 April 1927 at Wake Co., North Carolina.

    569   ii   Atlas Stanton BAGWELL, born on 9 December 1846 at Wake Co., North Carolina; died on 16 December 1889 at Wake Co., North Carolina.

♥ Atlas Stanton BAGWELL married Susanna HOOD on 8 November 1865 at Wake Co., North Carolina. Susanna was born on 26 March 1848; died 5 October 1920.

    570   iii   William Burke BAGWELL, born on 25 December 1856 at Wake Co., North Carolina; died on 10 August 1947 at Wake Co., North Carolina.

    571   iv   Edward Hiram G. BAGWELL, born on 17 March 1858 at Wake Co., North Carolina; died on 15 January 1888 at Wake Co., North Carolina.

♥ Edward H.G. Bagwell married Marjorie Price O'NEIL in 1879 at Wake Co., North Carolina. Marjorie was born on 5 March 1854 at Fulton, Mississippi.

    572   v   Mary L. BAGWELL, born on 27 September 1864 at Wake Co., North Carolina; died on 1 May 1949 at Wake Co., North Carolina.

Descendants of Richard Arrow Smith

   573 vi Arthur Pritchard BAGWELL, born on 23 January 1869 at Wake Co., North Carolina; died on 31 May 1870 at Wake Co., North Carolina.

♥ Green Berry BAGWELL married Rhodie PETTIGREW on 4 September 1875 at Wake Co., North Carolina. She was born on 30 May 1840 at Wake Co., North Carolina; died on 12 March 1929 at Wake Co., North Carolina.

 They had the following children:

   574 vii Joanna BAGWELL, born on 12 July 1876 at Wake Co., North Carolina; died on 25 August 1928 at Wake Co., North Carolina.

♥ Joanna BAGWELL married Hubert HOLDER at Wake Co., North Carolina. Hubert died on 21 May 1934 at Wake Co., North Carolina.

   575 viii Priscilla Sullie BAGWELL, born on 15 September 1877 at Wake Co., North Carolina.

♥ Priscilla Sullie BAGWELL married Zeb Vance BELVIN on 7 December 1898 at Wake Co., North Carolina.

543 Mary Willie BAGWELL, born about 1820 at Wake Co., North Carolina; died before 19 June 1855 at Wake Co., North Carolina.

♥ Mary Willie BAGWELL married Cullen BAILEY on 20 December 1841 at Wake Co., North Carolina. Cullen was born in 1820 at Wake Co., North Carolina.

 They had the following children:

   576 i William BAILEY, born about 1842 at Wake Co., North Carolina; died 4 June 1864 at Richmond, Virginia.

Descendants of Richard Arrow Smith

William Bailey enlisted in Co.D, 31st Regiment NC Troops on 18 September 1861 at the age of 19. He listed his occupation as farmer. Present or accounted for until captured at Roanoke Island 8 February 1862. Paroled at Elizabeth City 21 February 1862. Returned to duty on or about 15 September 1862. Wounded in the left thigh at or near Drewry's Bluff, Virginia, 16 May 1864. His left leg was amputated. He was hospitalized at Richmond, Virignia, where he died 4 June 1864 of his wound.

577 ii Livana BAILEY, born about 1844 at Wake Co., North Carolina.

♥ Livana BAILEY married John Gaston STRICKLAND on 4 January 1871 at Wake Co., North Carolina.

578 iii Polly Ann BAILEY, born on 20 August 1845 at Wake Co., North Carolina.

Polly and her brother Willie were twins.

♥ Polly Ann BAILEY married Rufus POOLE on 18 December 1866 at Wake Co., North Carolina.

579 iv Willie Rann BAILEY, born on 20 August 1845 at Wake Co., North Carolina; died on 25 December 1924.

580 v Cebret Ann BAILEY, born about 1847 at Wake Co., North Carolina.

♥ Cebret Ann BAILEY married James POOLE in January 1868 at Wake Co., North Carolina.

581 vi Jean BAILEY, born about 1849 at Wake Co., North Carolina.

♥ Jean BAILEY married Mr. RIDLAND at Wake Co., North Carolina.

Descendants of Richard Arrow Smith

544   Andrew Jack BAGWELL, born in 1822 at Wake Co., North Carolina; died in 1904 at Wake Co., North Carolina.

A.J. "Jack" Bagwell served in Co. D, 31st Regiment NC Troops during the Civil War, enlisting 18 September 1861 at the age of 38. Present or accouted for until captured at Roanoke Island 8 February 1862. Returned to duty on an unspecified date. Discharged 15 September 1962 under the provisions of the Conscription Act. Re-enlisted in the company at Camp Holmes 26 October 1864 for the war. Deserted 29 Janaury 1865. Took the Oath of Allegiance at Raleigh on 25 May 1865.

♥ Andrew Jack BAGWELL married Martha PACE on 17 August 1839 at Wake Co., North Carolina. Martha was born about 1825; died before August 1873 at Wake Co., North Carolina.

They had the following children:

582   i   Polly W. BAGWELL, born in 1846 at Wake Co., North Carolina.

♥ Polly W. BAGWELL married Albert BUSBEE on 13 November 1872 at Wake Co., North Carolina. Albert was born in 1850 at Wake Co., North Carolina.

583   ii   Helen BAGWELL, born in 1842 at Wake Co., North Carolina.
584   iii   Eliza Ann BAGWELL, born in 1844 at Wake Co., North Carolina.

♥ Eliza Ann BAGWELL married George W. JOHNSON on 20 November 1867 at Wake Co., North Carolina.

585   iv   Martha J. BAGWELL, born in 1846 at Wake Co., North Carolina; died in 1916 at Wake Co., North Carolina.

Martha never married.

Descendants of Richard Arrow Smith

Martha never married.

  586   v   Rosanna BAGWELL, born in 1852 at Wake Co., North Carolina.

♥ Rosanna BAGWELL married William F. BROADWELL on 22 January 1873 at Wake Co., North Carolina. He was born in 1855 at Wake Co., North Carolina.

  587   vi   Erastus J. BAGWELL, born in 1852 at Wake Co., North Carolina; died in 1924 at Wake Co., North Carolina.

Erastus never married.

  588   vii   Arvestus BAGWELL, born in 1857 at Wake Co., North Carolina; died in 1918 at Wake Co., North Carolina.

♥ Arvestus BAGWELL married Amanda BAILEY on 24 December 1879 at Wake Co., North Carolina. Amanda was born in 1859 at Wake Co., North Carolina; died in 1908 at Wake Co., North Carolina.

  589   viii Josephine BAGWELL, born in 1861 at Wake Co., North Carolina; died on 1932 at Wake Co., North Carolina.

♥ Josephine BAGWELL married James HOLDER on 6 January 1880 at Wake Co., North Carolina.

545 Mason BAGWELL, born about 1830 at Wake Co., North Carolina.

♥ Mason BAGWELL married Willie JONES on 30 March 1851 at Wake Co., North Carolina.

They had the following children:

  590   i   Troy JONES, born in 1857 at Wake Co., North Carolina.

Descendants of Richard Arrow Smith

546 Needham Bryant BAGWELL, born on 29 January 1832 at Wake Co., North Carolina; died on 25 August 1903 at Wake Co., North Carolina.

♥ Needham Bryant BAGWELL married Isabella H. THOMPSON on 23 March 1854 at Wake Co., North Carolina. Isabella was born on 30 January 1836; died on 13 August 1900 at Raleigh, Wake Co., North Carolina; buried at Bagwell Cemetary, Raleigh, Wake Co., North Carolina.

They had the following children:

+ 591   i   Henry W. BAGWELL.
+ 592   ii   Mary Elizabeth BAGWELL.
  593   iii Calvin Berry BAGWELL, born in 1859 at Wake Co., North Carolina.

♥ Calvin Berry BAGWELL married Martha COOPER on 22 December 1880 at Wake Co., North Carolina. She was born about 1860.

  594   iv   Jenadius Jackson BAGWELL, born on 28 August 1862 at Wake Co., North Carolina; died on 14 December 1930 at Wake Co., North Carolina.

♥ Jenadius J. BAGWELL married Tina COOPER on 10 January 1884 at Wake Co., North Carolina. Tina was born on 6 February 1865 at Wake Co., North Carolina; died on 9 March 1945.

Tina was the granddaughter of Martha Bagwell and Hance (Hancock) Poole.

  595   v   Needham Bryant BAGWELL, Jr., born on 9 February 1865 at Wake Co., North Carolina; died on 4 June 1937 at Wake Co., North Carolina; buried at Ebeneezer Methodist Church, Wake Co., North Carolina.

Descendants of Richard Arrow Smith

♥ Needham B. BAGWELL, Jr., married Gabriella ALLEN on 10 November 1889 at Wake Co., North Carolina. She was born on 1 September 1870; died on 20 April 1951 at Wake Co., North Carolina.

      596   vi   Lonnie D. BAGWELL, born on 24 June 1867 at Wake Co., North Carolina; died on 6 May 1955 at Rustburg, Campbell Co., Virginia; buried at Lynchburg, Campbell Co., Virginia.

♥ Lonnie D. BAGWELL married Martha STEVENS on 9 August 1893 at Wake Co., North Carolina. Martha was born on 30 October 1875 at Wake Co., North Carolina; died at Rustburg, Campbell Co., Virginia; buried at Lynchburg, Campbell Co., Virginia.

547   Catherine GREEN, born in 1830 at Wake Co., North Carolina; died in 1861 at Wake Co., North Carolina.

♥ Catherine GREEN married Calvin POOLE on 14 October 1852 at Wake Co., North Carolina. The bondsman was Josiah King.
    This individual's information has already been printed.

    They had the following children:

+ 597   i   Sion R. POOLE.
  598   ii   Hezekiah POOLE, born on 15 September 1855 at Wake Co., North Carolina; died on 1 June 1932 at Wake Co., North Carolina.

♥ Hezekiah POOLE married Elizabeth STURDIVANT on 4 May 1876 at Wake Co., North Carolina. Elizabeth was born in 1852; died before 1884 in Wake Co., North Carolina.

♥ Hezekiah POOLE married Lillie FERRELL about 1884 at Wake Co., North Carolina. Lillie was born

Descendants of Richard Arrow Smith

on 10 October 1861; died on 31 March 1943 at Wake Co., North Carolina.

  599   iii   Christiana POOLE, born on 1 May 1857 at Wake Co., North Carolina; died about July 1876 at Wake Co., North Carolina.

♥ Christiana POOLE married Robert BOONE on 25 May 1876 at Wake Co., North Carolina. The marriage was performed by J.F. Ellington, Baptist Minister.

  600   iv   Rosannah POOLE, born on 3 March 1859 at Wake Co., North Carolina; died on 23 July 1920 at Wake Co., North Carolina.

♥ Rosa POOLE married William H. KELLY on 5 October 1886 at Wake Co., North Carolina.

  601   v   Catherine Elizabeth POOLE, born on 16 November 1861 at Wake Co., North Carolina; died on 3 August 1900 in North Carolina.

♥ Catherine "Katie" POOLE married Nicholas P. STALLINGS on 26 December 1884 at Wake Co., North Carolina. Nicholas was born on 29 December 1856; died on 7 August 1917.

 Nicholas P. Stallings was a Baptist minister.

550 Sarah Ann BAGWELL, born in 1832 at Wake Co., North Carolina.

♥ Sarah Ann BAGWELL married Cullen BAILEY on 19 June 1855 at Wake Co., North Carolina.
 This individual's information has already been printed.

 They had the following children:

  602   i   Octavius BAILEY, born in 1857 at Wake Co., North Carolina.

Descendants of Richard Arrow Smith

♥ Octavius BAILEY married Sarah PARRISH on 24 ApriL 1884 at Wake Co., North Carolina. Sarah was born in 1867 at Wake Co., North Carolina.

      603   ii   Alice G. BAILEY, born in 1858 at Wake Co., North Carolina.

♥ Alice G. BAILEY married Charles A. GOODWIN on 1 October 1879 at Wake Co., North Caroina; born on 1853 at Wake Co., North Carolina.

      604   iii   Amanda BAILEY.
This individual's information has already been printed.

♥ Amanda BAILEY married Arvestus BAGWELL on 24 December 1879 at Wake Co., North Carolina.
   This individual's information has already been printed (son of Andrew Jack Bagwell).

592 Mary Elizabeth BAGWELL, born on 6 February 1857 at Wake Co., North Carolina.

♥ Mary Elizabeth BAGWELL married Sion R. POOLE on 5 Decembber 1878 at Wake Co., North Carolina. Sion was born on 12 January 1854 at Wake Co., North Carolina; died on 20 September 1912 at Raleigh, Wake Co., North Carolina.

   Sion was the son of Calvin Poole and his second wife Catherine Green who was the daughter of Clara Bagwell and Jesse Green.

   Sion was a farmer in Wake County and later a storekeeper in Raleigh. His wife kept several boarding houses in Raleigh.

   They had the following children:

Descendants of Richard Arrow Smith

605 i Hattie Lee POOLE, born on 9 June 1880 at Wake Co., North Carolina; died on 16 May 1917.

♥ Hattie POOLE married Angus Archie MCDONALD on 18 December 1901 at Wake Co., North Carolina.

606 ii Alice T. POOLE, born about August 1883 in Wake Co., North Carolina; died in 1915.

♥ Alice T. POOLE married Sam HODGES about 1915.

607 iii Grover Cleveland POOLE, born on 26 January 1887 at Wake Co., North Carolina; died on 19 March 1961.

Grover was born deaf. His wife was also deaf as were some of their children.

♥ Grover Cleveland POOLE married Fannie Elizabeth NORRIS on 1 June 1911 at Wake Co., North Carolina.

608 iv Exter POOLE, born on 1 August 1890 at Wake Co., North Carolina; died on 15 January 1941.

609 v Ila Kathryn POOLE, born on 6 August 1891 at Wake Co., North Carolina; died on 1 April 1987.

♥ Ila Kathryn POOLE married William C. HOLDER on 10 December 1913 at Durham, Durham Co., North Carolina. William was born on 15 May 1884; died on 22 June 1959.

610 vi Eugene POOLE, born about 1892 at Wake Co., North Carolina.
612 vii Melvin POOLE, born about 1894; died about 1896 at Wake Co., North Carolina.
613 viii Carrie POOLE, born about 1896; died as a child.

Descendants of Richard Arrow Smith

614 ix Margie Louise POOLE, born on 12 December 1900 at Wake Co., North Carolina; died on 29 July 1986.

♥ Margie L. POOLE married Famous Mark MANN on 21 November 1922. Mark was born on 3 September 1890; died on 21 February 1951.

597 Sion R. POOLE.
This individual's information has already been printed (husband of Mary Elizabeth Bagwell.)

♥ Sion R. POOLE married Mary Elizabeth BAGWELL on 5 December 1878 at Wake Co., North Carolina.
This individual's information has already been printed.

Mary and Sion were married at the home of Needham Bryant Bagwell, either her father or her brother.

Descendants of Richard Arrow Smith

Descendants of John Baucom

First Generation

615 John Baucom, Sr., born 1 July 1725 in Baltimore, Baltimore Co., Maryland; died in Johnston County, North Carolina after 19 August 1797.

John's surname was sometimes called Baughcom in the county records. The spelling used here was more common.

Other sources give John Baucom's birthdate as 1732 and his birthplace as Craven County, North Carolina. In either case, his father was reportedly Nicholas Baucom who arrived in Johnston County prior to 1739. Nicholas died about 10 April 1762 in Johnston County, North Carolina. In his will, dated 14 July 1761, Nicholas mentioned wife Sarah, sons Nicholas, Aaron, Jacob and Moses and Thomas, daughters Susanna, Ann and Esther. The executors were John Lee, Sr., and James Watson. The witnesses were Elisha Thomas, William Simpson, and Mary Simpson.

John Baucom's will, written 19 August 1797 and recorded 2 July 1800 (Will Book F, p. 92) named wife Rachel who received the "plantation where I live" for her widowhood. John also mentioned his sons John, Cader, Lewis, Reece, Britain, Asa, Josiah and daughters Mary Beddingfield, Jemimah Brannan and Rachel Scott. He also stipulated that at his wife's death or remarriage all household stock and goods were to be divided among his sons. "If they cannot agree, sell and divide the money." The executors were son Britain and wife Rachel. The witnesses were Jesse Ellington (Jurat), John Russell, and John F. Ellington (Jurat).

Descendants of Richard Arrow Smith

♥ John BAUCOM married Rachel, surname unknown, about 1754. She was born about 1735 and died after 1800.

Could Rachel be the daughter of William Hardcastle who wrote his will on 8 October 1775 at Wake County? He mentioned a daughter whose first name is not legible but whose last name was Baucom. He also mentioned sons James, John, and Elisha, daughter Betty Adams and wife Mary. The executors were Mary Hardcastle and James Hardcastle. The witnesses were Demsey Welch and John Beddingfield. It was probated in May of 1777.

They had the following children:

+ 616   i   Britain BAUCOM.
+ 617   ii   John BAUCOM, Jr.
  618   iii   Mary BAUCOM, born in Wake Co., North Carolina.

♥ Mary BAUCOM married John BEDDINGFIELD in North Carolina before 1797.

+ 619   iv   Cader BAUCOM.
  620   vi   Jemimah BAUCOM.

♥ Jemimah BAUCOM married Mr. BRANNAN in North Carolina before 1797.

  621   vii   Rachel BAUCOM.

♥ Rachel BAUCOM married John SCOTT on 24 January 1791 at Wake Co., North Carolina.

+ 622   viii   James BAUCOM.
+ 623   ix   Reece BAUCOM.
+ 624   x   Asa BAUCOM.
+ 625   xi   Josiah BAUCOM.
+ 626   v   Lewis BAUCOM.

Descendants of Richard Arrow Smith

Descendants of John Baucom

Second Generation

616 Britain BAUCOM, born after 1754 in Wake Co., North Carolina.

♥ Britain BAUCOM married Mary before 1796 at North Carolina.

They had the following children:

    627   i   Britain BAUCOM, born in 1796 at Wake Co., North Carolina.
    628   ii   Tempy BAUCOM, born in 1799 at Wake Co., North Carolina.
    629   iii   Edmund BAUCOM, born in 1800 at Wake Co., North Carolina.
    630   iv   Avery K. BAUCOM, born in 1802 at Wake Co., North Carolina.
    631   v   Josiah C. BAUCOM, born in 1805 at Wake Co., North Carolina.

617 John BAUCOM, Jr., born about 1750 in Wake Co., North Carolina; died after 27 December 1834 in Wake Co., North Carolina.

John Baucom, Sr., of Wake County deeded 100 acres to John Baucom, Jr., of the same, on 21 July 1784. This land "..part of a certain tract...on the south bank of Nuce (Neuse) River and on the Shop Branch adjoining James Hinton, it being part of the tract whereon John Baucom (Senr.) now lives and was granted to him by Earl Granville by deed bearing date 11 January 1761 and registered in Johnston County." The witness was James Hinton.

John's will, written 27 December 1834 in Wake County, named daughter Sally (Sarah) Smith who was loaned "..one Negro girl named Phiriby (sic) to her use during her lifetime and after her

Descendants of Richard Arrow Smith

death the said Negro and her increase I give to my three granddaughters Gilly Dodd, Susan A. Smith, and Mariah A. Smith (Sarah Maria). In addition, John devised to Willis Dodd, son-in-law of Sally Smith "..the sum of four hundred dollars in trust for use of said Sally Smith that he shall pay to sd. Sally Smith annually thirty dollars out of the principal and the Interest of said Legacy to her own use as if she was not married until the whole is exhausted..But if she should die before it is all paid over to her, the balance to be equally divided between Gilly Dodd, Susan A. Smith and Mariah Smith." Apparently, John did not think much of his son-in-law Samuel A. Smith, son of Richard Arrow Smith! Perhaps Samuel was too tight with his money to suit John Baucom.

In the will, John also left to son Isham Baucom the sum of ten dollars; to grandson Allen Baucom two Negro men named Jack and Grand; to daughter Polly Johnson one Negro man named Phil; to grandson Berry Johnson one Negro man named Antony; to Bennet Baucom's children one hundred dollars; to Gilly Nutt one Negro man named Branch; to grandson Thomas Nutt one Negro man named Richmond; to daughter Lydy Dunn the tract called the "Penny Place except a small slip on the South side of the tract which I conveyed to Bennett Baucom...also the tract...on which I now live containing 130 acres I purchased from James Hinton; also to Lydy Dunn one Negro woman named Ambrose and her three children and one girl named Zilphy, a boy named Henry, and all my household and kitchen furniture; to grandsons Van Rensaler and Poindexter Dunn "...210 acres which I purchased of Henry Hinton and Ransom Hinton"; to son Urias Baucom "...all the balance of my land..also one Negro girl named Emmy"; the balance of the estate was to be sold and the proceeds divided among Gilly Nutt, Polly Johnson, Lydy Dunn, and Urias Baucom. Lastly, "...it is my will that Negro Nell may live with whichever of my children she pleases." Evidently, Nell was his favorite servant. The executor was son Urias Baucom. The witness was Thomas Busbee. Written on the bottom of this will is the interesting notation: "The above will Jn. Baucom told me to destroy before H. Ellington, 13 June 1839. T. Busbee." If the will was destroyed and another written to take its place, its existance has not been found by this researcher. This change in the will may be due to John's marriage to Fanny Jordan in January of 1839. John died shortly after his marriage as his estate was settled in 1840.

♥ John BAUCOM married an unknown woman before 1779 at Wake Co., North Carolina.

John Parker, Sr., of Wake County named his daughter Elizabeth Baucom in his will dated 11 September 1805. Could she have been the wife of John Baucom? John Parker's wife was named Chloah (Chloe?) and his other children were named as John, Willie, Allen, Harry, Susannah, Tellitha, Nancy Brannen and Polly Robertson.

They had the following children:

+ 632   i   Sarah or Sally Ann BAUCOM.
+ 633   ii   Isham BAUCOM.
  634   iii   Mary Polly BAUCOM, born about 1783 at Wake Co., North Carolina.

♥ Polly BAUCOM married Henry JOHNSON on 4 October 1805 at Wake Co., North Carolina. The bondsman was Samuel Johnson.

  635   iv   Gilly BAUCOM, born about 1784 at Wake Co., North Carolina.

♥ Gilly BAUCOM married James NUTT on 21 May 1807 at Wake Co., North Carolina.

Descendants of Richard Arrow Smith

James was the son of William Nutt who wrote his will on 19 January 1808 in Wake County. He also mentioned children named Elizabeth Hutchins, Kedar Nutt, Elhannon Nutt (son), John Nutt, Margaret Nutt, and Bennett Nutt. The executors were son-in-law Isaac Hutchins and son James Nutt. The witnesses were Moses Hutchins and Woodson Clements (Wake Co. Record Bk 7, p. 318).

      636   v   Lydia "Lydy" BAUCOM, born about 1785 at Wake Co., North Carolina.

♥ Lydia BAUCOM married Grey DUNN on 27 August 1826 at Wake Co., North Carolina.

     + **637**   vi   Urias BAUCOM.
     + **638**   vii   Bennett BAUCOM.

♥ John BAUCOM married Fanny JORDAN on 1 January 1839 at Wake Co., North Carolina. The bondsman was Johnson Busbee.

619 Cader BAUCOM, born in Wake Co., North Carolina.

♥ Cader BAUCOM married Susannah FOWLER on 21 July 1797 at Wake Co., North Carolina. The bondsman was Reece Baucom, his brother.

They had the following children:

      639   i   Wilson BAUCOM, born in 1799 at Wake Co., North Carolina.
      640   ii   Nancy Elizabeth BAUCOM, born on 3 August 1800 at Wake Co., North Carolina.
      641   iii   John BAUCOM, born on 23 September 1801 at Wake Co., North Carolina.
      642   ii   Willis BAUCOM, born on 14 February 1802 at Wake Co., North Carolina.

Descendants of Richard Arrow Smith

622 James BAUCOM, born about 1760 at Wake Co., North Carolina.

♥ James BAUCOM married Sarah "Sally" ROGERS on 30 January 1780 at Johnton Co., North Carolina. The bondsman was Green Rogers.

Sally was the daughter of Isham Rogers and wife Prudence. Isham wrote his will on 14 November 1804 in Wake County; it was probated in the same month. He mentioned wife Prudence, sons Green, Mede, Benazer and Cody, daughters Lucy Wadson and Sarah Baucom, son-in-law James Baucom, and grandsons Willie Baucom, James Baucom and Isham Penny Rogers, son of Benazer Rogers. The executors were Mede Rogers and Benazer Rogers. The witnesses were J.C. Brantley and Nathan Upchurch.

They had the following children:

    643 i   Willie BAUCOM, born about 1782 at North Carolina.
    644 ii   James BAUCOM, born about 1784 at North Carolina.

♥ James BAUCOM married Sucky HARWOOD on 12 November 1806 at Wake Co., North Carolina. The bondsman was Cordie N. Rogers

625 Reece BAUCOM, born in Wake Co., North Carolina.

♥ Reece BAUCOM married an unknown woman.

They had the following children:

    645 i   Britain Burwell BAUCOM, born in 1798 at Wake or Guilford Co., North Carolina.
    646 ii   Willis Asa BAUCOM, born in 1809 at Guilford Co., North Carolina.

Descendants of Richard Arrow Smith

626   Asa BAUCOM, born on 29 March 1771 at Wake Co., North Carolina.

♥ Asa BAUCOM married Elizabeth SCOTT in 1794 at Wake Co., North Carolina.

They had the following children:

    647   i   Willie BAUCOM, born on 14 May 1800 at Wake Co., North Carolina; died before 15 October 1803 at Wake Co., North Carolina.
    648   ii   Winifred BAUCOM, born on 9 March 1802 at Wake Co., North Carolina.

♥ Winifred BAUCOM married John YATES on 26 January 1820 at Wake Co., North Carolina.

  + 649   iii   Wiley or Willie BAUCOM.
    650   iv   Fanny BAUCOM.
This individual's information has already been printed (wife of Rigdon Johnson).

♥ Fanny BAUCOM married Rigdon JOHNSON on 13 April 1847 at Johnston Co., North Carolina.
This individual's information has already been printed (son of Sill Johnson).

  + 651   v   Levi BAUCOM.
    652   v   Mary Polly BAUCOM, born in 1810 at Wake Co., North Carolina.
  + 653   v   John BAUCOM.
    654   vi   Delaney BAUCOM, born 27 December 1817 at Wake Co., North Carolina.

627   Josiah BAUCOM, born in Wake Co., North Carolina.

♥ Josiah BAUCOM married Sally before 1793 at Wake Co., North Carolina.

They had the following children:

Descendants of Richard Arrow Smith

       655   i   Lucy BAUCOM, born in 1799 at Wake Co., North Carolina.
       656   ii   Wiley BAUCOM, born on 12 November 1793 at Wake Co., North Carolina.
+ 657   iii   Ransom BAUCOM.
       658   iv   Willis BAUCOM, born on 7 July 1809 at Anson or Wake Co., North Carolina.
       659   v   Green BAUCOM, born on 24 December 1816 at Wake Co., North Carolina.

628 Lewis BAUCOM, born about 1779 at Wake Co., North Carolina; died after 1870 at Union Co., North Carolina.

♥ Lewis BAUCOM married Purity BRANNAN on 19 May 1801 at Wake Co., North Carolina. The bondsman was Josiah Baucom, his brother.

They had the following children:

+ 660   i   Bryant BAUCOM.

♥ Lewis BAUCOM married Lucy ELLINGTON on 24 February 1803 at Wake Co., North Carolina. The bondsman was Asa Baucom, his brother.

Descendants of Richard Arrow Smith

Descendants of John Baucom

Third Generation

632 Sarah Ann BAUCOM, born in 1779 at Wake Co., North Carolina; died after 4 December 1850 at St. Mary's Township, Wake Co., North Carolina.

♥ Sarah Ann BAUCOM married Samuel A. SMITH on 10 August 1798 at Wake Co., North Carolina. The bondsman was Britain Baucom, her uncle.
This individual's information has already been printed (son of Richard Arrow Smith).

Descendants of this couple have already been printed.

633 Isham BAUCOM, born about 1781 at Wake Co., North Carolina.

♥ Isham BAUCOM married Aley PENNY on 11 June 1798 at Wake Co., North Carolina. The bondsman was Samuel A. Smith, husband of his sister Sally.

Aley Penny was the daughter of Penuel Penny and wife Martha. Penuel wrote his will 15 July 1806 at Johnston County. He also mentioned sons Penuel Penny, Jr., William Penny, daughters Edith Folsom, and Charity Penny. William Penny was appointed administrator. The witnesses were John Jones and Miles Sweaney. The will was probated in November of 1806.

They had the following children:

       661   i   Penuel BAUCOM, born on 7 October 1802 at Wake Co., North Carolina.

637 Urias BAUCOM, born on 19 April 1794 at Wake Co., North Carolina; died before September 18, 1879 at Johnston Co., North Carolina.

Descendants of Richard Arrow Smith

Urias wrote his will on 27 May 1873 at Johnson County. He mentioned second wife Sally, daughter Charity Rand and her children Ed, Charles and Thomas, son Troy, and deceased wife Betsy and her son Caswell, both of whom were to receive a marble head and footstone on their graves out of the proceeds of the estate. Urias apparently was quite wealthy as he left $1000 to wife Sally, and $1000 each to grandsons Charles and Thomas to be held by Troy Baucom until they were of age. Grandson Ed received 400 acres after the death of his grandmother, Sally, and $500. Troy received 700 acres on the Neuse River. Urias also stipulated that a solid rock wall was to be built around his graveyard. The remainder of the estate was to be divided "equally among my five children." The witnesses were J.B. Robertson and J.W. O'Neil. The executor was son Troy Baucom.

♥ Urias BAUCOM married Elizabeth "Betsy" LEE on 29 September 1815 at Johnston Co., North Carolina. He was erroneously called "Hurious" in the marriage bond. The bondsman was Bennett Baucom.

They had the following children:

+ 662   i   Mary Ann BAUCOM.
  663   ii   Martha BAUCOM, born in 1819 at Johnston Co., North Carolina.
Martha and Mary Ann were twins.
+ 664 iii   Troy BAUCOM.
  665   iv   Caswell BAUCOM, born on 17 June 1830 at Johnston Co., North Carolina; died before May 1873 at Johnston Co., North Carolina.
+ 666   v   Charity BAUCOM.

♥ Urias BAUCOM married Sally TURNER on 28 September 1853 at Johnston Co., North Carolina. The bondsman was W.H. McCullers.

Descendants of Richard Arrow Smith

638 Bennett BAUCOM, born about 1789 at Wake Co., North Carolina.

♥ Bennett BAUCOM married Delilah "Dilly" Ann DUNN on 7 May 1808 at Wake Co., North Carolina. The bondsman was James Nutt, his brother-in-law.

They had the following children:

    667 i   Candis BAUCOM, born on 8 October 1816 at Wake Co., North Carolina.

650 Wiley BAUCOM, born on 15 October 1803 at Wake Co., North Carolina.

♥ Wiley BAUCOM married Elizabeth Ann UTLEY on 17 October 1832 at Wake Co., North Carolina.

They had the following children:

    668 i   Frances Eleanor UTLEY, born on 24 October 1834 at Wake Co., North Carolina.
    669 ii   Elizabeth Jane UTLEY, born on 20 March 1949 at Wake Co., North Carolina.

652 Levi BAUCOM, born about 1805 at Wake Co., North Carolina.

♥ Levi BAUCOM married Elizabeth YATES at Wake Co., North Carolina.

They had the following children:

    670 i   Francis BAUCOM, born on 6 April 1829 at Wake Co., North Carolina.
    671 ii   James Matthew BAUCOM, born on 26 November 1837 at Wake Co., North Carolina.
+ **672** iii   Green Henderson BAUCOM.
    673 iv   Sidney Denver BAUCOM, born on 20 May 1843 at Wake Co., North Carolina.

Descendants of Richard Arrow Smith

654 John BAUCOM, born on 7 April 1812 at Wake Co., North Carolina.

♥ John BAUCOM married Caroline UTLEY on 22 February 1832 at Wake Co., North Carolina. The bondsman was Gray Jones.

They had the following children:

    674 i   Sarah Frances BAUCOM, born in 1854 at Wake Co., North Carolina.

657 Ransom BAUCOM married Sally BARNES in North Carolina.

They had the following children:

    675 i   William Ransom BAUCOM, born on 13 November 1822 at Anson Co., North Carolina.
    676 ii   Sanders BAUCOM, born on 25 February 1824 at Anson Co., North Carolina.
    677 iii   Annis BAUCOM, born in 1828 at Anson Co., North Carolina.
    678 iv   Elizabeth E. BAUCOM, born in 1831 at Anson Co., North Carolina.

♥ Elizabeth E. BAUCOM married John K. KERR on 3 March 1852 at Union Co., North Carolina.

    + **679** v   Alvis BAUCOM.

660 Bryant BAUCOM, born in 1801 at Johnston Co., North Carolina.

♥ Bryant BAUCOM married Spicey CURLEE in 1822 at Anson Co., North Carolina.

They had the following children:

Descendants of Richard Arrow Smith

  680   i   Lucinda BAUCOM, born in 1824 at Anson Co., North Carolina.
  681   ii   Louisa Curlee BAUCOM, born in 1829 at Anson Co., North Carolina.
  682   iii   William BAUCOM, born in 1835 at Anson Co., North Carolina.
  683   iv   Obediah BAUCOM, born on 22 June 1840 at Anson Co., North Carolina.
  684   v   Josiah BAUCOM, born on 22 June 1840 at Anson Co., North Carolina.

 Josiah and Obediah were either twins or the same person.

Descendants of Richard Arrow Smith

Descendants of John Baucom

Fourth Generation

662   Mary Ann BAUCOM, born in 1819 at Wake Co., North Carolina.

♥ Mary Ann BAUCOM married Hardy POOLE on 27 December 1837 at Johnston Co., North Carolina. Hardy was born in 1814, the son of William Poole and Aley Powell Poole. He was also the brother of Calvin Poole who married Sarah Maria Smith and Caroline Poole who married Caswell A. Smith.

They had the following children:

685   i   Salina POOLE, born in 1840 at St. Mary's Township, Wake Co., North Carolina.

♥ Salina POOLE married John JORDAN.

686   ii   Urias POOLE, born in 1842 at St. Mary's Township, Wake Co., North Carolina

687   iii   Evaline POOLE, born in 1844 at St. Mary's Township, Wake Co., North Carolina.

♥ Evaline POOLE married John D. STURDIVANT on 17 September 1857 at Wake Co., North Carolina. The bondsman was David Lewis. G.H. Fairbault, J.P., performed the ceremony.

688   iv   Delia V. POOLE, born in 1846 at St. Mary's Township, Wake Co., North Carolina.

♥ Delia V. POOLE married F.M. BUSBEE on 28 February 1861 at Wake Co., North Carolina. The bondsman was S.F. Johnson. Samuel G. Dupree, J.P., performed the ceremony.

689   v   Julian Coy POOLE, born in 1848 at St. Mary's Township, Wake Co., North Carolina.

690   vi   Camden POOLE, born in 1849 at St. Mary's Township, Wake Co., North Carolina.

Descendants of Richard Arrow Smith

  691 vii Josephine POOLE, born in 1851 at St. Mary's Township, Wake Co., North Carolina.
  692 viii Quinton POOLE, born in 1853 at St. Mary's Township, Wake Co., North Carolina.
  693 ix Nathan POOLE, born in 1855 at St. Mary's Township, Wake Co., North Carolina.

♥ Nathan POOLE married Amelia Victoria BAUCOM.

  694 x Hardy B. POOLE, born in 1858 at St. Mary's Township, Wake Co., North Carolina.

♥ Hardy B. POOLE married Eva M. BAUCOM.

  695 xi Mary POOLE, born in 1859 at St. Mary's Township, Wake Co., North Carolina.

♥ Mary, or Molly, POOLE married Leonard BARNES.

664 Troy BAUCOM, born on 19 January 1827 at Johnston Co., North Carolina; died in June 1899 at Wake Co., North Carolina.

  Troy was a single man living alone in the 1850 census of St. Mary's Township, Wake County. He had built a new home on the property given to him by his father. He lived there alone for two years until his marriage to Elizabeth Rand in 1852. The home, now known as the Stallings place, is on Rock Quarry Road outside Raleigh, North Carolina. After Troy's death, his oldest child, Addie, and her husband lived in the home and made several improvements, including a wrap-around porch on the front.

  When Troy was drafted into service in the Civil War, his wife was left with young children to care for alone, except for the family slaves who lived on the property. It has been reported that when the Yankees came through, Elizabeth gave her money and valuables to one of the slaves to bury for safekeeping. A Yank soldier accosted

Descendants of Richard Arrow Smith

the slave and threatened to hang him if he didn't tell where the valuables were hiding. He refused, surreptitiously digging them up and giving them to Mrs. Baucom through her window. The northerners took all the stock and all the meat except for one ham which a soldier placed under Elizabeth's chair, saying he wanted to leave her one. Addie, the oldest daughter, had three dresses her mother had made for her. When the northern soldiers came, her mother made her wear all three so the raiders would not steal them. Addie passed these remembrances down to her daughter, Maud. (*Heritage of Wake County*, p. 502).

See the notes for Rev. Joseph Edwin Smith for a reference to Troy Baucom.

♥ Troy BAUCOM married Elizabeth Ann RAND on 18 February 1852 at Wake Co., North Carolina. Elizabeth was born in 1837 according to the 1880 census. The bondsman was Caswell Sturdivant. The marriage was performed by John F. Ellington.

They had the following children:

    696   i   Mary Adeline BAUCOM, born on 26 April 1853 at St. Mary's Township, Wake Co., North Carolina; died on 19 July 1917 at Wake Co., North Carolina; buried at Mt. Moriah Baptist Church, Auburn, Wake Co., North Carolina.

♥ Addie BAUCOM married Joseph Alpheus STALLINGS at Wake Co., North Carolina. Alph was born on 4 October 1848 at Wake Co., North Carolina.

Alph was an identical twin of his brother, Thaddeus, sons of James Bryan Stallings and Elizabeth Ann Jones Stallings.

    697   ii   Milton BAUCOM, born in 1855 at St. Mary's Township, Wake Co., North Carolina.

Descendants of Richard Arrow Smith

Milton was 25 years old and a farm laborer in the 1880 census, living in the home of his parents.

  698 iii Urias BAUCOM, born in 1859 at St. Mary's Township, Wake Co., North Carolina.

Urias was 21 years old, a laborer and attending school in the 1880 census.

  699 iv Amelia BAUCOM, born in 1861 at St. Mary's Township, Wake Co., North Carolina.

Amelia was nineteen years old and living at home in the 1880 census.

  700 v Annie E. BAUCOM, born in 1866 at St. Mary's Township, Wake Co., North Carolina.

Annie was fourteen years old and attending school in the 1880 census.

  701 vi Eva M. BAUCOM, born in 1872 at St. Mary's Township, Wake Co., North Carolina.

Eva was eight years old and attending school in the 1880 census.

  702 vii Eliza W. BAUCOM, born in 1875 at St. Mary's Township, Wake Co., North Carolina.

Eliza was five years old in the 1880 census. She was not yet attending school.

666 Charity BAUCOM, born in 1842 at Wake Co., North Carolina.

♥ Charity BAUCOM married John B. RAND on 12 December 1860 at Johnston Co., North Carolina.

They had the following children:

Descendants of Richard Arrow Smith

  703 i Edward RAND.
  704 ii Charles RAND.
  705 iii Thomas RAND.

672 Green Henderson BAUCOM, born on 18 March 1839 at Wake Co., North Carolina.

♥ Green H. BAUCOM married Edna HOWARD on 17 December 1860 at Wake Co., North Carolina.

 They had the following children:

  706 i Ella BAUCOM, born on 8 November 1862 at Wake Co., North Carolina.
  707 ii James BAUCOM, born on 11 June 1866 at Wake Co., North Carolina.
  708 iii John BAUCOM, born on 3 November 1867 at Wake Co., North Carolina.
  709 iv Sally BAUCOM, born in 1868 at Wake Co., North Carolina.
  710 v William BAUCOM, born on 28 January 1871 at Wake Co., North Carolina.
  711 vi Fred BAUCOM, born on 22 February 1872 at Wake Co., North Carolina.
  712 vii Charlie BAUCOM, born on 23 February 1872 at Wake Co., North Carolina.

 Fred and Charlie were apparently twins. Either there is an error in their recorded birthdates, or Fred was born in the late evening, and Charlie was born in the early morning hours.

679 Alvis BAUCOM, born on 16 July 1833 at Anson Co., North Carolina.

♥ Alvis BAUCOM married Julian Josephine LONG on 7 February 1854 at Union Co., North Carolina.

 They had the following children:

Descendants of Richard Arrow Smith

    713   i   William S. BAUCOM, born in 1855 at Union Co., North Carolina.
    714   ii   Mary Ellen BAUCOM, born in 1856 at Union Co., North Carolina.
    715   iii   James Thomas C. BAUCOM, born in 1860 at Union Co., North Carolina.

♥ Alvis BAUCOM married Lydia Adeline MULLIS before 1863 at Union Co., North Carolina.

They had the following children:

    + 716   i   Alvis Alexander BAUCOM.
    717   ii   Sarah J. BAUCOM, born in 1872 at Union Co., North Carolina.
    718   iii   Temperance Caroline BAUCOM, born in 1874 at Union Co., North Carolina.
    719   iv   Martelia Catherine BAUCOM, born on 4 April 1876 at Union Co., North Carolina.
    720   v   Lydia Angeline BAUCOM, born in 1879 at Union Co., North Carolina.

Descendants of Richard Arrow Smith

Descendants of John Baucom

Fifth Generation

716 Alvis Alexander BAUCOM, born on 21 December 1863 at Union Co., North Carolina.

♥ Alvis Alexander BAUCOM married Ella Amarantha SMITH on 20 February 1885 at New Salem Township, Union Co., North Carolina.

They had the following children:

    721 i   Henry Marshall BAUCOM, born on 1 February 1887 at Union Co., North Carolina.
    722 ii   Retta Jane BAUCOM, born on 11 November 1888 at Union Co., North Carolina.
    723 iii   Belinda Adeline BAUCOM, born on 27 January 1891 at Union Co., North Carolina.
    724 iv   Charles Franklin BAUCOM, born on 10 September 1893 at Union Co., North Carolina.
    725 v   Joseph Pierce BAUCOM, born on 30 December 1902 at Union Co., North Carolina.
    726 vi   Lena Hester BAUCOM, born on 21 November 1905 at Union Co., North Carolina.

Descendants of Richard Arrow Smith

Descendants of George Poole

First Generation

727 George POOLE, born about 1720 in Virginia; died in 1773 at Wake Co., North Carolina.

George Poole and wife Mary apparently owned land in Isle of Wight County, Virginia, prior to moving south to what was then Craven County, North Carolina prior to 1741. On 4 August of that year, George Poole was granted 100 acres on the north side of the Neuse River by Gov. Johnston. In 1760 George sold this 100 acres on "Meadow Branch" and applied for a land grant south of the Neuse river "on both sides of the Great Branch of Walnut Creek." In 1761 Gov. Johnston granted him 540 acres he had requested and surveyed the year before. This land was in Johnston County; when Wake County was formed, his land became part of the new county. In 1762 George and wife Mary sold 200 acres in Isle of Wight County as they were now settled in North Carolina. (Clyde M. Stallings, *Calvin Poole: His Ancestors and Descendants*).

♥ George POOLE married Mary, surname unknown, in Virginia. Mary died about 1787 at Wake Co., North Carolina.

They had the following children:

+ **728** i Lewis POOLE.
   729 ii Hester POOLE, born before 1750 at North Carolina.

♥ Hester POOLE married Jacob STEVENS before 1772 at Wake Co., North Carolina.

   730 iii William POOLE, born before 1750 at North Carolina.

Descendants of Richard Arrow Smith

♥ William POOLE married Sarah at Wake Co., North Carolina.

+ 731   iv   Hardy POOLE.
  732   v   John POOLE, born about 1756 at North Carolina.
  733   vi   George POOLE, Jr., born about 1758 at North Carolina.
  734   vii   Mary POOLE, born about 1760 at North Carolina.

♥ Mary POOLE married John ELLIS before February 1796 at Wake Co., North Carolina.

  735   viii   Edee POOLE, born about 1762 at North Carolina.

Descendants of Richard Arrow Smith

Descendants of George Poole

Second Generation

728 Lewis POOLE, born before 1750 at North Carolina; died on 25 May 1809 at Wake Co., North Carolina.

♥ Lewis POOLE married Catherine at North Carolina.

They had the following children:

    736   i   William R. POOLE, born on 8 October 1796 at Wake Co., North Carolina; died 2 April 1889 at Wake Co., North Carolina.
    737   ii   Lewis POOLE, Jr., born in 1798 at Wake Co., North Carolina; died in 1845.

♥ Lewis POOLE, Jr., married Catherine SHAW on 15 June 1836 at Wake Co., North Carolina.

    738   iii   Ransom POOLE, born 4 February 1803 at Wake Co., North Carolina; died 20 December 1869 at Wake Co., North Carolina.

♥ Ransom POOLE married Sally LASSITER on 16 December 1828 at Wake Co., North Carolina. The bondsman was Robert Powell.

    739   iv   Martha "Molsey" POOLE, born in 1807 at Wake Co., North Carolina; died in 1860.

♥ Martha POOLE married James H. COOK in 1825 at Wake Co., North Carolina.

729 Hardy POOLE, born about 1754 at Wake Co., North Carolina; died after 8 May 1813 at Wake Co., North Carolina.

♥ Hardy POOLE married Edith at North Carolina.

Descendants of Richard Arrow Smith

They had the following children:

+ **740** i William POOLE.
741 ii Howard POOLE, born before 1790 at Wake Co., North Carolina; died about 1839.

♥ Howard POOLE married Mary Ann POWELL on 12 April 1806 at Wake Co., North Carolina. The bondsman was John Poole, Jr.

742 iii George POOLE,III, born about 1794 at Wake Co., North Carolina.

♥ George POOLE,III, married Sythey HUNICUTT on 14 December 1830 at Wake Co., North Carolina.

743 iv Hardy POOLE, born about 1798 at Wake Co., North Carolina.

♥ Hardy POOLE married Mary LASSITER on 30 July 1824 at Wake Co., North Carolina. The bondsman was William POOLE.

744 v Charlotte POOLE, born at Wake Co., North Carolina.
745 vi Polly POOLE, born at Wake Co., North Carolina.
746 vii Betsy POOLE, born at Wake Co., North Carolina.
747 viii Nancy POOLE, born at Wake Co., North Carolina.

Descendants of Richard Arrow Smith

Descendants of George Poole

Third Generation

740 William POOLE, born about 1779 at Wake Co., North Carolina; died in January 1834 at Wake Co., North Carolina.

♥ William POOLE married Aley POWELL on 12 April 1806 at Wake Co., North Carolina. Aley was born about 1779 at North Carolina; died about 1855 at Wake Co., North Carolina. The bondsman was John Poole, Jr.

Aley was the daughter of Moses and Prudence Garner Powell.

They had the following children:

    748 i   Jonathan POOLE, born about 1807 at Wake Co., North Carolina.
    749 ii   Anderson POOLE, born about 1810 at Wake Co., North Carolina.

♥ Anderson POOLE married Elizabeth BEDDINGFIELD in 1829 at North Carolina.

    750 iii   Lewis POOLE, born about 1812 at Wake Co., North Carolina.
+ **751** iv   Hardy POOLE.
    752 v   William POOLE, born about 1816 at Wake Co., North Carolina.

♥ William POOLE married Martha POWELL on 2 October 1843 at Wake Co., North Carolina. The bondsman was Hardy Poole.

♥ William POOLE married Mary STANCIL on 11 April 1853 at Wake Co., North Carolina. The bondsman was Albert J. POOLE. The marriage was performed by William R. Poole, J.P.

Descendants of Richard Arrow Smith

♥ William POOLE married Cornelia TURNER on 28 February 1868 at Wake Co., North Carolina.

Cornelia was the daughter of Wesley and Mary Turner.

      753   vi   Albert Jackson POOLE, born about 1818 at Wake Co., North Carolina.
+ 754   vii   Caroline POOLE.
+ 755   viii Calvin POOLE.

Descendants of Richard Arrow Smith

Descendants of George Poole

Fourth Generation

751 Hardy POOLE, born about 1814 at Wake Co., North Carolina.
This individual's information has already been printed (See Baucom Section).

♥ Hardy POOLE married Mary Ann BAUCOM on 27 December 1837 at Johnston Co., North Carolina.
This individual's information has already been printed.

Descendants of this family have already been printed.

754 Caroline POOLE, born about 1821 at Wake Co., North Carolina.

♥ Caroline POOLE married Caswell A. SMITH on 19 September 1843 at Wake Co., North Carolina.
This individual's information has already been printed (son of Samuel A. Smith).

Descendants of this couple have already been printed.

755 Calvin POOLE, born on 22 April 1822 at Wake Co., North Carolina; died in 1908 at Wake Co., North Carolina; buried at Mt. Moriah Church, Auburn, Wake Co., North Carolina.
This individual's information has already been printed.

♥ Calvin POOLE married Sally Maria SMITH on 21 December 1841 at Wake Co., North Carolina. The bondsman was Hardy Poole, Jr.
This individual's information has already been printed.

Descendants of Richard Arrow Smith

Descendants of this couple have already been printed (daughter of Samuel A. Smith).

♥ Calvin POOLE married Catherine GREEN on 14 October 1852 at Wake Co., North Carolina. The bondsman was Josiah King.

This individual's information has already been printed (daughter of Clara Bagwell and Jesse Green--see Bagwell Section).

Descendants of this couple have already been printed.

♥ Calvin POOLE married Elizabeth JONES on 1 April 1863 at Wake Co., North Carolina. The bondsman was James Bryant.

Elizabeth was reportedly a Civil War refugee who relocated to Wake County from Lenoir County, North Carolina, with her widowed mother and their former slaves. Her parents were Green Jones and Laney Tull Jones.

They had the following children:

756 i Joseph POOLE, born in 1864 at Wake Co., North Carolina; died in 1943.

♥ Joseph POOLE married Edie JONES in 1890 at Wake Co., North Carolina.

757 ii Icana POOLE, born in 1866 at Wake Co., North Carolina; died in 1918.

♥ Icana POOLE married Adeline JONES in 1889 at Wake Co., North Carolina.

758 iii Alie POOLE, born in 1868 at Wake Co., North Carolina; died in 1956.

♥ Alie POOLE married John W. HONEYCUTT in 1890 at Wake Co., North Carolina.

Descendants of Richard Arrow Smith

  759   iv   Addie POOLE, born in 1870 at Wake Co., North Carolina; died in 1942.

♥ Addie POOLE married E. Marcus FERRELL in 1887 at Wake Co., North Carolina.

  760   v   James Wilder POOLE, born in 1872 at Wake Co., North Carolina; died in 1942.

♥ James W. POOLE married Emma about 1910 at Wake Co., North Carolina.

Descendants of Richard Arrow Smith

Family Charts

First	Second	Third
Richard ARROW SMITH m. Esther Johnson	William ARROW SMITH m. Phereby Ferrell	Edwin A. SMITH Benjamin A. SMITH Ephraim A. SMITH Bryant A. SMITH Willey A. SMITH William A. SMITH
	Samuel A. SMITH m. Sarah Ann Baucom	Calvin A. SMITH Zachariah A. SMITH Gilly A. SMITH Susan A. SMITH Clement A. SMITH John A. SMITH Abner A. SMITH Richard A. SMITH Sally Maria SMITH Caswell A. SMITH
	John A. SMITH m. unknown	Eliza A. SMITH
	Richard A. SMITH Jr. m. Elizabeth Wren	Burchett SMITH Esther A. SMITH Oswell A. SMITH Julia SMITH Mary Ann SMITH Simeon A. SMITH Catherine A. SMITH
	Clary A. SMITH m. John White	Elizabeth WHITE
	David A. SMITH m. Parthena Rogers	
	February A. SMITH m. William Etheridge	
	Winny A. SMITH m. Mr. Powell	
	Elizabeth A. SMITH m. Samuel Slaughter m. Mr. Hill	Rebecca HILL
	Aaron A. SMITH m. Gilly Ellis	

Descendants of Richard Arrow Smith

Third	Fourth	Fifth
Edwin A. SMITH m. Elizabeth Taylor	Orrin A. SMITH m. Elizabeth Terrell	Laura SMITH Albert B. SMITH Mary O. SMITH David Thaddeus SMITH Roxanna SMITH Alvin E. SMITH Elizabeth O. SMITH
	m. Louisa Broughton	Joseph Edwin SMITH Marcus M. SMITH William O. SMITH John W. SMITH Carrie Etta SMITH Benjamin F. SMITH Corrinna L. SMITH Henry Burgwyn SMITH Nellie May SMITH
	Larkin A. SMITH m. Caroline Terrell	Sarah Jane SMITH Charles H. SMITH Martha L. SMITH Virginia SMITH Emma SMITH Claudius SMITH

Descendants of Richard Arrow Smith

Third	Fourth	Fifth
(Continued from previous page) Edwin A. SMITH m. Eliza A. Smith	Mary A. SMITH	
	Rufus A. SMITH m. Jane Terrell	Benjamin SMITH Thomas SMITH Elijah SMITH Leonora SMITH
	m. Elizabeth Young	Robert J. SMITH Emma SMITH Ella Elizabeth SMITH Elizabeth R. SMITH Acharel M. SMITH Alma SMITH Cornelia Amanda SMITH Edwin E. SMITH Frank Rufus SMITH Anna SMITH
	Luceus A. SMITH m. Rebecca Broughton	Leonard SMITH Ida SMITH Stella SMITH Walter SMITH Alonzo SMITH
	E. Jefferson SMITH m. Louisa Williams	Alonzo J. SMITH Cora SMITH Silas SMITH Julia SMITH Charlie SMITH Annie SMITH Lula SMITH Nathaniel SMITH

Descendants of Richard Arrow Smith

Third	Fourth	Fifth
Benjamin A. SMITH m. Susannah A. Beasley	Alfred SMITH Catherine SMITH Sophia SMITH William SMITH Simeon Marion SMITH m. Nancy Champion	Mary Susan SMITH Nancy E. SMITH Simeon Lonnie SMITH James Addison SMITH Edy Elendor SMITH Rose Ellen F. SMITH Richard Henderson SMITH William F. SMITH Ella Nettice SMITH
m. Karen Gower	James H. SMITH m. Martha Stephenson	Richard A. SMITH Delia SMITH Matilda SMITH Martha SMITH Emily SMITH

	Ridley SMITH
	Daniel Ruffin SMITH
	  m. Esther A. Smith
	  m. Julia Johnson
		
		Rozella SMITH
		Elizabeth J. SMITH
		Lula Ann SMITH
		Sallie SMITH
		Henrietta SMITH
		Mary Magdelene SMITH
		Minnie SMITH

	m. Sarah Carlisle	William Alfred SMITH Lonnie Hilliard SMITH Haywood Thomas SMITH

Descendants of Richard Arrow Smith

Third	**Fourth**	**Fifth**
William A. SMITH m. Candis Ellis	Elizabeth SMITH	
	Elender SMITH m. Henry Dodd	Medoar DODD Alonzo DODD Jenny DODD John DODD Malissa DODD
	Delia SMITH	
	William McRae SMITH m. Annie M. Jones	Baby SMITH James W. SMITH Garner Arrista SMITH Ida SMITH Leather B. SMITH Grover Thurman SMITH Coy SMITH
	Hercelia SMITH	
	Jesse A. SMITH m. Mollie L. Pleasants m. Lottie A. Branham	William Ruffin SMITH
	Sylvester A. SMITH m. Dezzie Jones	Elizabeth Hawkins SMITH Hattie Idella SMITH Mattie V. SMITH Vernon L. SMITH William Ivan SMITH Irene Lula SMITH

Descendants of Richard Arrow Smith

Fifth	**Sixth**	**Seventh**

Joseph Edwin SMITH
m. Mary Blanche
    Blackwell
	Ralph Payne SMITH
	m. Isabella M.
	    Cleveland
		Helen Arlyne SMITH

	m. Viola H. Hanes	Carl Taylor SMITH, II
	Roy Pomfret SMITH m. Elsie L. Jors	Glenn Carl SMITH Roy Pomfret SMITH, Jr. Gail Ruth SMITH
	Elmer Vernon SMITH m. Hazel M. Bundy	E. Vernon SMITH, Jr. David William SMITH Richard Bundy SMITH
	Joseph E. SMITH, Jr. m. Isabel Curtis	Barbara Isabel SMITH Curtis Blackwell SMITH Joseph E. SMITH, III
	Mary Blanche SMITH Robert Reece Tranter	Robert Reece TRANTER, Jr. Mary Anne TRANTER

Descendants of Richard Arrow Smith

Fifth	Sixth	Seventh
Lonnie H. SMITH m. Lillie Mitchell	Betty F. SMITH m. Charles G. Clark	Gloria Jean CLARK Charles R. CLARK Pamela Lynn CLARK
	Jesse W. SMITH m. Sarah Kitchens	Deborah Lynn SMITH Kenneth Alan SMITH
	Crama Lee SMITH m. Billy R. Graham	Steven Ross GRAHAM
	Lonnie R. SMITH m. Katrina Alford	Kitty Sue SMITH Donnie Ruffin SMITH Kathy Ann SMITH
	Jasper Glenn SMITH m. Rachel Rogers m. Clara L.B. Hope	Tammy Phyllis SMITH Sonya Irene SMITH
	Linda Carol SMITH m. Grady R. Creech	Timothy Ray CREECH Wanda Joy CREECH Rodney Alan CREECH Anthony Scott CREECH

Descendants of Richard Arrow Smith

First	Second	Third
Richard JOHNSON m. Phereby	Esther JOHNSON m. Richard Arrow Smith	(See Arrow Smith Chart)
	Samuel JOHNSON	
	Phereby JOHNSON m. Alexander Penny	Phereby PENNY
	Sill JOHNSON m. Eliz. Watkins	Richard JOHNSON Sarah JOHNSON Rigdon JOHNSON Daughter JOHNSON
	William JOHNSON m. Clary Gale	
	Philip JOHNSON m. Nancy Giles m. Lucy Copeland	

Descendants of Richard Arrow Smith

First	**Second**	**Third**
Phereby		
m. Richard JOHNSON————————(See Johnson Chart)		
m. Abner SAULS————————┬─Reuben SAULS ————————————— Phereby SAULS		
	│ m. unknown	
	├─Bellison SAULS	
	│ m. Theophilous Poole	
	└─David SAULS ————————————— Abner SAULS,II	
	m. Lydia Penny	

Descendants of Richard Arrow Smith

Third	**Fourth**	**Fifth**
Phereby SAULS m. Willie Johnson	Rigdon JOHNSON m. Emily Johnson Merritt JOHNSON m. Mary Holland Alec JOHNSON m. Ally Cotton Osborne JOHNSON Leacy JOHNSON Edmund JOHNSON m. Wilsey Johnson m. Ellizabeth Lassiter Carroll JOHNSON m. Polly West Louise JOHNSON	

Descendants of Richard Arrow Smith

Third	**Fourth**	**Fifth**

Abner SAULS, II
m. Nancy Horton
- Lydia SAULS
  - m. Edward Certain
- Sarah A. SAULS
  - Thomas Mitchell
- David SAULS
  - Louisiana Ford
- Troy William SAULS
  - m. Caroline Jones
- Reuben Seaton SAULS
- Rufus A. SAULS
- Theophilous Pope SAULS
  - m. Emiline Franks
- Elizabeth C. SAULS
  - m. Daniel Mathews
- Josephus SAULS
  - m. Amanda Ennis
  - m. Sarah Munns
- Ann Tilla SAULS
  - m. James Hearn
- John William SAULS
  - m. Annie E. Ennis
- Thomas Henry SAULS
  - m. Morning E. Brady
  - m. Addie Baker

Descendants of Richard Arrow Smith

First	Second	Third

Joseph BROUGHTON
m. Mary P. Stancil
	├ Elizabeth BROUGHTON
	   m. William Eason
	├ John BROUGHTON
	   m. Martha P. Boyette ────────
		┌ Penelope BROUGHTON
		└ Mary BROUGHTON

	├ Sallie BROUGHTON
	   m. William Eason
	├ Benjamin BROUGHTON
	├ Jesse BROUGHTON ─────────
	   m. Susan Bagwell
		┌ Martha BROUGHTON
		├ Rebecca BROUGHTON
		├ Catherine BROUGHTON
		├ William H. BROUGHTON
		├ Louisa M. BROUGHTON
		└ Joseph T. BROUGHTON

	m. Matilda Studivant───────	Mary Esther BROUGHTON
	├ Steven BROUGHTON ───────── m. Willey Stallings	┌ Sally BROUGHTON ├ Polly BROUGHTON ├ Elizabeth BROUGHTON ├ Nancy BROUGHTON ├ Tevilla BROUGHTON └ James BROUGHTON
	└ Joseph BROUGHTON ───────── m. Mary Bagwell	┌ Gaston H. BROUGHTON ├ Minerva BROUGHTON ├ Louisa BROUGHTON ├ Salina BROUGHTON ├ Needham Bryan BROUGHTON ├ Zachariah T. BROUGHTON └ Joseph M. BROUGHTON

Descendants of Richard Arrow Smith

First	Second	Third
John STANCIL —————————— John STANCIL, II —————————— John STANCIL, III		
m. Katherine Hardy	m. Sarah Smithwick	m. unknown

Descendants of Richard Arrow Smith

Third	Fourth	Fifth
John STANCIL, III m. unknown	┬─ John STANCIL, IV │ m. Zilpha Grice ├─ Mary P. STANCIL ─────────── (see Broughton Chart) │ m. Joseph Broughton ├─ Jonathan STANCIL ─────────── Rebecca STANCIL │ m. Priscilla ├─ Nathan STANCIL │ m. Clary Taylor ├─ Sally STANCIL ├─ Elizabeth STANCIL ├─ Godfrey STANCIL ─────────┬─ Erelina STANCIL │ m. unknown ├─ Polly STANCIL │ ├─ Godfrey STANCIL, Jr. │ ├─ Elizabeth STANCIL │ └─ Willie STANCIL └─ Rebecca STANCIL	

Descendants of Richard Arrow Smith

First	Second	Third
Daniel BAGWELL m. Elizabeth	Frederick B. BAGWELL m. Mary Hill William BAGWELL John Daniel BAGWELL m. Rachel Chamblee	John D. BAGWELL, Jr. Blake BAGWELL Reed BAGWELL William BAGWELL Robert BAGWELL Warren BAGWELL Larkin BAGWELL Clara Kitty BAGWELL
	James BAGWELL Nathan BAGWELL m. Sally Mainor	Littleberry BAGWELL Clara BAGWELL Bryant BAGWELL Susan BAGWELL Rebecca BAGWELL Nathaniel BAGWELL Mary BAGWELL
	Thomas BAGWELL m. Sarah Privitt	

Descendants of Richard Arrow Smith

Third	Fourth	Fifth
Littleberry BAGWELL m. Mary Walker	William D. BAGWELL m. Martha Poole	Minerva H. BAGWELL Martha H. BAGWELL Catherine B. BAGWELL
	Greenberry BAGWELL m. Ann C. King	John G. BAGWELL Atlas Stanton BAGWELL William Burke BAGWELL Edward Hiram G. BAGWELL Mary L. BAGWELL Arthur P. BAGWELL
	m. Rhodie Pettigrew	Joanna BAGWELL Priscilla S. BAGWELL
	Mary Willie BAGWELL m. Cullen Bailey	William BAILEY Livana BAILEY Polly Ann BAILEY Willie Rann BAILEY Cebret Ann BAILEY Jean BAILEY
	Andrew Jack BAGWELL m. Martha Pace	Polly W. BAGWELL Helen BAGWELL Eliza Ann BAGWELL Martha J. BAGWELL Rosanna BAGWELL Erastus J. BAGWELL Arvestus BAGWELL Josephine BAGWELL
	Mason BAGWELL m. Willie Jones	Troy Jones
	Needham Bryant BAGWELL m. Isabella Thompson	Henry W. BAGWELL Mary E. BAGWELL Calvin Berry BAGWELL Jenadius J. BAGWELL Needham B. BAGWELL, Jr. Lonnie D. BAGWELL

Descendants of Richard Arrow Smith

Third	**Fourth**	**Fifth**
Clara BAGWELL m. Jesse Green	Catherine GREEN m. Calvin Poole	Sion R. POOLE Hezekiah POOLE Christiana POOLE Rosannah POOLE Catherine E. POOLE
Bryant BAGWELL m. Aisley Bunch	Granberry R. BAGWELL William S. BAGWELL Sarah Ann BAGWELL m. Cullen Bailey	Octavius BAILEY Alice G. BAILEY Amanda BAILEY
	Alcy BAGWELL m. Edward Graham Salivan BAGWELL m. W.M. Carter Delaney BAGWELL m. John V. Weathers Nancy Catherine BAGWELL m. T.J. Brooks Vashti J. BAGWELL m. Sylvester Catlette	

Descendants of Richard Arrow Smith

First	Second	Third
John BAUCOM m. Rachel	Britain BAUCOM m. Mary	Britain BAUCOM Tempy BAUCOM Edmund BAUCOM Avery K. BAUCOM Josiah C. BAUCOM
	John BAUCOM,Jr m. unknown	Sarah BAUCOM Isham BAUCOM Mary Polly BAUCOM Gilly BAUCOM Lydia BAUCOM Urias BAUCOM Bennett BAUCOM
	Mary BAUCOM m. Mr. Beddingfield	
	Cader BAUCOM m. Susannah Fowler	Wilson BAUCOM Nancy E. BAUCOM John BAUCOM Willis BAUCOM
	Jemimah BAUCOM m. Mr. Brannan	
	Rachel BAUCOM m. John Scott	
	James BAUCOM m. Sally Rogers	Willie BAUCOM James BAUCOM, Jr.
	Reece BAUCOM m. unknown	Britain Burwell BAUCOM Willis Asa BAUCOM
	Asa BAUCOM m. Elizabeth Scott	Willie BAUCOM Winifred BAUCOM Wiley BAUCOM Fanny BAUCOM Levi BAUCOM Mary Polly BAUCOM John BAUCOM Delaney BAUCOM
	Josiah BAUCOM m. Sally	Lucy BAUCOM Wiley BAUCOM Ransom BAUCOM Willis BAUCOM Green BAUCOM
	Lewis BAUCOM m. Purity Brannan	Bryant BAUCOM
m. Fanny Jordan		

Descendants of Richard Arrow Smith

Third	Fourth	Fifth
Sarah Ann BAUCOM m. Samuel A. Smith	(See Smith Chart)	
Isham BAUCOM m. Alcey Penny	Penuel BAUCOM	
Urias BAUCOM m. Elizabeth Lee	Mary Ann BAUCOM m. Hardy Poole	Salina POOLE Urias POOLE Evaline POOLE Delia POOLE Julian Coy POOLE Camden POOLE Josephine POOLE Quinton POOLE Nathan POOLE Hardy B. POOLE Mary POOLE
	Martha BAUCOM	
	Troy BAUCOM m. Elizabeth A. Rand	Mary Adeline BAUCOM Milton BAUCOM Urias BAUCOM, II Amelia BAUCOM Annie E. BAUCOM Eva M. BAUCOM Eliza W. BAUCOM
	Caswell BAUCOM	
	Charity BAUCOM m. John B. Rand	Edward RAND Charles RAND Thomas RAND
John BAUCOM m. Caroline Utley	Sarah F. BAUCOM	
Ransom BAUCOM m. Sally Barnes	Elizabeth E. BAUCOM	
Bryant BAUCOM m. Spicey Curlee	Lucinda BAUCOM Louisa Curlee BAUCOM William BAUCOM Obediah BAUCOM	

Descendants of Richard Arrow Smith

First	Second	Third
George POOLE m. Mary	Lewis POOLE m. Catherine	William R. POOLE Lewis POOLE, Jr. Ransom POOLE Martha POOLE
	Hester POOLE m. Jacob Stevens	
	Elizabeth POOLE	
	William POOLE m. Sarah	
	Hardy POOLE m. Edith	William POOLE Howard POOLE George POOLE Hardy POOLE Charlotte POOLE Polly POOLE Betsy POOLE Nancy POOLE

Descendants of Richard Arrow Smith

Third	**Fourth**	**Fifth**
William POOLE m. Aley Powell	Jonathan POOLE m. Polly Ellington m. Mary Temple Anderson POOLE m. Eliz. Beddingfield Lewis POOLE m. Mary Turner Hardy POOLE m. Mary Ann Baucom —————— William POOLE, Jr. m. Martha Powell m. Mary Stancil m. Cornelia Turner Albert Jackson POOLE m. Sally Baucom Caroline POOLE —————————— m. Caswell A. Smith Calvin POOLE m. Sarah Maria Smith —————— m. Catherine Green —————— m. Elizabeth Jones ——————	 (See Baucom Chart) (See Smith Chart) (See Smith Chart) (See Bagwell Chart) Joseph POOLE Icana POOLE Alie POOLE Addie POOLE James W. POOLE

Descendants of Richard Arrow Smith

Bibliography

Books

Bagwell, Pamela Murrell. *Bagwell: The Family History Book.* Published privately, 1976.

Belvin, Lynne and Riggs, Harriette, editors. *The Heritage of Wake County North Carolina, 1983.* Winston-Salem, NC: Wake Co. Genealogical Society, Hunter Pub. Co.

Bible and Family Records, Johnston County North Carolina Genealogical Records Committee, Smith-Bryan Chapter, NSDAR. Smithfield, North Carolina.

City Directory, Raleigh, North Carolina, 1881, 1887, 1888, 1896, 1899.

Dorman, John F.. *Westmoreland County Deeds and Wills Series.* Falmouth, VA: Published privately.

Holcomb, Brent. *Marriages of Johnston County, North Carolina 1762-1868.* Baltimore, Maryland: Genealogical Publishing Co., Inc. 1985.

Haun, Weynette Parks. *Records of Estates in Johnston County, North Carolina, Vol. 1. 1781-1807.* Smithfield, NC: Published privately, 1988.

Holcomb, Brent. *Marriages of Wake County, North Carolina, 1770-1868.* Baltimore, Maryland: Genealogical Publishing Co., Inc. 1986.

Manarin, Louis H. *North Carolina Troops, 1861-1865: A Roster.* Raleigh, North Carolina: State Department of Archives and History, 1966-1990.

Massengill, Steven, and Robert K. Tompkins. *Death Notices 1883-1893, Raleigh State Chronicle.* Raleigh, North Carolina: Published privately, 1992.

Ross, Elizabeth E. *Johnston County Will Abstracts, Vol. I, 1746-1820.* Smithfield, NC: Published privately, 1975.

Ross, Elizabeth E. *Johnston County Will Abstracts, Vol. II, 1820-1870.* Smithfield, NC: Published privately, 1977.

Ross, Elizabeth E. and King, Ray. *Marriage Registers of Johnston County, North Carolina, Vol. I and II.* Smithfield, NC: Published privately, 1986.

Stallings, Clyde M. *Calvin Pool, His Ancestors and Descendants.* Clayton, NC: Published privately, June 1991.

Watson, Joseph W. *Abstracts of the Early Deeds of Wake County, North Carolina, 1785-1802.* Rocky Mount, NC: Published privately, 1978.

Wynne, Frances Holloway. *Abstracts of Records of Wills, Inventories, and Settlements of Estates, 1771-1802.* Fairfax, VA: Published privately, 1985.

Wynne, Frances Holloway. *Wake County, North Carolina, Census and Tax List Abstracts, 1830-1840.* Fairfax, VA: Published privately, 1985.

County Records

Cumberland County, North Carolina
    Land Entries
    Deed Books
    Loose Wills and Estate Papers

Johnston County, North Carolina
    Loose Wills and Estate Papers
    County Court Minutes
    Marriage Bonds

Descendants of Richard Arrow Smith

Deed Books
Orphan Books

Wake County, North Carolina
  Loose Wills and Estate Papers
  County Court Minutes
  Marriage Bonds
  Deed Books
  Orphan Books
  Confederate Pension Applications

Census and Tax Records

Tax Records:
1783-90 Virginia Tax Schedules.
Census Records:
1790 North Carolina.
1800 North Carolina, Virginia.
1810 North Carolina, Virginia.
1820 North Carolina, Virginia.
1830 North Carolina, Virginia.
1840 North Carolina.
1850 North Carolina.
1860 North Carolina.
1870 North Carolina.
1880 Indiana, North Carolina.
1890 Indiana, North Carolina.
1900 Indiana, North Carolina.

Newspapers and Periodicals

The News and Observer, Raleigh, North Carolina.

Johnson, William Perry, editor. *The North Carolinian, A Quarterly Journal of Genealogy and History*, Vol. IV, No.3, September 1958. Raleigh, North Carolina.

Dees, Elizabeth and Jamison, Madlyn, editors. "Wake County Bastardy Bonds." *Wake County Treasures*, Vol. 1, No. 4. Raleigh, North Carolina: Wake County Genealogical Society.

Descendants of Richard Arrow Smith

Personal Papers, Letters, Bible Records

Blackwell Bible, in possession of Albert Earle Garrett.
Smith, Joseph Edwin, Reverend. Sermon books and scrapbooks, in possession of Rebecca L. Blackwell.
Smith, Mary Blanche Blackwell. Letters.
Smith, Joseph Edwin, II. Letters.
Smith, E. Vernon, Jr. Family records, Notes and Legal Papers.

Maps

Bevers, Fendol, County Surveyor. *Map of Wake County, 1870.* Raleigh, North Carolina: Nichols & Gorman Publishers.

Descendants of Richard Arrow Smith

Index of Names

Surnames in ALL CAPITALS are birth and/or marriage entries. Other surnames are anecdotal.

ADAMS, Alfred Weldon, 90
ADAMS, John W., 12
Adams, John W., 32
ADAMS, Robin Frances, 90
ALFORD, Katrina, 92
ALLEN, Ann, 88
ALLEN, Gabriella, 167
ANDREWS, Marshall, 102
Aperson, Richard, 3
Ar. Smith, Calvin, 5
Ar. Smith, Samuel, 5
Ar. Smith, Richard, 5
ARROW SMITH, Richard, 116
Arrow Smith, Richard, 1, 3, 175
ARROW SMITH, William, 6, 8
Atkins, Rodham, 4
ATKINSON, Ethel May, 48
ATWOOD, Christopher Brandon, 104
ATWOOD, Eddie, 104
Avera, John, 18
AVERA, Kedar, 117
Avera, Thomas, 117
AVERA, Thomas H., 112
AYCOCK, Daniel, 148

Babb, Christopher, 13
BAGWELL, A. Jack, 156
BAGWELL, Alcy, 157
BAGWELL, Andrew Jack, 164
BAGWELL, Arthur Pritchard, 162
BAGWELL, Arvestus, 165, 169
BAGWELL, Atlas Stanton, 161
BAGWELL, Blake, 154

BAGWELL, Bryant, 155, 156
BAGWELL, Calvin Berry, 166
BAGWELL, Catherine B., 160
BAGWELL, Cherry Cara, 159
BAGWELL, Clara, 155, 156
Bagwell, Clara, 169, 200
BAGWELL, Clara Kitty, 154
BAGWELL, Daniel, 149
BAGWELL, Delaney, 157
BAGWELL, Edward H.G., 161
BAGWELL, Eliza Ann, 158, 164
Bagwell, Elizabeth, 150
BAGWELL, Erastus J., 165
BAGWELL, Frederick, 150, 151
Bagwell, Frederick, 149
BAGWELL, Granberry Ross, 157
BAGWELL, Green Berry, 156, 160, 162
BAGWELL, Hardy Bryant, 46
BAGWELL, Helen, 164
BAGWELL, Henry B., 159
BAGWELL, Henry W., 166
Bagwell, Iano, 11
BAGWELL, James, 152
BAGWELL, Jenadius Jackson, 166
BAGWELL, Joanna, 162
BAGWELL, John, 159
Bagwell, John, 149
BAGWELL, John Daniel, 152, 153
BAGWELL, John Daniel, Jr., 154
BAGWELL, John G., 161
BAGWELL, Josephine, 165

227

Descendants of Richard Arrow Smith

BAGWELL, Larkin, 154
BAGWELL, Levy, 151
BAGWELL, Littleberry, 155, 156
BAGWELL, Lonnie D., 167
Bagwell, Lunsford, 149
BAGWELL, Margaret Nancy, 46
Bagwell, Martha, 166
BAGWELL, Martha H., 160
BAGWELL, Martha J., 164
BAGWELL, Mary, 131, 155, 159
Bagwell, Mary, 63
BAGWELL, Mary Elizabeth, 166, 169, 171
BAGWELL, Mary L., 161
BAGWELL, Mary Willie, 156, 162
BAGWELL, Mason, 156, 165
BAGWELL, Minerva H., 160
BAGWELL, Nancy, 159
BAGWELL, Nancy Catherine, 157
BAGWELL, Nathan, 152, 154, 159
Bagwell, Nathan, 151
BAGWELL, Nathaniel, 155, 158
BAGWELL, Needham B., Jr., 166, 167
BAGWELL, Needham Bryant, 156, 166
Bagwell, Needham Bryant, 171
Bagwell, Phereby, 158
BAGWELL, Polly W., 164
BAGWELL, Priscilla Sullie, 162
BAGWELL, Rebecca, 155
BAGWELL, Reed, 154
Bagwell, Richard, 149
BAGWELL, Robert, 154

BAGWELL, Rosanna, 165
BAGWELL, Salivan, 157
BAGWELL, Sally A., 159
BAGWELL, Sarah Ann, 157, 168
BAGWELL, Susan, 129, 155, 158
BAGWELL, Susan F., 159
BAGWELL, Thomas, 152
BAGWELL, Vashti Jackson, 158
BAGWELL, Warren, 154
BAGWELL, William, 151, 154
BAGWELL, William Burke, 161
BAGWELL, William D., 156, 160
BAGWELL, William G., 159
BAGWELL, William Sidney, 157
BAILEY, Alice G., 169
BAILEY, Amanda, 165, 169
BAILEY, Cebret Ann, 163
BAILEY, Cullen, 162, 168
BAILEY, Jean, 163
BAILEY, Livana, 163
BAILEY, Octavius, 168
BAILEY, Polly Ann, 163
BAILEY, William, 162
BAILEY, Willie Rann, 163
BAKER, Addie, 126
BAKER, Irma Mae, 79
Barbee, G.O., 51
BARBOUR, Roger, 82
BARNES, Leonard, 187
BARNES, Sally, 184
Bass, Douglas, 103
Batten, Josiah, 146
Batten, Patsey, 146
Baucom, Allen, 175
BAUCOM, Alvis, 184, 190, 191

Descendants of Richard Arrow Smith

BAUCOM, Alvis Alexander, 191, 192
BAUCOM, Amelia, 189
BAUCOM, Amelia Victoria, 187
BAUCOM, Annie, 189
BAUCOM, Annis, 184
BAUCOM, Asa, 173, 179
Baucom, Asa, 180
BAUCOM, Avery K., 174
BAUCOM, Barline, 157
BAUCOM, Belinda Adeline, 192
BAUCOM, Bennett, 177, 183
Baucom, Bennett, 175, 182
BAUCOM, Britain, 173, 174
Baucom, Britain, 181
BAUCOM, Britain Burwell, 178
BAUCOM, Bryant, 180, 184
BAUCOM, Cader, 173, 177
BAUCOM, Candis, 183
BAUCOM, Caswell, 182
BAUCOM, Charity, 182, 189
BAUCOM, Charles Franklin, 192
BAUCOM, Charlie, 190
BAUCOM, Delaney, 179
BAUCOM, Edmund, 174
BAUCOM, Eliza W., 189
Baucom, Elizabeth, 176
BAUCOM, Elizabeth E., 184
BAUCOM, Ella, 190
BAUCOM, Eva M., 187, 189
BAUCOM, Fanny, 117, 179
BAUCOM, Francis, 183
BAUCOM, Fred, 190
BAUCOM, Gilly, 176
BAUCOM, Green, 180
BAUCOM, Green H., 190
BAUCOM, Green Henderson, 183

BAUCOM, Henry Marshall, 192
BAUCOM, Isham, 176, 181
Baucom, Isham, 175
BAUCOM, James, 173, 178, 190
BAUCOM, James Matthew, 183
BAUCOM, James Thomas C., 191
BAUCOM, Jemimah, 173
BAUCOM, John, 176, 177, 179, 184, 190
Baucom, John, 11
BAUCOM, John, Jr., 173, 174
BAUCOM, John, Sr., 172
Baucom, John, Sr., 174
BAUCOM, Joseph Pierce, 192
BAUCOM, Josiah, 173, 179, 185
Baucom, Josiah, 180
BAUCOM, Josiah C., 174
BAUCOM, Lena Hester, 192
BAUCOM, Levi, 179, 183
BAUCOM, Lewis, 173, 180
BAUCOM, Louisa Curlee, 185
BAUCOM, Lucinda, 185
BAUCOM, Lucy, 180
BAUCOM, Lydia, 177
BAUCOM, Lydia Angeline, 191
BAUCOM, Martelia C., 191
BAUCOM, Martha, 182
BAUCOM, Mary, 173
Baucom, Mary, 174
BAUCOM, Mary Adeline, 188
BAUCOM, Mary Ann, 182, 186, 199
BAUCOM, Mary Ellen, 191
BAUCOM, Mary Polly, 176, 179
BAUCOM, Milton, 188

Descendants of Richard Arrow Smith

BAUCOM, Nancy Elizabeth, 177
Baucom, Nicholas, 172
BAUCOM, Obediah, 185
BAUCOM, Penuel, 181
BAUCOM, Rachel, 173
Baucom, Rachel, 173
BAUCOM, Ransom, 180, 184
BAUCOM, Reece, 173, 178
Baucom, Reece, 177
BAUCOM, Retta Jane, 192
BAUCOM, Sally, 190
Baucom, Sally, 179
BAUCOM, Sanders, 184
Baucom, Sarah, 70
BAUCOM, Sarah Ann, 11, 176, 181
BAUCOM, Sarah Frances, 184
BAUCOM, Sarah J., 191
BAUCOM, Sidney Denver, 183
BAUCOM, Temperance C., 191
BAUCOM, Tempy, 174
BAUCOM, Troy, 182, 187
Baucom, Troy, 70
BAUCOM, Urias, 177, 181, 182, 189
Baucom, Urias, 70, 175
BAUCOM, Wiley, 180, 183
BAUCOM, William, 185, 190
BAUCOM, William Ransom, 184
BAUCOM, William S., 191
BAUCOM, Willie, 178, 179
BAUCOM, Willie Asa, 178
BAUCOM, Willis, 177, 180
BAUCOM, Wilson, 177
BAUCOM, Winifred, 179
Beasley, Daniel, 18, 20, 24
BEASLEY, Gabriel, 14
Beasley, Marshall, 18, 35
BEASLEY, Susannah Ann, 20
Beasley, William, 17

BEDDINGFIELD, Elizabeth, 197
BEDDINGFIELD, John, 173
Beddingfield, Mary, 172
Beddingfield, Sarah, 121
BELL, Lorna, 139
BELVIN, Zeb Vance, 162
BENSON, Pauline, 58
Bettis, John, 1
Bevers, Fendol, 18
Blackwell, John Pomfret, 71
BLACKWELL, Mary Blanche, 71
Blackwell, Mary Blanche, 70, 96
BLACKWELL, Rebecca Lynn (Smith), 96
BLAKE, J.C., 82
Blalock, Henry, 22
Bledsoe, Moses, 4
BOONE, Robert, 168
BOTTOMS, Vara Holland, 107
Bottoms, William D., 107
BOYETTE, Martha Patsy, 128
BRADY, Morning E., 126
BRANHAM, Lottie A., 25
Brannan, Jemimah, 172
BRANNAN, Purity, 180
Brewer, John, 151
BRITT, Nancy, 157
Britt, Nancy, 9
BROADWELL, William F., 165
BROOKS, T.J., 157
BROUGHTON, Sallie, 128
BROUGHTON, Alice Wilson, 142
BROUGHTON, Alma, 139
BROUGHTON, Anna, 135
BROUGHTON, Benjamin, 128
BROUGHTON, Caroline, 133
BROUGHTON, Carrie Lougee, 138

Descendants of Richard Arrow Smith

BROUGHTON, Catherine, 129
BROUGHTON, Charles, 135, 139
BROUGHTON, Edgar E., 138
BROUGHTON, Effie Lee, 138
BROUGHTON, Elizabeth, 128, 131
BROUGHTON, Ella E., 140
BROUGHTON, Frances Susan, 134
BROUGHTON, Gaston H., 132, 135
BROUGHTON, George H., 69
BROUGHTON, Helen Irma, 135
BROUGHTON, Ida M., 139
BROUGHTON, J. Leonard, 135
BROUGHTON, James, 131
BROUGHTON, Jesse, 128, 129, 158
Broughton, Jesse, 48, 130
BROUGHTON, John, 128
BROUGHTON, John F., 134
BROUGHTON, Jos. Melville, 140
BROUGHTON, Jos. Melville, III, 142
BROUGHTON, Jos. Melville, Jr., 141, 142
BROUGHTON, Joseph, 127, 128, 131, 147, 159
Broughton, Joseph, 33, 49, 63
Broughton, Joseph M., 40
BROUGHTON, Joseph Melville, 132
BROUGHTON, Joseph Thomas, 130, 133
BROUGHTON, Jospeh, 135
BROUGHTON, Leonard G., 69
BROUGHTON, Lillie, 135
BROUGHTON, Louisa, 39, 132, 135
Broughton, Louisa, 62

BROUGHTON, Louisa M., 129
BROUGHTON, Martha, 129
BROUGHTON, Marvin J., 135
Broughton, Mary Bagwell, 134
BROUGHTON, Mary Esther, 130
BROUGHTON, Mary N., 138
Broughton, Minerva, 36
BROUGHTON, Minerva A., 112, 132
BROUGHTON, Nancy, 131
Broughton, Needham B., 64, 65
BROUGHTON, Needham B. III, 138
BROUGHTON, Needham Bryan, 132, 137
BROUGHTON, Needham L., 135
BROUGHTON, Numa R., 135
BROUGHTON, Philip H., 139
BROUGHTON, Polly, 130
BROUGHTON, Rebecca, 49, 52, 129, 133
BROUGHTON, Robert Bain, 142
BROUGHTON, Rosa C., 138
BROUGHTON, Sadie A., 140
BROUGHTON, Salina, 63, 132, 136
Broughton, Salina, 131
BROUGHTON, Sally, 130
BROUGHTON, Steven, 128, 130
BROUGHTON, Tevilla, 131
BROUGHTON, Thomas J., 134
BROUGHTON, William F., 134
BROUGHTON, William H., 129
Broughton, Willie, 25
BROUGHTON, Woodson Harris, 142
BROUGHTON, Zachariah T., 132, 139, 140

Descendants of Richard Arrow Smith

BROWN, Janice LaRue, 89
Bryant, James, 200
Bryant, Needham, 26, 136
Bryant, Samuel, 35
Bryant, Sarah, 136
Bryant, William, 40
BRYANT, William R., 136
Buffalow, Henry, 4
BUI, Tuyet Thi, 101
BUNCH, Aisley, 157
Bunch, Thomas, 150
BUNDY, Hazel Muriel, 85
Bundy, Mollie Susan Fultz, 86
Bundy, Willam Grant, 86
Bunting, J.N., 59
BURGE, Helen, 74
BURNETTE, Dan Thomas, 89
BURNETTE, Michael Dale, 89
BUSBEE, Albert, 164
BUSBEE, F.M., 186
Busbee, Johnson, 13, 17, 177
Busbee, Thomas, 8, 176
Busbee, W.A., 19
Busbee, W.I., 33, 62
Busbee, W.J., 45
BYRD, Martha, 59
BYRD, Paula Mae, 103

CARLILES, Sarah, 55
Carroll, Benjamin, 123
CARROLL, Dolly, 26
CARROLL, James Pinkney, 101
CARROLL, Jamie Lynn, 101
CARROLL, Jason Michael, 101
Carroll, John, 26
CARROLL, Jonathan Wayne, 101
Carroll, Labon, 55
Carroll, Sterling, 1

Carroll, Vina, 55
CARTER, W.M., 157
Carter, W.M., 112, 132
Caswell, Richard, 119
CATLETTE, Sylvester, 158
CERTAIN, Edward S., 124
CHAMBLEE, Rachel, 154
CHAMPION, Nancy Emily, 53
Chappel, Edward, 36
CLARK, Charles George, 90
CLARK, Charles Richard, 90, 101
CLARK, Frances Tuyet, 101
CLARK, Gloria Jean, 90, 100
CLARK, Pamela Lynn, 90, 101
CLARK, Victor Alan, 101
Clements, Woodson, 177
CLEVELAND, Isabelle Maude, 84
CLIFTON, Elizabeth, 60
COATES, John, 39
Cokely, John, Capt., 151, 153
COLLINS, Elizabeth, 22
Collins, Elizabeth, 23
COLLINS, Matilda, 23
Collins, Uriah D., 22
COOK, James H., 195
Cooper, David, 150
COOPER, Martha, 166
COOPER, Tina, 166
Cope, Henderson A., 113
Copeland, Charles, 115
COPELAND, Lucy, 115
COTTON, Ally, 123
COWARD, Hattie, 47
COX, Carol Ann, 93
CREECH Timothy Ray, 93
CREECH, Anthony Scott, 93
CREECH, Grady Ray, 93
CREECH, Jennie, 59

Descendants of Richard Arrow Smith

CREECH, Rodney Alan, 93
CREECH, Wanda Joy, 93
CROWDER, Emily Edwina, 106
CROWDER, Julia Ann, 113
Crowder, William D., 31
CROWTHER, Edward A., 94
CROWTHER, Edward A. Jr., 94, 105
CROWTHER, Kristine, 105
CROWTHER, Sandra F., 94, 105
CROWTHER, Wayne Edward, 105
CURLEE, Spicey, 184
CURTIS, Isabel, 87

DAUGHTRY, Miriam, 83
DAUGHTRY, William Bonnie, 83
DAUGHTRY, William Bonnie Jr., 83
David KING, 66
DAVIS, Robert Sanders IV, 100
DAVIS, Ronald Clayton, 99
DENBY, Isabella, 125
DODD, Alonzo, 56
Dodd, Elender Smith, 53
Dodd, Gilly, 175
DODD, Henry, 56
Dodd, Henry, 53
DODD, Jenny, 56
DODD, John, 56
DODD, Malissa, 56
DODD, Medoar, 56
DODD, Medoar "Dora", 53
DODD, Willie, 11
DUCK, John, 146
Duck, Sally, 145
DUNN, Delilah Ann, 183
DUNN, Grey, 177
Dunn, Lydy, 175
Dunn, Poindexter, 175

Dunn, Van Rensaler, 175
Dupree, Samuel G., 186

Eason, Jesse, 128
EASON, William, 128
Eaton, Thomas, 153
Ellington, H., 176
Ellington, J.F., 168
Ellington, Jesse, 172
Ellington, John F., 172, 188
ELLINGTON, Lucy, 180
ELLIS, Candis, 25
ELLIS, Gilly, 7
ELLIS, John, 194
ELLIS, Winney, 151
ENNIS, Amanda, 125
ENNIS, Annie Eliza, 125
Ennis, Raymond, 126
Etheridge, February, 5
ETHERIDGE, William, 6

Ferrell, A.L. 1, 43
FERRELL, Alice Catherine, 76
Ferrell, Alphious Lucian, 76
FERRELL, E. Marcus, 201
FERRELL, Emma Rosa, 76
Ferrell, Ephraim, 3, 9
Ferrell, Ephraim, Jr., 9
FERRELL, Hattie Helen, 76
Ferrell, Jacob, 13
Ferrell, Laban, 76
Ferrell, Levi, 26
FERRELL, Lillie, 167
FERRELL, Maggie Dent, 76
Ferrell, Merritt, 9, 120
FERRELL, Nellie, 76
FERRELL, Phereby, 9
FERRELL, Waylan Lucian, 76
FERRELL, Willey, 29
Finch, H.H., 122

Descendants of Richard Arrow Smith

Flowers, E.M., 50
Folsom, Edith, 181
FORD, Louisiana, 124
Ford, Zack, 124
Fort, William, 26, 44
FOWLER, Susannah, 177
FOX, Angela Marie ., 111
FOX, Henrietta Penny, 105
FOX, Michael John, 111
FOX, Paul N., 105
FOX, Paula Ann, 105
FOX, William E., 105, 110
FRANKS, Emiline, 125
FRANKS, Louisa, 135
Friddle, Burl Rush, 98
FRIDDLE, Jo Ann, 98

GALE, Clary, 115
GARRISON, S.O., 138
GARRISS, Eliza, 151
GILES, Nancy, 115
Giles, William, 115
Gladys SMITH, 79
GODWIN, Raney, 148
Godwin, Simon, 147
Gooch, Pomfret, 15
GOODWIN, Charles A., 169
GORE, Louis, 65
GOUCH, Bennett, 15
GOWER, Karen, 21
Gower, Perrin, 63
GOWER, Thomas, 63
GRAHAM, Billy Ross, 91
GRAHAM, Edward, 157
GRAHAM, Steven Ross, 91, 102
GRAHAM, William Watson, 102
Granville, Earl, 174
GREEN, Catherine, 156, 167, 200
Green, Catherine, 169
GREEN, Jesse, 156

Green, Jesse, 169, 200
GRICE, Zilpha, 145
GRIFFIN, Alma Grace, 47
GRIFFIN, Charlie, 47
Griffis, Elizabeth, 18
Griffis, Haywood, 112
Griffis, John, 18, 35
GRIFFIS, Richard, 118
Griffis, Richard, 116
Gully, Robert N., 130

HAIR, John Knox, 76
HALCOMB, Chad Alan, 109
HALCOMB, Clint Alan, 109
Halcomb, David, 109
HALCOMB, Hilary Jo Ann, 109
Halcomb, Shirley, 109
HALCOMB, Tyler Burl, 109
Hall, John R., 72
HANES, Viola Hagerman, 84
Hardcastle, William, 173
HARDY, Katherine, 143
HARRELL, Frances, 94
HARRIS, Sallie, 140
Hart, Samuel, 2
HARWOOD, Sucky, 178
Hawkins, Elizabeth, 120
Hawkins, Philip, Lt., 153
HEARN, James, 125
HEIGHT, Jackie, 103
HEIMBACH, Roberta, 97
HERNDON, Benjamin, 13
Hicks, Catherine Broughton, 48
HICKS, Henry C., 133
HICKS, Henry Thomas, 133
HICKS, Steve, 99
HIGHTOWER, Mary Lynn, 100
HILL, Mary, 151
HILL, Rebecca, 15
Hill, Rebecca, 5
Hill, William, 4

Descendants of Richard Arrow Smith

HILTON, Iris Sue, 100
Hinton, Henry, 175
Hinton, James, 174, 175
Hinton, Ransom, 175
Hocut, Melvin t, 45
HODGES, Sam, 170
HOLDER, Hubert, 162
HOLDER, James, 165
HOLDER, William C., 170
HOLIFIELD, Demetrae Lynn, 93
HOLLAND, Mary, 122
HOLLAND, Vara S., 107
Holland, Willis, 13
Homes, Benjamin, 145
Homes, Frederick, 145, 146
HONEYCUTT, John W., 200
HONEYCUTT, Rufus, 34
HOOD, Mattie E., 43
HOOD, Susanna, 161
HOPE, Clara Lee Blackburn, 92
Hornbuckle, Stella, 50
HORTON, Nancy, 124
HOSKINS, Barbara Jo, 109
Hoskins, Bobby Joe, 109
Hoskins, Marcia P., 109
HOWARD, Edna, 190
Hubbard, Henry, 3
HUNICUTT, Sythey, 196
HUNNICUTT, Lester, 66
Hunter, Col., 3
Hunter, Theophilius, 2
Hutchins, Elizabeth, 177
Hutchins, Isaac, 13, 17, 177
Hutchins, Moses, 177

Ivey, William, 13

JACKSON, Brittany Lynn, 105
JACKSON, Kent, 105

Jinks, Seth, 13
Jinks, Thomas, 4
Johns, Betty, 62
JOHNSON, Alexander, 122, 123

Johnson, Alsey, 117
Johnson, Amos, 122
Johnson, Berry, 175
Johnson, Billy, 33
JOHNSON, Carroll, 123
JOHNSON, Daughter, 118
JOHNSON, Edmund, 123
JOHNSON, Emily, 122
JOHNSON, Esther, 115, 116
Johnson, Esther, 1, 5
JOHNSON, George W., 158, 164
JOHNSON, Henry, 176
Johnson, Henry, 9, 10, 117
JOHNSON, Julia, 55
JOHNSON, Kindred, 13
JOHNSON, Leacy, 123
Johnson, Littleton, 37
JOHNSON, Louezur, 112
JOHNSON, Louise, 123
JOHNSON, Martha, 117
JOHNSON, Merritt, 122
Johnson, O.B., 23
JOHNSON, Osborne, 123
JOHNSON, Phereby, 115, 116
Johnson, Phereby, 114
JOHNSON, Philip, 115
Johnson, Philip, 120
Johnson, Polly, 175
Johnson, Reddin, 12
Johnson, Reuben, 123
Johnson, Reynold, 5
JOHNSON, Richard, 114, 117, 119
Johnson, Richard, 119
JOHNSON, Rigdon, 117, 122, 179

Descendants of Richard Arrow Smith

Johnson, Rigdon, 5
Johnson, Rubin, 2
JOHNSON, Samuel, 115
Johnson, Samuel, 176
JOHNSON, Sarah, 117
JOHNSON, Sill, 115, 116
Johnson, Sill, 5
JOHNSON, Thomas, 65
JOHNSON, William, 115
JOHNSON, Willie, 122
JOHNSON, Wilsey, 123
Johnston, Joseph, 1
Johnston, Robert, 8
Johnston, Simon, 2
JONES, Adeline, 200
Jones, Allen, 19
Jones, Allen, 112
Jones, Anita Crider, 96
JONES, Annie Maria, 57
Jones, Calvin, 20
JONES, Caroline, 125
JONES, Christine Joyce, 95
JONES, Corinna, 60
JONES, Dezzie, 57
JONES, Edie, 200
JONES, Elizabeth, 200
JONES, Geraldine, 83
Jones, Gray, 184
Jones, Green, 200
Jones, Hubert C., 96
Jones, Isaac, 120
Jones, John, 32, 181
Jones, John H., 25
Jones, Laney Tull, 200
JONES, Margaret, 60
JONES, Myrtie Irene, 81
JONES, Norman Gaston, 83
JONES, Norman Woodrow, 83
JONES, Troy, 165
Jones, William, 36
JONES, Willie, 165
JORDAN, Ananias, 24
JORDAN, Calvin, 155

JORDAN, Fanny, 177
Jordan, Fanny, 176
JORDAN, John, 186
JORS, Elsie Loraine, 84
Justice, Richard, 36

KELLY, Arlie, 104
KELLY, Brandon Todd, 104
KELLY, Crystal Grace, 104
KELLY, William H., 168
KENNEDY, Damiam Jason, 110
KENNEDY, Krista Meagan, 110
KENNEDY, Perry Eugene, 110
KENNEDY, Rodney J. W., 110
Kenyon, J.T., 147
KERR, John K., 184
KING, Ann C., 161
KING, C., 22
King, Josiah, 167, 200
KITCHENS, Sarah Gwendolyn, 90
KNIGHT, Henry Haywood, 47
KUESTER, Louise Elizabeth, 75
KUESTER, Raymond, L., 75
KUESTER, William H., 75
Lassiter, Alfred, 123
LASSITER, Elizabeth, 123
LASSITER, Mary, 196
LASSITER, Sally, 195
LEE, Elizabeth, 182
LEE, Sarah S., 59
Lewis, David, 36
Lewis, John, 17, 18
LEWIS, Paul, 104
LINCHON, Gussie, 41
Little, Barbara S., 110
Little, Dorman F., 110
LITTLE, Lisa Ann, 110
LONG, Julian Josephine, 190
LOUGEE, Caroline, 137

Descendants of Richard Arrow Smith

LYE, James, 99
LYE, Kevin Daniel, 99
LYE, Stephen Walter, 99
LYNN, Jason Matthew, 108
LYNN, Jason Scott, 108
LYNN, Jeffrey Scott, 108
Lynn, Luther C., 108
LYNN, Megan Elizabeth, 108
LYNN, Robert Christopher, 108
LYNN, Ryan Michael, 108

MAINOR, Sarah, 154
MALINKA, Amy Lynn, 98
MALINKA, Julia Ann, 98
MALINKA, Mary Laura, 98
MALINKA, Robert Martin, 98
MANN, Famous Mark, 171
MARTIN, Edwina, 82, 93
MARTIN, Miriam Frances, 94
MARTIN, Santford Frank, 94
MARTIN, Santford W., 82
MARTIN, Santford Wingate, 82, 94
MATHEU, Patty Smith, 99
MATHEU, Richard, 99
MATTHEWS, Daniel, 125
MATTHEWS, Haywood Isaac, 54
McCullers, Abraham, 49
McCullers, John, 3
McCullers, W.H., 182
MCDONALD, Angus Archie, 170
MESSER, Carrie Elizabeth, 77
MILLER, Thomas, 64
MITCHELL, Frederick Earl, 76
MITCHELL, Lillie Irene, 80
MITCHELL, Thomas, 124
Mitchener, James, 18
Montague, Geo. B., 51

Moore, Carr, 72
Moore, Elizabeth, 145
MOORE, Randolph, 146
Moore, Randolph, 145
Morris, James, 120
MOYE, Pattie, 79
MULLIS, Lydia Adeline, 191
MUNNS, Sarah, 125
MURRAY, Sally Lou, 88
MYATT, Amelia, 78

NORRIS, Fannie Elizabeth, 170
Nutt, Bennett, 177
Nutt, Elhannon, 177
Nutt, Gilly, 175
NUTT, James, 176
Nutt, James, 183
Nutt, John, 177
Nutt, Kedar, 177
Nutt, Margaret, 177
Nutt, Thomas, 175
Nutt, William, 177

O'Neal, Rebecca, 145
O'Neil, J.W., 182
O'NEIL, Marjorie Price, 161
Ogburn, Joseph, 23
Olive, Johnson, 70
OLIVER, Mark, 104
Overly, Jackson, 50

PACE, Martha, 164
PACE, Mary Gray, 81
Pace, William, 1
PARK, Charles Benjamin, 138
PARKER, Bernard, 75
PARKER, Claude L., 75
PARKER, Evelyn, 75
Parker, John, Sr., 176
PARKER, Lewis, 75

Descendants of Richard Arrow Smith

PARKER, Michael, 92
PARKER, Robert, 75
PARKER, Virginia, 75
Parker, Weston, 48
PARRISH, Sarah, 169
Pearce, Evelina, 147
PEARSON, Wayne, 104
PENDER, Nancy, 146
PENNY, Alexander, 116
Penny, Alexander, 6
PENNY, Aley, 181
Penny, Caleb, 3, 32, 116
Penny, Charity, 181
Penny, Charles, 121
Penny, Elizabeth, 6
PENNY, Henrietta, 61
Penny, Jacob, 116
PENNY, Lydia, 121
Penny, Penuel, 181
Penny, William, 120
Penny, Willliam, 181
PERRY, Judy, 89
PERRY, Miona J., 139
PETTIGREW, Rhodie, 162
PIPER, Linwood Sherrill, 90
PLEASANTS, Mollie L., 25
Polk, John, 50
Polk, William, 17
Pollard, Caswell, 50
POOLE, Addie, 201
POOLE, Albert J., 197
POOLE, Albert Jackson, 198
Poole, Aley, 32
Poole, Aley Powell, 186
POOLE, Alice T., 170
POOLE, Alie, 200
Poole, Alonzo, 160
POOLE, Anderson, 197
POOLE, Ava, 61, 82
POOLE, Betsy, 196
POOLE, Calvin, 31, 167, 198, 199, 200

Poole, Calvin, 69, 169, 186
POOLE, Camden, 186
POOLE, Caroline, 32, 198, 199
Poole, Caroline, 186
POOLE, Carrie, 170
POOLE, Catherine, 195
POOLE, Catherine Elizabeth, 168
POOLE, Charlotte, 196
POOLE, Christiana, 168
POOLE, Delia V., 186
POOLE, Della, 61, 83
POOLE, Edee, 194
Poole, Edith, 195
POOLE, Emeline, 32
Poole, Emma, 201
POOLE, Eugene, 170
POOLE, Eulalia, 61
POOLE, Evaline, 186
POOLE, Exter, 170
POOLE, George, 193
POOLE, George, III, 196
POOLE, George, Jr., 194
POOLE, Green, 62
POOLE, Grover Cleveland, 170
POOLE, Hancock, 160
Poole, Hancock, 166
POOLE, Hardy, 186, 194, 195, 196, 197, 199
POOLE, Hardy B., 187
Poole, Hardy, Jr., 199
POOLE, Hattie Lee, 170
POOLE, Hester, 193
POOLE, Hezekiah, 167
POOLE, Howard, 196
POOLE, Icana, 200
POOLE, Ila Kathryn, 170
POOLE, James, 163
POOLE, James Wilder, 201
POOLE, John, 194

Descendants of Richard Arrow Smith

POOLE, Jonathan, 197
POOLE, Joseph, 200
POOLE, Josephine, 187
POOLE, Julian Coy, 186
POOLE, Lewis, 193, 195, 197
POOLE, Lewis, Jr., 195
POOLE, Margie Louise, 171
POOLE, Martha, 62, 160
POOLE, Mary, 187, 194
Poole, Mary, 193
POOLE, Mary A., 113
POOLE, Melvin, 170
POOLE, Molsey, 195
POOLE, Nancy, 196
POOLE, Nathan, 187
POOLE, Paschal, 32, 61
POOLE, Polly, 196
POOLE, Quinton, 187
POOLE, Ransom, 195
POOLE, Rosannah, 168
POOLE, Rufus, 163
POOLE, Salina, 186
POOLE, Sallie, 61
Poole, Sarah, 194
POOLE, Sion R., 167, 169, 171
POOLE, Theophilous, 120
POOLE, Urias, 186
POOLE, Vasti, 113
POOLE, William, 62, 193, 196, 197, 198
Poole, William, 186
POOLE, William R., 61, 195
Poole, William R., 26, 59, 113, 120
POWELL, Aley, 197
POWELL, Martha, 197
POWELL, Mary Ann, 196
Powell, Winny, 5, 7
PRICE, Perrin, 28
PRIVETTE, Bessie Gray, 79

PRIVETTE, Cindy Evonne, 101
PRIVETTE, Debbie Lorraine, 101, 110
PRIVETTE, Nancy Michelle, 101
PRIVETTE, William Frederick, 100
PRIVITT, Sarah, 152
Privitt, William, 150
Pullen, R.S., 37
Pullen, Richard S., 4

RAINES, Helen Gold, 82
RAND, Charles, 190
Rand, Dallas, 48
RAND, Edward, 190
RAND, Elizabeth Ann, 188
RAND, John B., 189
Rand, Nathaniel G., 18
Rand, O.R., 48
RAND, Thomas, 190
Rand, William, 2
Reynolds, William, 149
Rhodes, Jesse, 152
Richards, Jesse, 150
Richardson, L., 146
RIVERS, Elizabeth, 12
Robertson, J.B., 182
ROBINS, James Hardwick, 103
ROBINS, Joshua James, 103
Rogers, Cordie N., 178
ROGERS, Emeline, 112
Rogers, Green, 178
Rogers, Isham, 178
ROGERS, Martha Patsy, 33
Rogers, Parthena, 6, 10
Rogers, Prudence, 178
ROGERS, Rachel, 92
ROGERS, Sarah, 178
Rogers, Sarah, 25
ROONEY, Katherine, 111

ROWLAND, Addie F., 140
RUSLIN, George, 65
Russell, John, 172

Sanders, Lewis B., 122
Sanders, Reuben, 10, 120
SATTERFIELD, H. J., 42
SAULS, Abner, 119
Sauls, Abner, 1, 3, 114, 117
SAULS, Abner II, 121, 123, 124
SAULS, Ann Tilla, 125
SAULS, Bellison, 120
SAULS, David, 120, 121, 124
SAULS, Elizabeth C., 125
SAULS, John William, 125
SAULS, Josephus, 125
SAULS, Lydia, 124
SAULS, Phereby, 121, 122
Sauls, Phereby Johnson, 1
SAULS, Reuben, 120, 121
SAULS, Reuben Seaton, 125
SAULS, Rufus A., 125
Sauls, Rufus A., 123
SAULS, Sarah A., 124
SAULS, Theophilous Pope, 125
SAULS, Thomas Henry, 126
SAULS, Troy William, 124
SCHRIVER, Rosa Ellen, 42
Schwarzenboeck, August, 97
SCHWARZENBOECK, Linda Louise, 97
Schwarzenboeck, Maria Gar, 97
SCOTT, Elizabeth, 179
SCOTT, John, 173
Scott, Rachel, 172
Seaborn, Benjamin F., 4
SEYMOUR, S. Romelus, 47

SHAW, Catherine, 195
Simpson, Mary, 172
Simpson, William, 172
Skinner, Thomas E., 112, 132
Slaughter, Elizabeth, 5
SLAUGHTER, Samuel, 16
Slaughter, Samuel, 17
SMITH, 64
Smith, Aaron, 5
SMITH, Aaron A., 7
SMITH, Abner A., 12, 28
Smith, Abner A., 18, 29, 32, 60
SMITH, Acharel M., 47
SMITH, Addison Glenn, 78
SMITH, Albert B., 39, 68
Smith, Alexander, 2
SMITH, Alexander A., 27
SMITH, Alfred, 21
SMITH, Alfred Daniel, 79, 88
SMITH, Alma, 47
SMITH, Alonzo, 49
SMITH, Alonzo J., 51
SMITH, Alton, 67
SMITH, Alvin E., 39
SMITH, Amanda Brooke, 103
SMITH, Anna, 48
SMITH, Anna Christina, 100
SMITH, Annie, 51
SMITH, Annie Estelle, 82
SMITH, Avis, 79
SMITH, Baby, 57, 81
SMITH, Barbara Isabel, 87
SMITH, Barthenia A., 112
SMITH, Benjamin, 45
Smith, Benjamin, 120
SMITH, Benjamin A., 9, 20
Smith, Benjamin A., 17, 21, 23, 60
SMITH, Benjamin F., 42

Descendants of Richard Arrow Smith

SMITH, Betty Frances, 80, 89
SMITH, Billy Thomas, 81, 93
SMITH, Brenda Joyce, 88, 99
SMITH, Bryant A., 10, 23
SMITH, Burchett, 13
SMITH, Burt E., 29
SMITH, Calvin A., 11, 26, 59
Smith, Calvin A., 10, 18, 32, 35, 55
SMITH, Carl Taylor, 73
SMITH, Carl Taylor II, 84
Smith, Carrie E., 38
SMITH, Carrie Etta, 42, 74
SMITH, Caswell A., 12, 32, 199
Smith, Caswell A., 35, 186
SMITH, Catherine, 21, 34, 62
SMITH, Catherine A., 14
SMITH, Charles H., 43
Smith, Charles H., 43
SMITH, Charlie, 51
SMITH, Chester B., 78
SMITH, Clary A., 6, 14
SMITH, Claudius, 44
SMITH, Clay Blackwell, 97, 107
Smith, Clem A., 23
SMITH, Clement A., 12, 27
SMITH, Cora, 51
SMITH, Corina Maude, 78
SMITH, Cornelia Amanda, 47
SMITH, Corrinna L., 42
SMITH, Coy, 57
SMITH, Crama Lee, 80, 91
SMITH, Curtis Blackwell, 87
SMITH, Daniel Ruffin, 54, 55, 60

Smith, Daniel Ruffin, 21
SMITH, Danny Marcus, 88
SMITH, Darius, 28
Smith, David, 5
SMITH, David A., 6
Smith, David A., 10
SMITH, David Thaddeus, 39
SMITH, David William, 86
SMITH, Deborah Lynn, 91
SMITH, Delia, 25, 54
SMITH, Delia Irene, 82
SMITH, Dock Garner, 82
SMITH, Donald Duane, 93
SMITH, Donna Lynn, 93, 104
SMITH, Donnie Ruffin, 92, 103
SMITH, E. Vernon, 86, 95, 97
Smith, E. Vernon, 70
SMITH, Early, 67
SMITH, Edwin A., 9, 17, 33
Smith, Edwin A., 35, 48, 73, 112
SMITH, Edwin E., 47
SMITH, Edwin Jefferson, 20, 49, 51, 52, 133
SMITH, Edy Elendor, 53
SMITH, Elender, 25, 56
SMITH, Elijah, 45
SMITH, Eliza A., 12, 19, 33
SMITH, Elizabeth, 25
SMITH, Elizabeth A., 7, 15, 16
Smith, Elizabeth A., 13
SMITH, Elizabeth Hawkins, 58
SMITH, Elizabeth Jane, 55
SMITH, Elizabeth O., 39
SMITH, Elizabeth Rufus, 46
SMITH, Ella Amarantha, 192
SMITH, Ella Elizabeth, 46
SMITH, Ella M., 53

Descendants of Richard Arrow Smith

SMITH, Ella Nettice, 54
SMITH, Elmer Vernon, 73, 85
Smith, Elmer Vernon, 41
SMITH, Emily, 54
SMITH, Emma, 44, 46
Smith, Ephraim, 23
SMITH, Ephraim A., 9, 21
SMITH, Eppie, 69
SMITH, Ernest, 66
SMITH, Ernest Gray, 81
SMITH, Vernon L., 58
SMITH, Esther, 13, 74
SMITH, Esther A., 27, 55, 60
Smith, Esther P., 59
SMITH, Eugene, 28
SMITH, Eva, 65, 69
SMITH, Fanny, 23
Smith, Fanny, 22
SMITH, February A., 6
Smith, Fereby, 24, 25
Smith, Flora V. Byrd, 59
Smith, Francis, 2
SMITH, Frank Rufus, 48
SMITH, Gail Ruth, 85
SMITH, Garner Arrista, 57, 81
SMITH, Gertrude, 68
SMITH, Gilly A., 11
SMITH, Glenn Carl, 84
SMITH, Grace, 82
SMITH, Grover Artimas, 77
SMITH, Grover Thurman, 57
Smith, Hardy, 2
SMITH, Harlan, 68
SMITH, Harvey Moody, 78
SMITH, Hattie Idella, 58
SMITH, Haywood Thomas, 56, 80, 81
SMITH, Helen, 74
SMITH, Helen Arlyne, 84
SMITH, Henrietta, 55

SMITH, Henry, 74
SMITH, Henry Burgwyn, 42
SMITH, Hercelia, 25
SMITH, Herman, 67
SMITH, Ida, 49, 57
SMITH, Irene, 79
SMITH, Irene Lula, 58, 83
SMITH, Irvin Lorenza, 60
SMITH, Isabel, 34, 67
Smith, James, 36
SMITH, James A., 24, 26, 30, 58
SMITH, James Addison, 53, 77
SMITH, James B., 53
SMITH, James Haywood, 54
Smith, James Haywood, 21
SMITH, James M., 60
SMITH, James Maylon, 80, 89
SMITH, James W., 57
SMITH, Jason Odell, 100
SMITH, Jason Ruffin, 103
SMITH, Jasper Glenn, 80, 92
Smith, Jefferson, 18, 19, 37, 49
SMITH, Jennifer Bundy, 97
SMITH, Jeremiah Blackwell, 108
SMITH, Jesse A., 25
SMITH, Jesse Willard, 80, 90
SMITH, Jessica Holland, 108
SMITH, Jimmy, 74
Smith, John, 1, 120
SMITH, John A., 6, 12, 26, 30, 33, 112
Smith, John A., 29, 35
SMITH, John B., 59
SMITH, John W., 42, 74
Smith, Jonathan, 4

Descendants of Richard Arrow Smith

SMITH, Joseph Edwin, 40, 69, 71
Smith, Joseph Edwin, 22, 41, 53, 138, 188
SMITH, Joseph Edwin II, 73, 87
SMITH, Joseph Edwin III, 87
SMITH, Julia, 14, 51
SMITH, Katherine Gar, 97
SMITH, Kathy Ann, 92, 103
SMITH, Kenneth Alan, 91
SMITH, Kimbrael A., 112
Smith, Kimbrough A., 8, 17, 18
SMITH, Kindrick, 34
SMITH, Kitty Sue, 92, 102
SMITH, Larkin A., 19, 42
Smith, Larkin A., 35
SMITH, Larkin C., 53
SMITH, Laura, 39
SMITH, Lawrence Glenn, 89, 100
SMITH, Lawrence Odell, 79, 89
SMITH, Leather B., 57
SMITH, Leonard, 49, 77
SMITH, Leonard W., 76
SMITH, Leonora, 46
SMITH, Leonora "Nora", 64
SMITH, Levi, 22
Smith, Liddy, 17
SMITH, Lillie, 64
SMITH, Linda Carol, 80, 93
SMITH, Lonnie, 65
SMITH, Lonnie Hilliard, 56, 80
SMITH, Lonnie Ruffin, 80, 91
SMITH, Louisa H., 29
SMITH, Lucetta, 34
SMITH, Lucetta A., 28
Smith, Lucius, 18, 36
SMITH, Lucius A., 20, 48, 133
Smith, Lucius A., 52
SMITH, Lucy, 68
SMITH, Luenza, 24
SMITH, Lula, 68
SMITH, Lula Allen, 55
SMITH, Lula B., 64
Smith, Lula E., 38
Smith, M.A., 62
SMITH, Macy, 67
SMITH, Marcelia, 22
SMITH, Marcellus A., 34, 66
SMITH, Marcus, 66
SMITH, Marcus M., 40
Smith, Marcus M., 38
SMITH, Margaret, 67, 78
Smith, Mariah A., 175
SMITH, Martha, 54
SMITH, Martha A., 34
SMITH, Martha L., 44
SMITH, Mary A., 20
SMITH, Mary Ann, 14
Smith, Mary Ann, 4
SMITH, Mary Blanche, 73, 88
SMITH, Mary Magdalene, 55
SMITH, Mary O., 39, 69
SMITH, Mary Susan, 53
SMITH, Matilda, 54
SMITH, Matthew, 22
Smith, Matthew, 21
Smith, Mattie A., 66
SMITH, Mattie V., 58
SMITH, Mayton, 78
SMITH, Melvin H., 79
SMITH, Menzia, 112
SMITH, Michael Loren, 104
Smith, Minerva, 34
SMITH, Minnie, 55, 66
SMITH, Mollie L., 63
SMITH, Muriel, 74

Descendants of Richard Arrow Smith

SMITH, Myrtle, 78
Smith, Nancy, 19, 20
SMITH, Nancy Elizabeth, 53
SMITH, Nathaniel A., 51
SMITH, Nellie May, 42, 75
SMITH, Norman, 66
SMITH, Ola, 65
SMITH, Olivia Jean, 100
Smith, Orrin, 19
SMITH, Orrin A., 19, 35, 136
Smith, Orrin A., 4, 18, 38, 45, 48, 53, 62
SMITH, Oscar N., 52, 56
Smith, Oswell, 62
SMITH, Oswell A., 14, 33
Smith, Oswell A., 24, 136
SMITH, Palmer, 74
SMITH, Patricia Mae, 80, 89
SMITH, Paul L., 78
SMITH, Peggy Lou, 88, 99
Smith, Penelope, 4
Smith, Perillia, 22
SMITH, Perrilla, 22
SMITH, Phereby, 22
Smith, Phereby, 9, 21
SMITH, Phil, 104
SMITH, Philip S., 112
SMITH, Phillip S., 132
Smith, Phillip S., 36
SMITH, Ralph Payne, 73, 84
SMITH, Ransom A., 112
Smith, Ransom A., 8, 28
SMITH, Rexie Jane, 88, 99
Smith, Richard, 4
SMITH, Richard A., 27, 34, 54
Smith, Richard A., 8, 10, 15, 17, 19, 30, 114
SMITH, Richard A., III, 12
SMITH, Richard A., Jr., 6, 12, 13

SMITH, Richard Bundy, 86
SMITH, Richard Henderson, 53, 78
SMITH, Ridley, 21, 27
Smith, Ridley, 27, 35
SMITH, Robert J., 46
SMITH, Rose Etta Florence, 53
SMITH, Roxanna, 39
SMITH, Roy Pomfret, 73, 84
SMITH, Roy Pomfret Jr., 84
SMITH, Rozella, 55
Smith, Rufus, 37
SMITH, Rufus A., 20, 44, 46
Smith, Rufus A., 19, 112
SMITH, Rufus Millard, 67
SMITH, Rufus W., 29, 60
Smith, Rufus W., 29
SMITH, Russell Keith, 89, 100
SMITH, Salley, 33
SMITH, Sallie, 55
Smith, Sally A., 10, 27
SMITH, Sally Maria, 12, 31, 199
Smith, Sally Maria, 70
SMITH, Samuel, 32
SMITH, Samuel A., 6, 10, 27, 30, 181
Smith, Samuel A., 3, 4, 5, 6, 9, 18, 20, 115, 181
SMITH, Sandal, 29
Smith, Sarah, 77
Smith, Sarah A., 28
SMITH, Sarah Jane, 43, 75
Smith, Sarah Maria, 186
SMITH, Silas, 51
SMITH, Simeon A., 14
SMITH, Simeon Lonnie, 53, 77
SMITH, Simeon Marion, 53
Smith, Simeon Marion, 21

Descendants of Richard Arrow Smith

SMITH, Sonya Irene, 92, 104
SMITH, Sophia, 21
SMITH, Stella, 49
SMITH, Susan A., 11
Smith, Susan A., 175
SMITH, Sylvester A., 26, 57
SMITH, Tammy Phyllis, 92
SMITH, Tempy, 24
SMITH, Texanah A., 30
Smith, Thaddeus, 37
SMITH, Thomas, 45
SMITH, Thomas A., 30
SMITH, Timothy Wayne, 89
Smith, Tranquella, 21
SMITH, Tranquilla, 22
SMITH, Troy Gaston, 68
Smith, Turner, 4
SMITH, Ugenia, 112
SMITH, Valley, 67
SMITH, Vernon, 67
SMITH, Virginia, 44
SMITH, Virginia "Jennie" 65
SMITH, Walter, 49
Smith, Wesley, 29, 60
SMITH, Wesley A., 112
Smith, Wesley A., 8, 28
SMITH, Wesley O., 113
SMITH, William, 21, 22, 24, 33
Smith, William, 21, 120
SMITH, William A., 24, 25, 33, 113
Smith, William A., 4, 9, 20, 23, 24, 32, 70
Smith, William A., Jr., 10
SMITH, William Alfred, 56, 79
SMITH, William F., 53
SMITH, William Gaston, 52
SMITH, William Ivan, 58

SMITH, William McRae, 25, 56
SMITH, William O., 41, 73
SMITH, Willie Gray, 79
SMITH, Winny A., 7
SMITH, Yancy L., 136
Smith, Yancy L., 33
SMITH, Yancy L., 34, 62
SMITH, Zachariah A., 11
Smith, Zachariah A., 17
SMITH, Willey A., 10
SMITHWICK, Sarah, 144
SNELLING, Martha Helen, 134
Snellings, William, 48
Spence, B.A., 113
Stallings, James, 25, 33, 62
STALLINGS, Joseph Alpheus, 188
STALLINGS, Nicholas P., 168
STALLINGS, Willey, 130
STANCIL, Elizabeth, 146, 148
STANCIL, Evelina, 148
STANCIL, Godfrey, 146, 147
STANCIL, Godfrey, Jr., 148
STANCIL, John, 143
STANCIL, John, III, 144, 145
STANCIL, John, IV, 145
STANCIL, John, Jr., 143, 144
STANCIL, Jonathan, 145
STANCIL, Martha, 148
STANCIL, Mary, 197
STANCIL, Mary Polly, 127, 145, 147
Stancil, Meriah, 147
STANCIL, Nathan, 146
STANCIL, Polly, 148
Stancil, Priscilla, 146

Descendants of Richard Arrow Smith

STANCIL, Rebecca, 146
STANCIL, Sally, 146
Stancil, Sarah, 147
STANCIL, Willie, 148
Stancil, Willie, 147
STEPHENSON, Martha Ann, 54
Stevens, Irby, 122
STEVENS, Jacob, 193
STEVENS, James M., 46
STEVENS, Martha, 167
STONACHER, Willie Lee, 81
STONE, Elizabeth, 154
STOTT, Alsey, 148
Stott, Polly, 147
Strain, J.B., 24
STRICKLAND, John Gaston, 163
Studivant, Allen, 35
Sturdivant, Allen, 18
Sturdivant, Caswell, 32, 36, 44, 188
STURDIVANT, Elizabeth, 167
Sturdivant, Esther, 44
STURDIVANT, John D., 186
STURDIVANT, Matilda, 130
Sugg, Aaron, 3
Sweaney, Miles, 181

TALTON, Thomas J., 58
Taunt, J.M., 133
TAYLOR, Clary, 146
Taylor, Ed, 72
TAYLOR, Elizabeth, 19
Taylor, Elizabeth, 73
TAYLOR, Rebecca, 112
Teeples, Ethel, 85
TEMPLE, Alvie Healon, 78
TEMPLE, Caswell Putnam, 54
TEMPLE, Everlina Elendor, 77
TERRELL, Caroline, 43
TERRELL, Elizabeth, 38
Terrell, Elizabeth, 37

Terrell, Jackson, 37, 38, 39, 42, 43, 45
TERRELL, Jane, 45
Terrell, Solomon, 44
THOMPSON, Isabella H., 166
Thomas, Elisha, 172
THOMAS, Jessica Lynn, 111
THOMAS, Melissa, 111
THOMAS, Ronald, 111
TODD, Fannie, 67
TODD, Otho, 67
TRANTER, Alison N., 110
TRANTER, Amanda M., 109
TRANTER, Cynthia Ann, 98, 108
TRANTER, Deborah, 98
TRANTER, Debra Jo, 108
TRANTER, John Richard, 98, 110
TRANTER, Mary Anne, 88, 98
Tranter, Robert, 71, 85
TRANTER, Robert Reece, 88
TRANTER, Robert Reece II, 88, 98
TRANTER, Robert William, 109
TRANTER, William Robert, 98
TRANTER, Zachary W., 110
TRULOVE, Anita Beth, 103
TURNER, Cornelia, 198
TURNER, Daisy, 74
Turner, Henry, 36
Turner, Mary, 198
TURNER, Sally, 39, 182
Turner, Wesley, 198

UTLEY, Caroline, 184
UTLEY, Elizabeth Ann, 183
UTLEY, Elizabeth Jane, 183
UTLEY, Frances Eleanor, 183

Descendants of Richard Arrow Smith

WALKER, Mary, 156
WALL, James D., 131
WALL, James M., 130
WALL, Jesse Bunion, 160
WALTERS, Elizabeth, 11
Walton, Jos. A., 48
Warnock, Benjamin, 2
Warren, Daniel, 36
WATKINS, Elizabeth, 116
Watkins, Reece, 116
WEATHERS, John V., 157
Webb, John, 73
Welch, Demsey, 173
West, Noel, 123
WEST, Polly, 123
White, Clary, 5
WHITE, Elizabeth, 15
White, Elizabeth, 4, 5
WHITE, John, 14
White, John, 4, 8
Whitesides, Anna Margaret, 98
Whitfield, William, 17, 20
WHITLEY, Paul Edwin, 58
Whitley, Rebecca, 146
WILLIAMS, Arthelia, 44
WILLIAMS, Corinna, 94
Williams, F.M., 50
WILLIAMS, Louisa A., 51
WILLIAMS, Mary J., 24
Williams, Polly, 36, 50
Williams, S.W., 50
Williams, Samuel W., 51
WILLIAMS, Sidney, 160
Williams, W.G., 29
WILLIAMSON, James R., 48
WILSON, Alice Harper, 142
Wilson, Clementine, 71
Wilson, William R., 71
WINSLOW, Patricia Ann, 102
WISEMAN, Carla, 105
WOODS, Maggie, 14

Wortham, Richard Jordan, 71
Wortham, Sallie Green, 71
WREN, Elizabeth, 13

YATES, Elizabeth, 183
YATES, John, 179
Yates, William A., 14
Yearby, Hutson, 6, 10, 15
Young, Elijah, 42
YOUNG, Elizabeth, 46
Young, Francis, 68
Young, Joe, 42
Young, Lucy Ogburn, 68
YOUNG, Sandal D., 68
Young, Y.E., 45

www.ingramcontent.com/pod-product-compliance
Lightning Source LLC
Chambersburg PA
CBHW071329190426
43193CB00041B/1046